ABOUT THE
MIND CHRONICLES TRILOGY

This series is based on the Hermetic Principle: "As Above, So Below."

The goal of the series is to experience and chronicle the story of humankind since the primeval fireball, as found in the depths of one human mind—my own. The Hermetic assumption is that all places, times, and beings we have ever known exist now in the memory bank. If the key can be found to unlock this primordial memory bank, then light can shine into the records of time.

There have been many times in our history when it seemed the end of the world was upon us. These potential End Times often came at the end of an astrological age or millenium. Perhaps this twentieth-century period is unusually threatening because the end of an age coincides with the end of a millenium. In times past, we have thought the disaster was caused by moral depravity, war, or catastrophe. What is essential to understand is that all those fears *were a failure of the imagination.* Matter is never destroyed, it just changes form. In times past, we knew little about the planet as a whole, but our inner resources were richly developed. Now we know much about the whole planet, but almost nothing about our inner minds, which are creating inexplicable agents of destruction on the Earth. The Bomb, like the medieval dancers of death, confuses inner and outer. We thought our salvation was in knowing more about the world, so we did this. We must now explore the landscape of our inner selves.

Past-life regression under hypnosis, and other altered states of consciousness for deep exploration, are the methods I have used to obtain the material for this series. Ancient initiatory religions used these techniques to bring the initiate to his or her highest potential for living, and the techniques in these books are as old as the first human awareness. This series attempts to go even further, however. It recaptures the phylogenetic Earth mind records, including all the influences on this planet from other galaxies and planets. We contain all this knowledge deep within ourselves, and this series recovers the long-forgotten Earth story.

We are now precessing from the Age of Pisces into the Age of Aquarius. Thirteen thousand years ago, Earth precessed from the Age of Virgo into the Age of Leo. The Age of Leo—Atlantis—was an age of creativity, and the Age of Aquarius will be the full expression of cosmic consciousness. This Golden Age will be aborted, however, unless we recapture our story, our myth. Knowing this great myth will awaken our souls. Like the initiated bards of old, I unfold my tale for you. Together, let us awaken to full planetary consciousness.

EYE OF THE CENTAUR
Volume One of
The Mind Chronicles
Trilogy

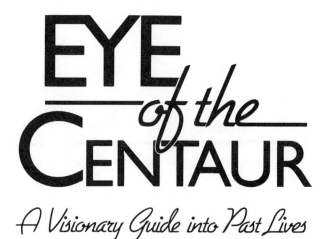

EYE _of the_ CENTAUR

A Visionary Guide into Past Lives

Barbara Hand Clow

INTRODUCTION
by therapist, Gregory Paxson

FOREWORD
by physicist, Brian Swimme

ILLUSTRATIONS
by Angela C. Werneke

BEAR & COMPANY
PUBLISHING
SANTA FE, NEW MEXICO

LIBRARY OF CONGRESS CATALOGING-IN-PUBLICATION DATA
Clow, Barbara Hand, 1943-
    Eye of the centaur / by Barbara Hand Clow; illustrations by
Angela C. Werneke.
    (The Mind chronicles trilogy)
    Reprint. Originally published: St. Paul, Minn. U.S.A. : Llewellyn
Publications, 1986. (The Mind chronicles trilogy)
    Bibliography: p.
    1. Clow, Barbara Hand, 1943-   . 2. Reincarnation —
Biography. 3. Reincarnation therapy — Case studies. I. Title. II. Series:
Clow, Barbara Hand, 1943-   Mind Chronicles trilogy.
[BL520.C56A3   1989]   133.9'01'3
ISBN 0-939680-60-2   89-6929

Bear & Company
Santa Fe, New Mexico 87504-2860

Cover illustration: Karl Meschbach
Cover design & interior illustration by Angela Werneke
Printed in the United States of America by R.R. Donnelley

9 8 7 6 5 4

To Gerry Clow

ACKNOWLEDGMENTS

I would like to thank Gregory Paxson for being my guide as I became a whole person and for his excellent introduction. I would like to thank Brian Swimme for his unrelenting pursuit of the truth and his comments on the scientific implications of this book. I would like to thank Kurt Leland for his readings of the Akashic records of my incarnations, Matt Fox for being my teacher while I wrote the master's thesis which resulted in this book, and Jungian analysts, John Giannini and Diane Nelson for reading my thesis and encouraging me to publish it in book form. I would like to thank my editors Sue Kurman and Gerry Clow for their technical assistance and unflagging enthusiasm. And I would like to thank my illustrator Angela Werneke, for her remarkable visualizations of the text. Her visualization of the text added all the extra detail surrounding the spoken words on tape. I am grateful to my grandfather Hand, my brother Robert, to my uncle Charles Wilkinson, and to my mother who all accepted me as a child. I would also like to acknowledge my readers who offered me hours of their time and advice. They are Larry Dieckmann, Carolyn Arcure, Beatrice Briggs, Lynn Andrews, Briane Swimme, Linda Goldman, Frederick Franck, Gerald Hausman, Robert Boissiere, Georgia Kelly, Chris Griscom, and Michael Talbot. I would like to give special thanks to Steve Bucher, Carl and Sandra Weschcke, and Terry Buske, and the other people at Llewellyn for making this book possible.

CONTENTS

"The mission of our times is to reinvent the human at the species level reflexively within the community of life systems in a time-developmental universe by means of story and shared dream experience."
—**Thomas Berry**

INTRODUCTION
by therapist, Gregory Paxson

You are about to begin a remarkable story; Barbara Clow's inner journey, and if you attune to it, a journey of your own. Out of her journey into the past to find herself, she has found that Greater Self who transforms and reaches forth, to touch and transform all who would have it.

The vehicle for this journey is Past-Life Regression, a technique for accessing memories from past incarnations. Many books have been written on the subject, examining past-life memories statistically, therapeutically, metaphysically and emotionally. As far as I know, this is the first account of a series of regressions by the subject, rather than by the therapist or researcher.

This is Barbara's story, told as an integral step in her own path of creation. My job is to describe the working approach that unfolded what Barbara found within herself, and to unveil some of the thinking behind that approach.

This book is unique in a number of ways. It emerged from a new approach to past-life regression; we were using past-life memories as a direct vehicle for transformation, for taking major evolutionary steps. Here Barbara has shared verbatim the most powerful of those past-life experiences. Her story shows how a series of Past-Life Regressions, guided to seek out the highest in self, brings forth the miraculous: a balanced, powerful, efficient technique for quantum growth that is at one with the integrity of the person.

Through the eyes of Barbara's past incarnations you'll be able to enter the minds and lives of both mundane and extraordinary personalities. But, in this approach, the extraordinary personalities are purposely sought out: they are the ones who hold the energies of initiation, the keys that open the doors into transmutation. As you journey with Barbara into the life and work of Aspasia, consulting the Oracle at Delphi in 1400 BC; and Ichor, Initiate of Osiris in the reign of Amenhotep II; and the Roman Catholic priest in his true work, as a Celtic seer; with these, and with others even more ancient, you will enter the interior of mysteries as old as life on earth.

Enter the mysteries freshly here, recounted through the voices of those who lived them, in the context of their own time. In times when high spirituality was seen as a technical capability, working cooperatively with the higher energies of Creation, and contributing that capability to the well-being of society.

In these ancient lives, you'll find a model of spirituality different from our own. One having little to do with safety from sin or inner peace, but everything to do with practical service at a literally spiritual level. Here we see, spanning thousands of years, a model of spirituality in integral relation to society, having objective, rather than subjective, value in daily life. As you and I now step onto the threshold, or precipice, of the change of the Age, this "mystical" model of spirituality as an objective, technical capability is essential.

Based on transcripts of 18 Past-Life Regression sessions Barbara and I did in 1982-84, Barbara selected scenes from these regressions with the most direct bearing on her own process of growth. These scenes were transcribed directly from tape recordings of the sessions, and edited only for readability. She has succeeded in sending the powerful energies of her experiences throughout this book. For all my own experience in these areas, and having already journeyed with Barbara, I was knocked unexpectedly into a deep meditational state while reading her manuscript. Be prepared, and enjoy!

Eye of the Centaur tells a wonderful story of personal and spiritual evolution, as it illustrates a new approach to the practice of Past-Life Regression as a vehicle for spiritual growth and transformation. Through a direct collaboration with the Higher Self, past lifetimes of high development and the original experience of initiatory energies are brought into the mind and body of the present self. These memories holographically attune the present personality with its own history as a being. Because these past experiences are of one's own being, they are pre-integrated with the energy patterns of the present person, they emerge as quickly as the Higher Self will allow, and they show a contextual framework for putting transformation into practice.

This process allows one to achieve a transformation of one's life quickly, while in the midst of all the demands of ordinary life. Totalling less than 30 hours of hypnosis time, our sessions took place in the midst of Barbara's astrological practice, her care for her family, and her completion of an unusually demanding Master's program. I make note of the circumstances because the reach and depth of our work and its results would, by other means, probably involve either disengagement from ordinary life in a retreat, or a lengthy process of some form of spiritual discipline.

In reading *Eye of the Centaur*, you are looking directly into the way Past-Life Regression can connect past and present into a whole greater than its parts; as meanwhile you enter into the inner experience of those skilled in ancient mystery practices of cultures going back through the Celtic, Ancient Greek, Egyptian, and on back into the involutionary times of Atlantis.

As Barbara's guide through these journeys, I'm moved that she, as a person, has found it within herself to publish such an intimately personal venture. I think of her sharing her story, and the courage with which she has told it, as an expression of her Being, one who has worked in many lifetimes serving the evolution of humankind.

Barbara and I both felt a certain excitement during our initial interview. I recall my own, and she showed hers in coming, suddenly, almost brusquely, over to my chair to show me a diagram. I'm often reminded of how the karma business calls back one's old friends. Joy and responsibility rise as one, as a great dome of light floating high above our minds.

In our work together Barbara and I have come great distances. She is and is not the woman I first met in 1982, or perhaps I should say she is a very different manifestation of that woman. She has worked through many goals, exploring, releasing, expanding and moving deeper into the energies and the nature of her being. My life is deepened with what she has shared with me.

Implicit in Past-Life Regression is the notion of reincarnation, the idea that one has a soul, an ongoing conscious energy field that enters the physical body to experience and grow, departs at death to another realm, and returns into another physical form for further growth. Karma is the mechanism for this growth, a process of natural balancing through which unfinished business and learnings can be completed elsewhere in the cycle of lifetimes. This cycle occurs many times. The Buddha is said to have recounted 649 such earthly adventures of his own, so his students might better understand the cycles of their own existence.

Our own Judeo-Christian culture has by and large been the historical exception in the avoidance or denial of reincarnation and karma, while philosophers of most other cultures, like our own early Christians, debate only the implications rather than the validity of the subject. However, every religion has an "inner teaching," and within that inner teaching, reincarnation and its evolutionary implications have been regarded as fact among Jews and Christians for millenia.

So, while Past-Life Regression is only a few decades old in our culture, it is in fact a practice with an ancient and sacred tradition, and that tradition has great resonance in this book. Through the ages there have been a few individuals who have entered the inner teachings of their spiritual form, and within those rarified and restricted milieu, past-life remembrance played an important part in the training of those adepts.

Based on both firsthand regression accounts and the little available historical record, past-life remembrance was used by the Ancient Celts, the Egyptians, the Tibetans, the Hebrew Cabalists, and various mystical orders of Christians. Keep in mind that the most powerful teachings are typically sacred secrets, passed on orally, or experientially, from teacher to student. That is because information and energy are one force, and the vehicle—the person—must be able to absorb and integrate that information/energy without harm, and use it without harming others.

The many sides of the mountain vary in their terrain and paths of ascent, while at the peak one can look in all directions from one place. Likewise the inner teachings of all the religions have more in common with each other than each has with the popular religion it seems to spring from. Thus having climbed upon that mountain through several lifetimes, one may be karmically drawn once again to the ascent, taking up whatever path one's culture presents. Through *Eye of the Centaur*, you'll see several sides of the mountain, and enjoy an extraordinary view.

In the training of adepts, Past-Life Regression serves as a shortcut, allowing the trainee to recapture the steps toward mastery already taken in previous incarnations. This same act of remembering opens a doorway that enters into the realms of higher vibration, the understanding of those realms of our source, and a working relationship with the Beings of those realms. Ultimately, through repeated practice, the past-life remembrance functions as training in the mental penetration of the substance of time and distance, essential to the mastery of physical substance.

The modern history of Past-Life Regression is, relatively speaking, comic. Since Bridey Murphy arrived with a splash in American awareness in the mid-50's, reincarnation and Past-Life Regression have emerged as a minor genre, having been celebrated in a variety of novels and movies of generally questionable accuracy or artistic merit. Coincidentally, a number of serious books of either spiritual or psychotherapeutic orientation have appeared, a substantial body of research has been developed, and the practice of Past-Life Regression and its psychotherapeutic cousin, Past-Life Therapy, is developing as an area of specialization.

A number of psychotherapists, Fiore, Wambach, and Netherton among them, have written about their accidental discovery of past incarnations as they took patients back in time to the cause of a symptom. They wrote of finding the symptoms abating as a result and found that belief or disbelief in reincarnation, on the part of either therapist or patient, played no great part in the therapeutic effectiveness of Past-Life Therapy.

Some therapists, while using Past-Life Therapy, have disclaimed that symptom relief is a verification of reincarnation. The implications of their discovery landed them on some rather shaky ground within their profession, which prompted some very useful research. However, the focus of their research has stayed within the bounds of symptom relief.

The therapeutic approach has been demonstrated to be astonishingly effective. It is also an astonishingly limited sort of thinking. While that approach does accomplish immediate therapeutic goals, it beggars the Being at the very threshold of opportunity. That opportunity is one of spiritual and psychological transformation, based on the ancient model, and adapted to modern needs.

Other research involving Past-Life Regression has focused mainly on examining the validity of reincarnation using tools of scientifc orientation. The usual approach has been to take a case of past-life recall with a lot of detail, and then investigate the details and see if they can be verified. There are at least a dozen such books, and Dr. Ian Stevenson's *Twenty Cases Suggestive of Reincarnation* (1966), takes this approach to its most thorough and painstaking level. This kind of research is as easy to think up as it is hard to do well, and so far no one has exceeded Dr. Stevenson's execution. With diffidence perhaps appropriate to a professor of psychiatry, he finds the evidence suggestive, rather than definitive. In any case, verifiable past-life detail has been a substantial means for building a body of evidence supporting the reality of reincarnation.

The late Dr. Helen Wambach applied a statistical approach to reincarnation research. Travelling across the country, she regressed over 1100 subjects in groups of 10 to 100. By limiting her subjects to a choice of a half-dozen time periods, asking about the most mundane details of daily life and death, and statistically comparing their details with known historical fact, she developed the first broad overview of reincarnation memory. Her *Reliving Past Lives* (1978), was the first research that allowed us to comparatively view the memories of many different people, substantiating the accuracy of even the most un-dramatic memories, and showing us how past lifetimes play a normal part in the lives of ordinary people.

This same statistical thinking is always important when explor-ing past lifetimes. When the regression involves ancient mystical teachings, historic events and cultures we know only vaguely, and prehistoric cultures like Atlantis, statistical consistency of detail may be the only verification available. It is often more reliable than surviving historical accounts, many of which were recorded second or third hand, translated through several languages, edited in later centuries, or recounted by propogandists.

Through the course of our sessions, Barbara did her own verifica-tion, which gave her a greater sense of solidity about the whole process. Her past life as Erastus Hummel was sufficiently obscure to require some deep, but productive, digging. Aspasia's account of the destruction of her island could be historically verified and was con-firmed again for me by another client, unknown to Barbara, who recounted a life as a young seer/priestess on that island, who died in the same apocalyptic destruction. The "Victorian woman's" story, being quite recent, was verified to the last detail. As for the ancient mystery teachings; the energy work of Ichor, the Atlantean, the Celtic priest: the evidence was mostly statistical, based on the many accounts of Egyptian priesthood, Gaul, Atlantis and so on as related to me by many clients.

I still marvel at the consistency of the descriptions of ancient and unrecorded practices and techniques, coming from so many people who are so different in their knowledge and beliefs. Or their accounts of cultures like Atlantis, so advanced it could self destruct thoroughly enough to leave no trace, yet described in consistent detail by a hundred different people. Barbara's accounts of the energy work, the mysterious inner teachings, the ancient cultures, all are consistent with the accounts of many others. Even the extraordinary events of the the last chapter are paralleled in my files. In that, the most startling of all our regressions, I heard my midwestern, Catholic client speak in Hebrew, as that past incarnation read to me from his sacred book.

Probably the most exciting approach to verifying the reality of past lifetimes is bringing forth a skill or ability from a past life, one that can be used by the present self. Since any one human contains so many variables, this is the least scientific approach; but since each one has a life to live, it's the most rewarding. It is also the most personally substantial, since in the expression of a past life capability in this lifetime, verification and growth are integral. My own experience, in remembering how to ski from an incarnation ended years before my birth, was what moved me to begin my work in regression. For me, it raised the question of what great leaps might suddenly be feasible for any person—what wealth of possibility lies within such easy reach? For Barbara, her first experience of that phenomena occured in a TV appearance, as she attuned to the robust enthusiasm of Erastus Hummel in making her presentation come alive as never before. The longterm changes in her life and work attest to the inherent power of attuning with the best in one's past incarnations.

In working with any client, I look to all four venues of verification: symptom relief, accuracy of detail, statistical consistency, and the ease of reproducing past abilities. Of course, for all the possible evidence, reincarnation is an unproven notion. The existence of God is equally troublesome because in either case, or in matters of similar magnitude, there is no physical proof. It's rather like trying to prove your love for someone. The circumstantial evidence, even though there be a wealth of it, is the best one's heart and mind can do. Past-Life Regression holds far more promise than the verification of reincarnation.

Past-Life Regression is a unique process in its own right, going beyond symptom relief or validation of belief. Regression gives us a means to explore a larger realm of reality, from a personal point of view. That personal reality connects with a cosmic reality that is constant. That connection, and the power, authenticity and efficiency of the process when rightly guided, distinguishes past-life work from psychotherapy on one hand, and from familiar techniques for spiritual development on the other. Therapy focuses on the personal; spiritual disciplines focus on the cosmic. Regression focuses both by connecting them, integrating personal healing and spiritual growth into one spontaneous process.

You are far more than this lifetime has yet shown you. Historically, each culture favors certain human possiblities at the expense of others. You can know your own possibilities only by going back into lifetimes lived in other cultures, in order to find the resources fostered by cultures that saw life in ways fundamentally different from our present time. In accurately seeing, sensing, feeling those other realms of oneself, the resonance of that long forgotten power awakens again in the present. That is the mysterious power of memory, and it is a power of refreshment, of new life in harmonic resonance with the ancient earth of the heart. And such lifetimes become one's teachers, most personal and direct, in a time when worthy teachers are hard to come by.

My personal bias is that we are evolving creatures, and that problems are not to be solved: they are triggers for our transformation. So while lifetimes from which limitation still emanates must be explored, and limitation cleared away, those painful experiences also contain gifts, and those gifts transmute pain into value, even wisdom. Likewise there are lives which illuminate, inspire and invigorate. In remembering, all those incarnations can lift us, move us through a transcendence of known self, and into a fresh and larger life.

In the motion of reincarnation, the individual is seen as having a larger self, or soul, which continues to exist after death, and returns to inhabit another human form, repeating this cycle many times. The purpose for this cycle is traditionally said to be that through earthly life one may improve the quality of that soul, or essence of self, ultimately to further the progress of one's Creator. Through the long course of those cycles there occur turning points, events of personal discovery and choice, which determines one's position in the cycles to come. Choice could be said to be an assertation of one's attunement to certain values, and a value could be said to be a vibration, having a certain periodicity, a certain pulse-length in its frequency band. Thus, a given value has a specific energy resonance, a felt-sense in the body when tuned in. In that way choice, experience and energy are one, and our present and past lives are a variable gestalt.

My essential objective in regression is to clarify the frequency of that gestalt, by enlightening one's longterm choice of values, as they emerge from millenia of experience, and thus alter the attunement, or energy-quality, of one's life.

Energy is what we are and what surrounds us in infinite range of frequencies as Creation. Energy manifests in several discrete levels of density: physical, emotional, mental, soul and spiritual. The realms of the solid, the feeling, the thinking, the identity, the source. In the person, these are holograms of different densities, co-occupying the same physical space, vibrating independently and in harmonic interaction around the reference-frequency of Self. And, in constant interaction with larger hologram systems, the most comprehensive of which we call God, in a paradoxical interplay both inside and outside the realm of time. From here, the purpose of our existence is to play a conscious part, a knowing and committed part, in the interplay of the energies of creation in all of its realms, including this one.

Memory functions like musical resonance, notes from past and present forming a chord; thus we then seek, within a past life, resonant experience. Since the power of resonant experience is the heart of my approach to regression, I seek out intiatory experiences in the past lives of my clients.

Generally, the term initiation is used to refer to a variety of rituals, symbolic events of religious or social importance. "Symbolic" is what we call rituals that have survived after their power to change us is lost. Referring to initiation here, I refer specifically to an event in which higher energies are received into the person, permanently changing the energy frequency and functioning of that personality. In ancient times, these energy-events were often generated through a ritual, or energy-technique. However, the energy-event may also occur without a ritual to evoke it. There may be few or many initiations in one's life, each one generating another evolutionary step. In past cultures whose spiritual technology was more developed than our own, initiation was used to attune and empower an individual into spiritual service and continuing growth.

Initiations as energy-events are essential to feed our own personal evolution and they resonate powerfully, as Barbara's many accounts demonstrate. Our present dilemma, in a culture whose rituals are largely empty or mindless, is how to supply ourselves with the higher energies we need to grow. Lack of them may throw personality functions out of balance, and initiations borrowed from foreign cultures, may be dissonant or indigestible.

Through the ritual, so to speak, of Past-Life Regression, one may recover and re-experience initiations of other incarnations, which are already attuned to one's own frequencies. Thus one's present self can be nourished naturally, and only as one is ready to receive a given initiation. Past-Life Regression itself might be seen as an initiation as it is an access point for higher energies.

With that intention I have made countless journeys with my clients to ancient Egypt, early Greece, pre-Roman Britain and Gaul, Atlantis and Lemuria; into the cloisters of Tibet and the mystery orders of Medieval Europe, and flowed through the global underground river of shamanic practice and tradition. In recalling these experiences of initiation into higher energies and expanded consciousness, one is not only able to recall the memory, but also to "bring back" the totality of the original experience, including the higher energies involved, into one's present body and consciousness.

My own goal in doing Past-Life Regression is to use as many facets as possible, and take the process as far as my client and I can find a way to go. Goals within that process include symptom relief, discovery and development of past skills and capacities, observation of life patterns, and eliciting personal values that have evolved through lifetimes. The purpose of these goals is to solidify a larger sense of self. The objective is actually a reorientation of one's life; turning one's life in the direction most true to oneself. To attain that objective, one must step outside the contextual set pieces of one's cultural conditioning, release the limitations created in the past, find and create relationship with one's own models of the highest in oneself, and enter into an alignment with the self that lives in The Light.

There is another level in the process, more easily achieved than it is explained. I think of it as the "systems" view of incarnations. While it is true, from a physical point of view or "3-D reality", that time is quite real, and that these other lifetimes of ours are in the past, there is another, paradoxical, equally-true point of view. From the viewpoint of the soul, projecting its energies into the holograms we call personalities, each incarnation occupies a different point on a sphere we call "time". Imagine a network of lines connecting points on a sphere, and imagine energy/information pulsing through that network of lines. Remember that the energy/information may be quite complex, including a great variety of vibrations, some dissonant, some harmonious, and carrying both general and specific messages. That is an "incarnation system". Now imagine that one of those points on the sphere becomes consciously aware of the others, and can tune in to the energies/informations of the others. Immediately, fresh resources become available to the conscious one, very possibly in such character and force to bring about substantial change. By definition, a change in any aspect of a system alters the whole system. Such is the power of consciousness, and its ability to integrate energies into new forms of living.

It is this view of connections that shapes the order of the scenes in Barbara's story. Rather than recalling each lifetime in a linear chronological progression, there is a fluid movement through time along the energy connections between lifetimes. You may find it difficult to follow the story rationally, but that is only of secondary importance. This story makes sense from the point of view of a higher aspect of consciousness, and in reading it, you are invited to make similar leaps in consciousness.

Lifetimes are interactive. As one contacts one's other incarnations, the awareness, at some level, is mutual. They are able then to help each other, refining the energy quality of the whole. One may not change the physical events in the life of another incarnation, but one may alter advantageously the emotional and conceptual value of those events. Therein lies the transmuting power of Past-Life Regression.

As persons of spiritual intention, we remain persons caught up in histories, aspirations and obligations: childhoods, parents, loves, spouses, children, careers, monthly payments, and dreams. All of that is with us as we long for God and the something-beyond within ourselves. We seek a source of vision, and direction for our growth, and a place within ourselves where decision and transformation can occur. Our other incarnations, linked together in a system, are such a source and consistently true to who we are. That system is linked to others like our own, and to others greater than our own.

By becoming conscious of one's past, resonating to one's own personal archetypes, one achieves an inner alignment. More advanced goals are initiation (receiving higher energies and an expansion of consciousness) and integration (spontaneous expression of initiation in daily life), the steps from which personal transformation naturally emerges. And through that transformation may come the return, in this lifetime, to the "Greater Path" of the soul.

So through regression we can see and feel our lives, deaths, loves and ventures beyond time. We can make connection with the system of selves which we have been, and paradoxically, are now being. And we can know the greater purpose of the lives we have lived, a principle I call the Greater Path. From the several thousand regressions I've guided, I've observed that souls choose certain areas of expertise, or avenues for learning and development, that take lifetimes to complete. Each path takes shape as some form of service to the humans around us: as healers, channels for higher energies; as politicians, channels for order; as warriors, channels for justice and safety; as artists, channels for vision; and so on. In discovering the nature of that path, attuning to that energy/intention frequency and aligning one's life with it, one finds peace and purpose and the power to be: lifted outside the personal history of this life, transformed by a larger self, an authentic yet fresh creation.

This notion of the Greater Path is illustrated in Barbara's story, in the path of the the priestly worker. You'll notice that the lives of the greatest development are those in which she engaged self in working with energy/information in behalf of the planet and its people.Just as the endeavors of Ichor, or the Priest of Enoch, or Aspasia, seek to serve the collective well-being of humankind with higher energies, so are her present daily endeavors as astrologer, as a publisher, and her offering of this book, an expression of that same path.

The Process

How all this is done is worthy of its own book. Philosophy and practice are one in this sort of work, and having stated some philosophy, some technical notes might help you understand what Barbara has shared. I think of Past-Life Regression as a very specialized field in its own right, distinct from psychotherapy, spiritual practice, hypnosis or whatever, and my technical observations apply accordingly.

Hypnosis is the most commonly used means of accessing past-life memories. Past-life memories can be brought forth without hypnosis, and there are a variety of methods, claiming to be something other than hypnosis, which bring about the necessary altered state of consciousness. However induced, an altered state in which the mind is open and receptive makes possible a "tuning in" to a particular frequency in the realism of the astral (feeling) or mental (thinking) awareness. It's analogous to having a multiband radio: after selecting, say the short-wave band, one then tunes to a specific station or signal. Or, in this case, to a specific time-band of one's experience.

The structure of a regression session is fairly consistent. With the client reclining on the couch and wired for sound, I ask for specific guidance and higher energies; that is, I pray. Then I do a rather long induction during which the felt sense in my body signals the depth level of the client, and I feel a distinct surrendering of myself into a kind of active trance. Then we go back, into an earlier incarnation. After completing the grounding process, my client and I are both tuned in, and my own visual and intuitive attunement allows me to see the past with my client, and sense the kind and timing of the questions, flashbacks and flashforwards that best elicit the story of a lifetime, and focus on the events of karmic importance. Before the last of those comes death.

Guiding the remembrance is the heart of the job. While skills in psychotherapy and healing are critial to effectiveness, it is the philosophical character, intuitive wisdom and clairvoyance of the regressionist that shapes the quality of the work. In entertaining the sacred presences of a client, the regressionist must then be therapist, philosopher, and shaman; for his biases about reality will come forth in the directions chosen, the questions asked, the powers of penetration and connection brought to the exploration. As the guide, I choose our destination and the course of our journey through it. I am also the teacher, training my client to allow the memory to come through, then to focus on precise detail within the memory.

The client is asked to go back to a lifetime before birth, and that it is possible to recall as though it is now taking place. There follows an interview of the client, in which essentially neutral questions are asked, directing the subject's attention to various elements of self and environment, and important events within that environment. The client may view the self from outside, as though watching a movie of itself, or, more effectively, from inside, with subjective awareness of its own experience. Thus the client enters a body of memory, and the regressionist guides the focus of the client through various aspects of that memory.

Once we are tuned in, we lock in the signal. I call that step "grounding", a means of achieving a clear focus, a solid sense of being there. For the first ten minutes of the regression, I ask a format of questions asking for visual and tactile information about the body, face, hair, clothing, jewelry, immediate surroundings; then expanding out into looking at the broader environment. Grounding is essentially a focus on the mundane, which keeps the attention of the client on observable facts—and away from speculation and interpretation. Through focusing on the mundane, the client becomes able to bring specific items of experience forward with great clarity, so that soon even "inner experience" becomes as clear-cut as the cobblestones underfoot.

In reading Barbara's story, you will notice that nearly every scene will begin with this grounding as she describes her physical body, dress and surroundings before describing the events and experiences themselves.

We start with the physical facts, then move to the feelings (using all sensory modalities), and can then enter the very thoughts of another human being, a past self. The importance of entering the thoughts can't be overemphasized, because the conscious and intuitive functions reveal basic attitudes, critical decisions, the keys to past abilities, and past experiences of transcendental energy movement. Those energy experiences, more than any other, are the key resonances that will energize the process of change in the present, or presenting, self. In the meantime, having established the physical facts of the person, we move to find out about the mundane aspects of the daily life of that person, and from there to explore the significant experiences of that life. Because we know the mundane facts of that existence, the significant experiences have a context, which makes it relatively easy to make pattern connections to the present lifetime.

The majority of my clients amaze me with the ease and speed with which they are able to do this. It's as though the memories, and the past personalities who literally lived those memories, were just waiting for an opportunity to make themselves known to the client. Once the client has learned to allow an easy and accurate flow of memory to come through, we have turned memory into a vehicle of discovery.

Memory, like imagination, is a curious phenomenon. It is fiendishly difficult to be scientific about, if only because we haven't established its variables, or the boundaries of its variables, or—alas— how many dimensions its variables may be bounded in. Science or not, however, memory has power, giving continuity and form to our experience of being as individuals, lending place and purpose to our endeavors amongst humankind, breathing again on the embers of our longing to be with God.

Destination! With all these lifetimes to choose from, how do we decide where to go? That choice can be obvious or artful, depending on one's view of the possibilities. In doing symptom-oriented work, one asks the client to go back to the source of the symptoms. But, in working toward accelerated evolution, the greatest distance between two points is a straight line. One must attune the heart to an unseen peak, and commence a winding path.

As I begin working with an individual, my intention is to take an inventory; I choose destinations that will give us an overview of past lives of very different kinds. Specifically, my priority in session one is to "clear a space", and to do that I simply ask that the Higher Self of the client choose the lifetime we go back to. The Higher Self leads us to the past life most directly related to the top priority issue of the present moment. I started using this instruction many years ago, and found it works—independently of the subject's belief about, or ignorance of, the existence of a "Higher Self". Frankly, this can be a tough way to begin, and often very tricky to guide, but I think anything less is a waste of time. The past life first chosen by the Higher Self may carry a heavy emotional load, and usually involves a critical decision that must be found, carefully explored, related to the present, and revised according to present needs. After the regression, that remembrance occasions fresh reflection on one's present life. This first step is so effective that I begin with the guidance of the Higher Self even when there's a clear-cut presenting issue, for the issue will often be reframed in more accurate terms. Or be shown to be something quite different from what one would logically expect.

With respect to psychological symptoms, I share the persuasion of Roberto Assagioli, the founder of Psychosynthesis, which is that symptoms may derive from unresolved past events, OR from a process of growth that is having trouble being born. In the larger karmic cycle, it is usually both at once. for reasons already mentioned, Past-Life Regression makes it relatively easy to discover the actual nature of the "stuck place" in its original moment, *and* in the karmic pattern-repeats that have reinforced it, and present-life events that have triggered its reappearance. In going through this discovery process, much of the "stuck" energy will be released.

If the "stuck place" is actually in the realm of growth having trouble being born, the experiential mobility of Past-Life Regression leads through the necessary steps with extraordinary efficiency. One, it shows the nature of that growth, and brings the energy of past development along those lines into the present self. Two, we can discover just where that growth got stuck, and the specifics of what feeling, cemented with what decision, is keeping it stuck there. Three, it reveals the present-life experience that triggered the old stuck place. Four, regression is a situation where the whole gestalt can be viewed and revised according to present needs and vision. Thus a stuck place, from whatever past, becomes fuel for growth.

Beyond stuckness, past lives present an opportunity to experience lifetimes of contact with the highest in ourselves, showing the way to what we most profoundly resonate to, and indicating the Greater Path of our own unique possibility.

Having this point of view, I structure the flow of regression sessions so that both stuck places and transcendence are addressed; clearing a space, and moving beyond one's known self. A kind of alteration unfolds: clear some space, move beyond somewhat; clear some more space, move beyond even further. As simple and balanced as walking, when one foot is always behind, another in front, and as they take turns, they support something larger, moving it forward.

And so it is in Barbara's story. In working with Barbara, I began with respect for her unusually developed self-awareness. Nonetheless, the first step in a regression series is to allow the Higher Self, an aspect of consciousness that acts as an arbiter between the soul and personality, to choose the first lifetime we explore, in order to clear a space for further work. That brought us to the Syrian prostitute, and the karmic theme of resignation to circumstance. That theme recurred in the lives of the Roman farmer, the Victorian woman, and again, at the moment of moral choice, in the life of the 13th Century trader. It was presaged, subtly, in the life of Ichor, resigned to performing an exalted duty he did not enjoy, and in the life of Aspasia, with great delicacy, in her graceful witnessing of the destructive forces she could foresee but not change.

In the second regression, my goal is to expand our vision and achieve a positive counterpoint. As I guide the client back in time, I ask for a lifetime of a certain positive quality; a lifetime of service to others, or a life of some kind of high achievement, possibly related to some area of the present life. This will bring forth and energize some very positive attribute or expression of self, and lend strength for resolving negative experiences. Each of us, in our becoming, has relied more than we know on the models around us; in working toward one's evolution, the positive models from one's own past lives are invaluable.

With Barbara, our second regression took us into the life of Erastus Hummel, vibrant with life and ambition for fulfillment, as is Barbara, curious and creative. Hummel, an early astronomer, drew on his felt sense of the universal energies he knew, his sense of the planetary forces moving within his own body, for his sense of order, power and purpose. Variations of that theme, the empowering force of integration with the energies of creation, reoccur in the lives of the Celtic priest, the Atlantean priest, Aspasia, Ichor, as the example of static balance, and in diminuendo, in the life of the 13th Century trader, and in a poignant echo, in the Victorian woman's work in the soup kitchen.

After the second regression, the choosing of a destination becomes more subtle. One might now work directly with the source of a symptom, or some present-life issue, with a much better chance of resolving it—without having the whole process get caught up in that one issue. Certainly, the first two regressions will have provided a wealth of clues. For example, a past incarnation's traumatic response to an event might seem to be out of proportion to the event itself, implying an experience previous to that one, where that pattern originated. Other choices might be the most recent lifetime (typically unusually influential in the present), or I might refer to the client's personal history, or I might simply ask the client's Higher Self to tell me which past lives are important, and why.

In the course of a regression we explore the whole of a lifetime and use the range of opportunities it offers. Then there's dying. Not to be missed! Through thousands of descriptions, the transition is the same. As a rule, death is a moment of relief, unexpected objectivity and often pleasure. Yet, we go on. It seems there is a time, after returning to the realms of one's origin, when one is to review that departed incarnation in terms of what was learned and what was achieved. The environment where that review takes place varies, according to one's level of evolution. There, where the Being returns to itself, we might conclude. Or, as a further step, that personality might have some counsel for the personality of the client. Or, we might venture on into life in nonphysical realms.

I then return the client to the present time and present body, and we physically move from the subdued quiet of the hypnosis room into a bright airy space where we can discuss what was seen and felt, what it may be suggesting in terms of the present life. Thoughts and feelings are often at some distance from each other at this point, and I know that after the client has listened to the tape of the regression the experience will solidify, and further movement will occur. When we next meet, in a fortnight or so, I'll find out what energy moved within that person by where change showed up in daily life. Then we'll work out our next destination.

One's ordinary life on earth is a mirror, reflecting one's energy in events and reactions to one's actions. So I advise my clients to observe the practical changes in their lives, their jobs, relationships, social lives and financial affairs, that occur coincidentally with their exploration of past lifetimes. That is our means of staying grounded in the here and now, in relation to the growth in their karmic relationship with self. From my own perspective as a guide, it is my means of assessing the accuracy and value of the work I am responsible for. For when a genuine resonance is struck in the past, the present responds with practical growth and, at times, impractical joy.

With each new client I am meeting with a new mystery. As I take appropriate history, I know the person before me is probably not representative of the possibilities; I would rather be a detective than a diagnostician. However, I have noticed that a history of certain kinds of psychological or functional disturbance is characteristic of individuals who have come into this lifetime with higher levels of awareness intact. Barbara's early childhood experiences of "reality warp", and her attempted suicide at age five, are at the strong end of the range, but within it. My general notion is that the Being of this new client is working toward coming forth into the personality before me, and that a series of regressions will unveil the possibilities, and begin the making-whole.

Being born into this culture with one's higher energies awake is likely to lead into an early life of loneliness and a sense of being out of place, at the very least. Imagine a scenario in which Gulliver finds himself a child in a land populated by Lilliputian minds in Brobdignagian bodies. Growing up there, he might justifiably have some psychological symptoms. Or he might have weighed himself with some harsh self judgements for his inability to fit in.

Any one Being, through its various incarnations, lives far longer than any culture. Cultures, as expressions of the collective consciousness focused on specific areas of human evolution, vary in the kinds of learning and capability they favor. Thus conditions of any one culture may or may not be simpatico for one's essence, or for the expression of that essence one has chosen for this lifetime. The state of our own culture has a lot to do with the present importance of Past-Life Regression; because regression offers a means of discovering essence, and defining a genuine self notwithstanding the cacaphony of the moment, and because it allows for a step outside the moment into a personal experience of the larger order of Creation.

An existential schizophrenia has evolved in our own society which is manifested in the inner lives of many of its inhabitants. Judeo-Christian culture is founded on the accounts of men to whom God spoke directly, or through a burning bush, or prophesied through their dreams, and reaches its height of fervence in the Teacher who raised the dead, restored sight to the blind, and, as a climax in a long series of miracles, resurrected himself after death. The binding thread that runs throughout is that there is a higher source and value to our existence than we can perceive by physically objective means. The chasm between those fundamental roots in "the Seen and the Unseen" and the realm of scientific, rational knowledge of the tangible world "where we actually live" is broad and deep. This polarity in our minds and bodies has been expanding and intensifying for the last two centuries. As we sought to free ourselves of the control of the priesthood and the aristocracy, we surrendered into the mutual embrace of science and the will of the lowest common denominator. Our priesthoods wear long white smocks, and our options in life are chosen for us by the aristocracy of numbers. The faith that once shaped our assumptions about reality now decorates it, harmless to affect the reality that we collectively share and shape. It is as if we must individually and collectively choose between transcendant values and good sense—or attempt to hold these incompatible notions of reality within ourselves, and, pretending there is no conflict, distance ourselves from Self.

Our schizophrenic split arrays rationality vs. spirituality, and thus cannot be resolved by either of them. Meanwhile, the economic, political, ethnic and environmental forces on our planet are converging toward a critical mass; our values are so split we can barely make out what's happening, let alone what to do with it. Somehow we are never ready for the change of the Age.

The split is felt within our individual selves as conflict. The anxiety generated from that conflict seems to be coming from psychological, economic or political imbalance—your choice. As a generation we are more distant from the support systems of family and friends, we keep our jobs and spouses for shorter periods of time, while we are called upon to adapt more competitively to conditions that change faster. Our knowledge of the world has outgrown our knowledge of God. The traditional shorings of identity—love, work, and faith—shift and pull in the tides. Or go rigid.

And yet the conflict is false. There is a connective tissue between the realms of faith and the tangible, a connection that transforms conflict into a creative interaction of both realms. That connective tissue consists of a direct personal experience of higher reality, and the tissue strengthens to muscle as that experience is repeated, expanded and lived out, becoming a bridge that joins faith and tangible Creation into a usable whole. That is what miracles and the "ancient mysteries" are about. That is what healers demonstrate in their daily work. That experience is one that Past-Life Regression reliably generates: coming from openness rather than theory and belief, starting from right where you are.

That is the essential value of what Barbara is sharing with you. Her personal experience of higher reality, including all of its wonder and technical virtuosity; and how that bridged and integrated her rational and faithful selves, is her gift to you here.

Gregory Paxson
Chicago, Illinois
October, 1985

FOREWORD
by physicist, Brian Swimme

In "Eye of the Centaur" Barbara Hand Clow fearlessly follows the memories of ancient times that flood her. How are we to regard these stories? As the past actually remembered? As a former consciousness brought into present awareness? As past lives seemingly forgotten and now suddenly brought back?

Of course, each reader will respond differently. As a physicist, perhaps I should be regarded as representing the most skeptical sector of modern society. What could one trained in mathematics and the controlled experiment make of these stories? Does scientific honesty compel me to regard them as simply "made-up"? Or has science's conception of reality stretched to the point where we can encounter the astrological tradition in an entirely new light?

In order to offer my own view, I need to report what I regard as the central scientific discovery of the twentieth century. I am referring to the discovery of cosmic background radiation. Scientists interpret this radiation—these photons in the microwave region of the electro-magnetic spectrum—as the last light from the primeval fireball at the beginning of time, eighteen billion years ago. We are so accustomed to such vast statements coming out of the sciences that we need to pause a moment and wonder about this. Indeed, for the first time in all of mod-ern science astrophysicists have claimed in full confidence that we can now see the actual beginnings of the whole universe.

What needs emphasis here is the fact that these lowly photons arrive soaked in news. These photons, invisible to the eye, carry a story. Certainly it is not an easy story to read, requiring much stringent training on the part of the scientists. But the photons arrive and tell something wondrous, speak to us of the birth of the universe in a vast firey explosion. Thus, we need to break free of our old habit of think-ing of photons as "just physical". At the very least we need to regard them as "informed" for they come shaped by information that a heightened sensibility can respond to.

The light from the beginning of time comes bearing news. That is the first step, seeing matter as more than just physical. But the second step involves seeing this information as activated. When these photons arrive and the scientific sensitivity is there, the news is spoken forth.

What are the scientists experiencing and feeling? They are experiencing the realization that the past has come alive in and through them. The photons by themselves would say nothing. It is only through the scientist's awareness that the past can live again, now in a new form. The light from the primeval fireball suddenly lights up in human awareness.

But wouldn't information be lost over the eons? Wouldn't what was once crisp and fresh slowly become worn out and diffuse, all but totally eroded? Wouldn't the sort of crystal-sharp presentation of consciousness such as we find in *Eye of the Centaur* be impossible? On this point too, contemporary science has a suggestive discovery, the soliton. The soliton is an extraordinary phenomenon. This particular wave-packet of energy does not die out. No matter how far it has travelled from its sourcepoint, it remains as sharply defined as if it were freshly formed.

Contemporary physics contemplates a universe in which the past permeates the present, a past that can be evoked into a new form. That is, science offers a different world from the newtonian universe where bits of matter were swirling about each other in the great dead void. We may have to accustom ourselves to living in a universe where all that has gone before swirls in and through everything existing in the present. Where not only news from the beginning of time, not only news of the vertebrate eye, but news from every drop of experience floods us silently, invisibly, just as the cosmic background radiation. Not only do we entertain the idea of a universe as a realm that cherishes all experience of the past; we must also wonder about the possibility that each and every drop of experience has an eternal dimension.

Such are the musings of a physicist confronted by this remarkable book. But enough of my scientific speculations. Enter this world yourself: the past comes alive here and teaches us life in the present; and time is no longer a single strand stretched out and forbidding but is rather a vast spaciousness all are invited to explore.

Brian Swimme, Physicist
Institute of Culture and Creation Spirituality
Holy Names College
Oakland, California.

PREFACE

Many people encountering *Eye of the Centaur* may wonder why anyone would expend such great time and effort to explore the central reality of existence: What does it mean to be human? Going through the experience you are about to encounter in this work left me so passionately attuned to this reality, that I was literally forced to create this book for you. But there are personal reasons which began the journey in the first place.

When I was under six years old, I had strong and recurrent memories of other times and places. I now understand that these memories came from previous lives. However, the result of these powerful feelings as a child was that I had great difficulty handling reality. The present life is all that really matters. I was quite sure that whatever was the matter was not my parent's fault, that it was deep within myself. But, this insistent memory-voice inside caused me to be more attuned to it, than to the real people around myself. Frequently, I experienced *deja vu*, feeling like I'd been in a place before, but that was merely a matter of idle curiosity. It was the urgency and power of the inner voices that moved me to take action. As I got closer to being forty, I began to fear that the inner voices would shatter me into pieces. I feared psychological chaos. So, I decided to get to know them, to ask them to tell me what I seemed to need to hear.

It had been a severe psychological threat to discover that I was empty inside, when I had nearly succeeded in permanently entering the void when I was five and seventeen by means of committing suicide. Suicide was no longer an option: I am a mother. Finally I walked into Gregory Paxson's office in a state of sheer desperation. I began regression and quickly discovered that this wasn't even going to be enough! Even though I was a happily married woman with four children, I was in grave danger. So, I left my family each day and attended Matthew Fox's master's program in creation-centered spirituality at Mundelein College, Chicago. I spent that entire year living without a "why" as Matt Fox puts it. This was not a case of a woman rediscovering herself after the normal immersion in family: I was a woman who never knew herself in the first place.

During the seventies and early eighties, I was an astrological

23

counselor heavily influenced by C.G. Jung. As my work at school deepened with Matt Fox while I was also doing two regressions per month, I began to see that the material I was accessing was of universal interest. It never mattered to me whether the lives I found were actual past lives or whether a voicing of subconscious needs was occurring. But, whatever I was discovering, it was definitely similar to the level of depth experienced in Jungian analysis, but it was faster, cheaper, and more effective on the physical body. Therefore, I devoted my master's thesis to a comparison of past life regression under hypnosis to Jungian analysis as a technique for finding the archetypal self.

I chose to work with Gregory Paxson in particular after interviewing many past-life regression therapists because he is very grounded in this reality. Like many young healers today, he works with an energy until it is fully integrated into the body, or he works with a trauma until it is completely cleared from the body. Since hypnosis could potentially be a very mental or psychic journey, I wanted a person who was very grounded on the physical plane. With Greg I found a potent fusion of mind and body because hypnosis itself is a laser beam directly into the right brain memory bank. With Greg's guidance, that powerful recall essence was transferred fully into me. Every cell got the energy, and fundamental growth and change was the result. In fact, I found I could taste the food thousands of years ago, hear the wind again in the Aegean, see the colorful medieval woodwork in the Rhineland. One night after a regression with Aspasia, I swam in the Aegean in phosphorescent waters with dolphins.

The direction of choosing which lifetime to explore is taken by the client in consultation with the therapist, and by learning to dialogue with the higher self. I discovered that we all have a higher self that is the guiding principle of all incarnations, and the higher self leads the incarnated self through whatever experiences are required at a given time. The result of working with the higher self as a guide with Greg is a fully conscious and complete investigation of each lifetime from birth to death. Greg pays particular attention to past-life trauma or to uplifting experiences that have bearing on the present physical and psychological state. I found fears and physical problems mysteriously disappearing a few weeks or months after a regression.

Much of the content of the lives we explored is fantastic, and the farther we went back in time, the more bizarre became the realities we explored. Much of what we found far back in time is consistent with the ancient teachings of native peoples and occultists. This technique is a potent tool for exploring very ancient and destroyed civilizations such as Atlantis. And, now that the theory of a consistent and unifying ancient culture is gaining increased respect in academic circles, possibly this technique could be used, along with more conventional forms of archeology. At the very least, I found my own pleasure and fascination with ancient cultures greatly enhanced and developed. Before doing regression, I knew very little about occult material outside of astrology, although I had been curious about it, but my background in ancient history and cultures was extensive and mainly from traditional sources. I think this background greatly enhanced my skill at accessing memory. Once hypnotized, I tended to explore lifetimes lived in historical periods and cultures which have fascinated me in this life. But, often I found things which contradicted what I had been taught, or I wandered into such detail that I learned things which would have taken me many years of study to discover. I now believe that children are drawn to certain subjects because they are already familiar with them; that they mainly learn by recollecting something from the past, and that our educational techniques ought to deal with the implications of this possibility.

The accounts of past lives in *Eye of the Centaur* exist complete on tape. Later I checked sources for verification, and I found that my reports from under hypnosis were rarely at variance with mythology, historians, or archeologists. I was either effectively re-experiencing the past or somehow time-traveling to that past. Or, perhaps the answer in physicist, Brian Swimme's comments is it: Perhaps it is possible for humans to "read" the solitons? However it is, I would be genuinely pleased to see academics open themselves enough to consider more unconventional sources.

I worked through many stages of methodology for this book. At first, I was inclined to heavily footnote the regression with ancient sources and opinions of modern scholars which would shed even more light on the subject matter. But, I decided against that because I want the readers to enter into the experience with me so that it can trigger inner transformation. The experience is more important than the material, just as this life is more important than the past. I went to a great deal of trouble to verify and search deeply into the lives I had found. I even consulted an excellent channel and reader of the Akashic records, Kurt Leland of Boston, who amplified each lifetime for me so that I could see more. In regression I was simply one person in the middle of a complex and fast moving scene, just as I am today. Kurt helped me to see wider, to know the historical and political fabric around myself. Further proof that these are actually past lives lies in the fact that we see those lives then as we see life now. Consequently, one does not know about politics or history unless one is informed at the time. I did everything I could to make myself into a better camera so that possibly the reader can see with me. The resulting text contains almost all the past lives from the tapes. I did not alter the material on tape even if I thought a date, name, or place was inaccurate. For readers who want to explore the periods by further reading, I have included an annotated bibliography at the end of the text.

The most meaningful result of this work was the overall integration of my personality, which was my original goal. I leave it to the reader to decide whether such an experience would also cause them to grow. Finding my higher self and learning what is needed for me in this life has opened me to greater happiness, freedom, balanced sensuality, success in work, and even a recent initiation into the mysteries. And, this book is the first book in a trilogy because the implications of the material encountered in the last chapter will require further work.

Doing past-life regression was not always pleasant and it was never easy. It was not an indulgence in idle curiousity. I got no "ego boost" from accessing a lifetime or two that could be labeled "famous". In fact, all that has done is raise really critical questions in this life about my path this time. It was peculiar to walk out of Greg's office onto the streets of Chicago after spending a few hours thousands of years ago. But, there was always constant humor in the situation. One day at graduate school, Matt Fox, who is a Dominican priest, commented that I looked tired after class. I told him he'd be tired too if he'd just gone through a witch burning during the Albigensian Crusades. Yes, I did wonder whether I was ready for the little men in white coats during those two years. But, my friend Murray Prosky said it all when he commented to my husband after hearing I was doing past-life regression; "You mean you have to get to know all of *them*, too?"

Chapter One

THE COURT JESTER, THE VICTORIAN LADY, AND THE ROMAN

I remember exactly what it felt like to be an infant with clenched fists and kicking feet. All things were primal; emotions and actions were one. As I clenched my fist and pushed it out, it was the same as being angry. Energy moved in my system freely, and my system responded automatically. There was no understanding of fear; there was no will and no self-awareness. There was no difference between myself and the things around me. It was ecstasy.

I'm dancing in court! My outfit is tight around the waist with a skirt of bell-tipped points. It is green felt alternating with grey, and my shoes are the same. The bells ring as I jump and stomp my feet. My outfit looks like fish scales. The Gothic ceiling is high and ornate, and the arches are carved of brightly painted wood. Everything is carved, and painted red, green, yellow, and blue. There are lots of people around me, and I'm moving fast. I'm highly trained as a dancer. I'm kicking my feet and bending over and swooping with my hands. I'm twirling around fast, stomping my feet hard on the floor. The pointed shoes with bells are like moccasins, and I'm thumping! Thumping my heels. Music is ringing to the high ceilings as I hit my tambourine on my knee, shaking it and stomping hard and whirling almost out of balance. I am laughing as I swirl close to the people.

There are beautiful ladies here, and I'm paying a lot of attention to them. Dangerously close, I smile at them. They pay no attention to me, but I'm free to look at them all I want. I can look at anybody I want to look at as long as I keep dancing with the rhythm of the musicians.

I'm fourteen, and I leave when the dancing ends. My eyes are rolling around in my head because there is so much to see.

The musicians file out, and I dance along behind them. There are

27

·Und der lacht·

ten or twelve of them, and they are all older than me. We pass through a beautiful hallway with highly decorative green, red, and yellow floor tiles and carved wainscoting on the walls. The ceiling is still high with vaulting arches carved and painted in bright colors. We step down into an archway and enter the servants' quarters. Now the hall is narrow, the floor is wooden, and down a few stairs is the servants' kitchen. The others put their instruments down on the way in as I take my pointed hat, heavy with bells, off. The table is long with a bench on each side, and we sit down awaiting our supper. We will be served supper now that we have entertained the court.

This room is long and narrow with a high ceiling of dark wood. The walls are stone, the beams heavy, and it feels like a church. Everybody is in a festive mood, and we laugh and talk about the scenes in the court. The women musicians are older than me, and they love to tease. They wear low-necked dresses for the pleasure of the Count, and they tease me because I look at their breasts pushed up high. They laugh and pinch my cheeks. The food is carried in on large platters. It is pork roast slathered with sticky marmalade and surrounded by thick carrots. The black bread is thick, fruit is piled high in heavy bowls, and we drink wine out of metal stemmed goblets.

Later I stumble to the place where I sleep, down a narrow hallway with stone floors. The arches are triangular and made of wood. the walls are stucco with heavy tapestries hanging on them to help absorb the relentless cold and dampness, and the vaulted ceilings are dimly visible from the light of the burning sconces on the walls. The heavy wooden doors have large iron rings, and they creak when opened. It is damp, even though I sense this is the dry time, and I open the door of my room. I walk in and go to the end and push aside a fabric covering on the window opening. The window is small with a thick sill, but the sunlight outside is very bright. The stone walls are so thick that I cannot reach through to the outside wall. It is the sixteenth century in Leipzig, and this building is already more than four hundred years old. There are bars in the opening, and as I look out, I see yellow grass and intensely green trees. My thoughts turn to my studies.

My room has a small cot close to the floor, a dark wooden chair with a high back, a trunk with a few clothes in it, and there is a large leather-bound book on the trunk. I don't spend much time in here, and the books for the house are in the Count's library. The heavy book on the trunk is a Bible. I open it, and it begins with "Und der lacht," and I do not like it. The opening letters are large and ornate and drawn with blue and red. I like other books better.

This is not where I spend my time. I like to dance in the court and study in the large library. My name is Erastus Hummell.

As I lie in my crib in the fifth month of this life, I feel Erastus as I swing my feet around and bump them hard on the side of my crib. I wonder if there is more I can do to awaken this Renaissance jester into my muscles to counteract the paralysis I feel in the air. During those early months, as my new reality as Barbara organized my nervous system, I re-experienced a systemic ecstasy from Erastus. As my new reality of this incarnation thickened and threatened to overwhelm my fragile thread to consciousness, it was the jester, the clown in me, who lit the candle of my spirit— for, next I was temporarily blinded by a rare eye disease.

My eyes were sealed shut for four days and nights, and I was left alone to cope in my crib. No one around me seemed to be aware of my terror as my world sunk into blackness. It was too much for my mother to cope with, and the nurses did not care. Suddenly it was as if the gates of Hades had engulfed me! I was just left in my crib in the midst of inexplicable blackness! Within hours, I was gripped by massive anxiety and terror, a terror so great that I lay awake continuously for four days and nights. All the deepest inner fears played through my system in this incarnation, reaccessing past life terrors on a scale so intense and so early that my will to live was challenged too soon. The voices began echoing from the deepest recesses of my brain as I lay helpless and sightless in my crib.

They are taking me down this hallway. It is a prison. The cells are crowded with people; there are even people lying in the halls outside the cells who seem to be sleeping in their rags and fleas. I cannot imagine who they are. The soldiers stumble over them and kick them. They do not rise out of their stupor. I thought they'd put me in one of those cells but they don't. They lead me pulling my limbs so roughly that I wonder if the sockets will hold, down to the end, to the round room. I am a small man, I am 21 or 22, and I am in a prison in Rome. I am frightened by the change from the country to the city. It smells. See those bars. They lead me in; there is no one in there, only a wooden flat table. And I know what they're going to do to me. They're going to castrate me! That's what the table with surgical instruments is for. I only realized what they were going to do to me as I passed through that door with bars. And I start thrashing! I am suffocating! The lights turn to thick grey fog. It is as if adrenaline shoots through every cell of my body so that all my senses are obliterated. There are five or six soldiers; I am pushing and shoving like a cornered wild animal. And I bite, I snap my head back! One of them has golden blond hair and vacuous blue eyes, and he is enjoying it. The others don't want to do this to me. But the little blond one leers at me in his clutches. I try to bite him, claw him; it is hopeless.

I am lying on the table, and I also feel like I am above my body watching it. They have removed my pants, and my genitals are exposed. I feel a naked terror, and my mind is exploded by bright light mixed with a deafening humming, as if existence ceases. A man comes in who wears a long white tunic, and he gets out a thin knife about four inches long. It is as if I see it from the outside, but not completely. The pain is incredible! The holding down of my legs is almost as bad. I can't even move to release the shock in them. He cuts off one ball. The blood spurts out like thick warm water, like my sap splashed on the floor. It is my Ichor.

Next, I am overwhelmed by a sickeningly relieving passivity. They lift me and haul me out of the room quickly and put me in one of the cells in the hall. There is a woman in the cell. As if she is one of the mothers, I collapse next to her, writhing in pain, with my knees doubled up. She strokes my back with long slow strokes as she stares at the ceiling with no expression on her face. She strokes me until I black out.

But in this life during my blindness, no one stroked me, and I relived my castration scene many times over during the four days in 1943. And there was another memory that flooded from the deep during the time of blindness, the memory of my lifetime as a Victorian lady, just before my birth in 1943.

First, I begin to merge into her body, but it is too close, and she is my shadow. It is like having two bodies in one. I could see her sagging brown-eyed face drift through my reality, but then I was confused again. Just as I always see my own mother's face now when I look in the mirror, so also I saw myself as her face. The drifting was agony, the feathery images moving like dust so I could not grasp them. And then, as if only compressed terror could move me into her memory, I fought not to know the ultimate terror. I was going to suffocate in the spinning trap of the female spider.

As if only a female can know the full horror of the silken thread spun endlessly out of the female spider, in my blindness I pushed frantically against my arachnid prison crib. My breathless nightmare mercilessly moved out of

*soft grey pillows of throat-catching sticking saliva into the black pitiless tum-
bling. The last picture my sightless brain activated was my crib spun into the
nest of the female black widow, and then I became her. I broke all the rules of
karma. I passed into her and became her, the woman I was who had died eleven
years before I was born in 1943.*

The Victorian shadow speaks. I am a tall bony woman with slightly
curled medium-length hair. My skin is soft and loose, my nose is large
with a bump on the ridge, and my eyes never focus directly on anyone. I wear a light-blue wool sweater with a brown cardigan over it.
My skirt is brown-and-beige plaid and made of wool from Scotland. It
is dowdy looking, but I will never throw it out because it makes me
secure. I wear brown leather shoes with blue stockings. I am about 40
years old. I stand on a large Oriental rug in an elegant wood-panelled
room filled with heavy furniture. Everyone in the room is dressed in
heavy winter clothes, and they are all very rich.

I look out of a bay window from the first floor, and I see a street
scene of two and three-storied brownstones and grey cut stone
buildings with small wrought iron fences surrounding small yards in
front. There is no snow, but the earth is frozen. There are a few leaves
left on the ground from fall still blowing around or sticking wet to stiff
grass. Chevrolets and Packards, and a few Fords are parked here and
there, and the wavy glassed window surface is cold and damp.

It is Chicago in November. This house is a large corner house
from the 1880s, and it is rigid and unbending like my relatives born
during those years. The house is a prison to me. I am not allowed to
say that to anyone, and so my soul is imprisoned in my body like my
body in that house. There is a clock on the mantel in the room I stand
in, and it says 9 am. I walk into the library across the hallway. There is a
New Yorker on the table, and the date is November 17, 1928. I walk into
the hallway and look into the mirror, and I see my mother's face
instead of my own. I always do. She died when I was 17, just when I
wondered if I was beautiful or not. It is a haughty face I see with a
velvet feather-plumed hat, but behind that face I see my own face. I
don't like to look at my face because I'm unhappy—I'm always
unhappy—so I look away. Like gazing into a smoky quartz crystal ball,
one could read much in the striations in those eyes.

I cannot tell you my name, so I am just the Victorian woman. I am not
around my children very much. Everything in this house is controlled
by other people: my husband's mother, the servants. I can't cook for the

children, I can't arrange their rooms. They're driven to where they go by the chauffeur. I am criticized by his mother because I want to spend time with them, relate to them. It is as if I am poison to my own children! The way she makes the children side with her family is to keep me away from them. But I am passive, I don't fight it. I let it all happen to me, and the cells deep within my body, even now, are cancerous.

My mother-in-law thinks I'll have a bad effect on the children. What matters are the structures that they have in their lives for dealing with children, not a mother's feelings or emotions toward her children. And my husband doesn't care; she has absolute control over him. And it's mostly through business. He either does as she pleases in the business or else she has financial control over him anyway. This house feels like it's her house. Not her house in actuality, but she owns everything. She controls all of the wealth; we exist on her gifts.

We're eating dinner, and it's a big table, very formal. And they're all there, groomed, dressed, having a nice time. And I just look at them. I feel very, very weak. I feel the children are stronger than me, have more power than I have. I know why I feel weak. I'm sick, very sick. Looking in the mirror, I feel like it shows. It shows in my face that I'm sick.

I feel like I've produced the children for somebody else. But I have really strong feelings about them. I really do love them very much. And I feel like I'm just trapped inside and can't reach out. And I feel very strongly that if I did really try to reach them they would reject me because they've been so conditioned.

I remember the first one when he was just an infant, a boy, wearing all white. I was 24, and the trouble from the very beginning was that somebody else was taking care of the baby. And oh, everyone was always so afraid of germs! There was a nanny. I have this impression of holding the baby for a little while and then somebody else cares for him. I have a sense that this is not a good thing. It never occurred to me before that that would be a problem, but I'm holding him. I'm all dressed up, and my son is all dressed up as usual. And I'm handing him back to the nurse, and I'm going out. And it strikes me right now that this is not right.

But I can't do anything about that. Everything is a sense of holding my arms out and letting it out, letting it go to someone else. And I'm dressed up as usual. Just a feeling of deafness, listlessness, automatic responses.

I like the lake a lot. I just had a flash of sailing, being in a boat. There are times when there's a little bit of a feeling of nature. But mostly it's a feeling of being in buildings and having everything—all these clothes, and everything's all tight.

Drifting, drifting, it is so oppressive. How can anyone stand to drift? I am lying still now on my back holding a blanket, and the oppressiveness has gone on so long now that I stop drifting and fall. I still cannot see. I fall softly like endless snow right back into my death in my last life. It is against all the rules of the human universe, but if a small baby suffers enough, it will die previous deaths in order to find a path. I had to break through the passivity of the Victorian Woman in order to even activate my lungs and utter my first cry in this life.

I'm lying in my bed, the cancer has finally won its pernicious battle, and I await my end with total resignation. I'm 43 years old, and I no longer care. But I wish she weren't here, my daughter. Her cornflower blue eyes make me feel so bad I choke. I am leaving her behind, and I wonder if anyone will hear me softly weeping. I wanted to be close to her, but I wasn't. Now she stands there like a moment in time. She's 8; she knows I'm dying. Like an animal, all I want to do is crawl away into a pit, but I can't reject her now. I weight 80 pounds. She has light all around her, but at that moment as she's with me, she decides she will never live! As if the cancer started when her female hormones were activated in my body, she captures everything of my passive deathliness within herself. I'm leaving her; she goes on, but I am aware that she decides to die in her mind. I am aware she will never even know the passion I felt when I was young.

It is as if we are both surrounded by deafness. She feels I am the only life she has known, so as the life passes out of me, a part of her dies too. I hated everything that was around me. She knew it, so all that is left behind are those structures. She tuned into who I really was, and she really understands that all that remains is the deathly structures. So, while she has the chance, she dies with me in her soul. And later, all the structures of society become her life.

And it was my vision of the light around her that terrified me. I knew her higher self decided to leave her then and not come back unless she could find a way later to take in her higher self again. I can go to the light, but she has to live her life without it. And so when my death hour arrived, I could not leave. I was imprisoned to hover on earth until I returned as Barbara and found my daughter again.

Chapter Two

THE PRIEST OF OSIRIS
AND THE DRUID

The blindness ceased, the blessed light filled my reality, my muscles strengthened, and my shadow withdrew to a place deep inside for a while. When I began to walk, the power surges intensified. It was a wonderful time of reckless surging forward, but then I finally fell often enough to learn that there is emptiness over the edges of the cliffs.

Adrenalin flooded in like an injection of heroin in the blood for the first time, and the intuitive part of my brain accessed such powerful memories that I still wonder how I lived.

Even now I wonder exactly how Ichor is a part of my essence. But knowing this strange Egyptian shadow, being able again to see through the Eye of Horus, somehow Ichor's energy has grounded me more firmly in present reality. Like all shadows, the dark side disappears when the sun shines. Now, my mind's eye moves back, back to a haunting mythic memory . . .

I'm riding in a small boat on a tributary of the Nile approaching a small temple near Philae. I am a male, and others row this little boat. My hair is encased in a cap which makes me look hairless. I wear sandals, and I wear a loin cloth with a wide leather belt at the waist and a tall and heavy headdress. I sense the energy of the uraeus, the serpent of early creation, above my third eye, and I see from another level the red, yellow, and gold stripes radiating out from the snake. I wear my gold initiation bracelets, and as I drift far back into time, I read the hieroglyphics indented deeply into the gold:

> Running eye of the serpent,
> The wind rushes like a chariot,
> The wind carries the grain and barley,
> Before Winter Solstice to the granary.

I am the Master of the Grain,
The grain comes from the people.
The grain comes with the sun.
Comes in the full time of the sun.

So these signs are the signs of who I am,
    Master Osiris.

I come here to make the energy connection, to begin the cycle of planting and harvesting. If I do not connect the energy, then the cycle will be broken in the Kingdom. I step out of the boat and walk up the path to the stone temple. The entrance is about six feet high, and the inside of the temple is about fourteen feet high. Everything I see is angular, sparse, and of stone. The light comes in through a large quartz crystal window above me on the left. In the center of the temple is the energy source. It is a pyramid about two feet tall, and the energy source is in the top of the pyramid.

It is almost time.

It is almost time for the sun to shine through the crystal above me on my left. I move forward now and stand in front of the short pyramid, and the top of it reaches my phallus. The light begins to illuminate the crystal above me to my left. The crystal is about a foot in diameter and the sun only shines through it like a laser beam and into the top of the pyramid when the sun is in the bull. It is time, it is happening; the light forms the beam into the top of the capstone.

I shut my eyes, and my head fills with blue energy, blue light. I stand very rigidly with my legs spread slightly apart and my hands back. I'm in the position with my chest pushed rigidly out, and I feel strong in this position. I don't look in the top of the pyramid yet, because the ray of light has not gone into it. Now the quartz crystal glows and begins to shine. The sun sends one strong beam into the top of the pyramid. Light and color are flashing all over the temple walls and floor, and I can't see anything. I can feel all the rays; it is like being jolted in an electrical generating station. I feel a piercing stab in my royal uraeus, and then it's time to look down, and I look down. There's a stone in the top, not an opal or a scarab. As the light intensifies, I see an eye in the stone. It's the side of a hawk looking sideways. It's an image of Horus.

Now I'm using all my power just to stand in place. It sends energy into my uraeus which feels like burning hot light, and then my royal uraeus comes alive in my third eye. Those who are not trained by the shining ones would be blinded at this point. I feel convulsed as my body goes rigid with a massive jolt. I feel a rod of golden energy in my spine, and then suddenly my phallus goes rigid and every cell in my body fuses. The energy is very physical and heavy, it pulls earth magnetism into my legs and thighs and shoots it into my phallus, and the muscles in my groin are like rock. And then I go limp, the magnetism dissipates, I let down. I feel tired and depressed as it passes away. I feel like a prisoner.

I never liked it, not at all. And yet I have to tell you why it obsesses me so. I am the instrument Osiris Min for the people of the Kingdom to get the energy from the root chakra at Philae and carry it up the Nile for the cocreation of the grain. But it is a form of madness, and it leaves an indelible impression in front of my vision throughout all my lives. It is the power of the Eye of God in the Eye of Horus. I stare into the top again. What is it? Many images rush through me: It is a convex crystalline surface, the inside of a shining beehive, a grey liquid in the center that resembles mercury but is only found on the Pleiades. It vibrates and emits power; it sends off a humming fusion of sound and light like sound vibrations in crystals.

I am the instrument of the waxing and waning of time as I hold out my hands to pull in the power so that the people can grow the plants. I am the master of the grain, I am Osiris. I feel the great power of the sun, I am the sun! The sun power comes to me from 360 degrees.

I have no dark side like the moon. I am the seed in the sun.

My bones feel like the marrow has been sucked out of them; I stand there with my head bowed as the sun power diminishes. But my soul is now energized for the inundation of the land by the Nile, and my phallic energy will germinate the seeds. I have told the gods that the cycle is to begin. All of our rituals are in advance of the cycles. We tell the gods what we need. I turn and walk out; no one speaks to me, and I walk back down the pathway through the palm trees and olive groves to the boat. I reach the tributary, it is muddy, and the boat is carved out of light-colored soft wood. It is about twenty feet long, twelve feet wide at the middle, and there are six oarsmen waiting in it. I do not see them because I do not know them. They push the boat down the narrow waterway with long poles as I sit in the middle. I just don't look at them. I am spaced, almost crazy, I am going into a trance. We go to the larger boat, the barque.

Now I see my boat. It is one hundred feet long and docked in the deep waters of the Nile. It has sixty oarsmen, fifteen pairs on each side, and it is made for the long journey. We will go over four hundred miles to Memphis Heliopolis on our way back, and I make this trip once a year. I walk across a plank and step down into the boat. The oarsmen move with swift silent power, but they are silent in my presence. It's as if they are in military position. There is one man who waits for me, my teacher Mena. He wears a long white robe with a rope at the waist, and he puts a fitted jacket with a long cloak on my back that matches my headdress. It's beautiful; it's made of gold and has green gold-leafed scales on the body of it. It makes me feel like I came from the sea. It has many bright red, green and blue decorations on it, and it is an honor to have him put the coat on me. He doesn't speak, he just waits for me and puts it on me when I sit in my chair in the front of the barque. Mena makes sure everything is arranged before we set out because I am in a deep trance.

Now I have to breathe with the wind and river currents, to experience all the forces of the cosmos on my journey. I will travel four hundred miles on the Nile fusing the earth energies with the sky forces. We will go past Thebes on the way to Memphis and even at that point the Sethian forces will hold in balance. As we move downriver toward the delta, I image all the canals and sacred lakes where I want the water to flow in the up-coming inundation. We image the water flow each year, and the priests monitor the level with the Nilometers. I will bless the sacred seed as I pass by Abydos, but we do not stop the boat. And as we are passing Abydos, I visualize the water flow into the sacred canal, and it encircles the Mound of Creation in my Temple. I think of myself as a straight line, a trajectory pulling the water forces with the lower part of my body, imploding the wind forces with my chest, and carrying the star plan in my head. The journey is many days, I never sleep, and as we draw near Memphis, I do not see the rabble on the river.

The moment I arrive is crucial. They are waiting for me at the causeway to the palace to see exactly when I arrive. My teacher stands behind me as we move in. There are seven gods waiting for me on the platform to the causeway. They wear bright robes with heads of animals. I see lime green, red, and gold, and they look like seven large birds standing there. They watch to see exactly when the prow touches land. It is very important.

I'm coming out of the trance, and the first thing I see as I come out of it is the Eye. I'm not aware of touching shore; that is to be determined by the astrologers. I'm carrying my consciousness in the eye that I saw in the top of the pyramid, and it is like the eye of a hawk. It's an eerie eye, not evil; it is just the eye of knowledge. I see the eye with the running serpent more clearly now, and as the visualization intensifies I see that one of the gods on shore has the head of a hawk. It is Horus! I approach him, I can't see a face, just a beak and feathers, and I pass my image of the Eye of Horus to this god.

As I pass the visualization of the eye to him, it goes into his head. The Eye becomes his eye. Just at that point I become conscious. I've done it and I'm relieved. I have done this seven times now, the first time when I was fourteen. I am to do this forty-nine times, seven times seven, if I live long enough. Only four have done it forty-nine times till now, and only three more will do so before the fall of the Kingdom. I know the future, that is the way it is, and it is 1423 B.C. at this time.

Next we walk as a group up some stone steps from the shore and no one watches us. It is not allowed. They can only gaze at the gods at certain times. I walk first, my teacher behind me, and then the seven follow us. We go up fourteen walled steps and the water level is about ten feet below the bottom step. Soon it will rise to the bottom step. I cannot look back at the Nile at this time, but I can always feel her beauty. Though this is a secret ceremony, we are all in ceremonial attire. As we ascend the fourteen steps to the top, none of us looks back. We pass through a double door into a covered causeway that leads into the palace. All doors are opened for us by people we can't see as we pass along. The first door is made of copper, and the causeway is dark. We walk along until we come to some stairs, and no one speaks.

We walk into the main reception room of the palace which is filled with people. We enter close to the Pharaoh's throne which is elevated, and the court is celebrating the time of the bull. It is the time of the flood of the spring energy. As soon as I gave up the Eye of Horus when we landed, the priests took my cloak and headdress. Now I wear a simple tunic of fine linen. Mena wears the same. I am a priest and a scribe.

This is a chaotic situation. We are very serious about our roles, but the Pharaoh is not very religious There are many soldiers and women in the room, the Pharaoh sits up high on his throne, and he's not waiting for us the way the seven gods were. But as we come into the room, the people become aware of our entrance. They begin to pound their staffs on the floor, the thumping intensifies, and the court quiets. Now it is Sacred Time.

I do not look at the Pharaoh, no one does. I go up in front of him, and I prostrate myself flat on the floor in front of him so I can only see his sandals. I turn my head to the side so I am flat on the floor, and I connect totally with the earth magnetism. Then Horus who received the Eye from me stands behind me and bows deeply and slowly. The other six gods gather behind him, then I begin to stagger up in a deep trance again. The six help me up. I am dense, I feel electrical vibration as I give all my energy to the Kingdom, to the Pharaoh. It has been done, and the court goes on.

I join the court. I have nobility. I am a member of the priestly caste. I am the energy of the dynasty. The Pharaoh is Amenhotep II, and I am Ichor.

I also felt powerful geomantic energy when I was very small, and I couldn't imagine what it was. Sometimes I could see blue-white energy around objects in the house or around the trees and rocks. But no one else seemed to see it. When I was older I found out that my house was located right in the middle of an ancient Sauk village. The land was alive with Indian spirits, and that may be one reason the subtle voices were opened in me when I was little. I always heard messages in the wind and trees that I thought no one else heard. Only my Irish grandmother knew about the spirits and kept it a secret with me. She introduced me to all the fairies in her old Victorian house.

One inner voice whispered at me over and over again:

> *"You were trained for special purposes by the Cretan Masters. There were tree oracles before the fall of Minos. This has been a method of divination which has been lost, which you were particularly talented for. It was possible during those periods to hear voices in the winds, and you were trained to make yourself accessible for what was an inborn talent, to hear the voices in the fluttering leaves communicating essential information to you as a rush or chorus. This hearing is initiated by wind, by hearing leaves fluttering in the trees. You were skilled at hearing voices in water, but you were not trained to do that by the Masters on Crete. You learned it in Thasos, Thracia because of the proximity of your temple to a waterfall. It was most frequently with the laurel tree that you felt your deepest affinity to the voices."*

The wind blowing the leaves seemed similar to the notes I played on my piano keyboard. I sensed that my inner self was like the inner strings of the piano, finely tuned, well strung, but sometimes out of tune. Like one who strikes a note not previously heard, I sensed that a memory is only reaccessed in this life if something happens this time around to make the note sound again. And my infantile crib was right next to a screened window with the tops of massive oaks, elms, and chestnut outside. I was a winter baby and listened intently during the summer that I was blinded for four days. And later I sat by the river behind our house and listened to the water messages for hours. I was allowed to wander at will when I was small, and I took to the river, marshes, ponds and trees. The rushing water and wind spirits retrained my ear well. The spirit by the river who called me almost daily was a powerful Druid brother . . .

I am twenty-eight years old, and I am a Druid priest in secret and a Roman priest in public. I wear the silver ring with the green stone in it, the symbol of my Brotherhood, the Liber Frater. Today I am with twenty people, and we all wear robes that are burgundy red, blue, brown or grey, and coarsely woven with hoods. Most of the women are young, and there is one old woman. We are an order, and the colors we wear depend upon our roles in the ceremony. This is an important day, and we have a little farther to walk now. We walk on a ley line, an energy line. The walk itself is transformative because we walk on the ley line, and now the ley line crackles with magnetic energy. This is not my country; it is Britain. We are all in a prayerful and altered state of mind, and we walk now because of the positions of the stars. It is the time of the Summer Solstice.

It is getting dark and the stars are appearing. This is the sixth century A.D., and we are walking in the end of the land in southern Britain going toward St. Michael's Circle. Now we call this place Avebury. The road is straight and marked with stones, and we have come here before. This is not my country. We stop by the side of the road and put down the things we are carrying. We proceed single file up the stone steps and into a circle of stones. As we move in, I go near the center with four other priests who wear brown robes; the grey robed figures move into the middle, and the people wearing burgundy robes go to the outer edge of the circle. It does not really matter whether one is male or female, but the five of us who move into position with the five stones in the center are male. I see all the formations with my inner

sight, but I am only aware of what I am doing.

Once in position, we begin raising the energy. We're very deliberate about how we walk into position, and once we are there we each gather the energy in our place. We bend our shoulders while tensing the muscles in our torso; rigidly we show our hands to the earth palms out, then we turn our hands and begin lifting the earth energy. As we slowly raise our hands in unison, the energy begins to form and rise like a pulsating cloud of mist. The vibrations are audible to the inner ear.

As we stand in the inner circle with an empty space in the middle behind us, the five of us face large stones that are taller than we are, each weighing a few tons, and we face the flat side. The outer side is rounded, like the back of a dolphin, and pulls in power from the outer star systems. We form a perfect pentagram. The stones are buried deep in the earth. Like an iceberg, only the tip is showing. The stones survived the flood and the earthquakes; they are ancient, and they are slightly tipped from their original position when they were built during the Age of the Double Lion. I put my hands to the side of my body as a rushing spiral of wind pushes my chest hard, and I take into my heart the etheric brand of a cross from the wind.

I feel a sickening dizziness as I pull my arms and elbows rigid, forward, and stretch out my palms facing upward. I am going to move the stone! Now the rushing wind energy moves into my third eye, and I begin to feel energy coming into my shoulder blades from the backs of the other priests forming the pentagram with me. I can't see their formation now because now I am connected to their power. We are the five points of the star with the stones in front of us. The linkage of the energy between the five of us starts to feel like a hot stabbing in my back. It shoots hot, right into my heart center.

I am rigid like steel. We are now resonators for the stones in order to energize them. We are vehicles for the power in the stones, and as it moves from us back into the stones, they seem to be thick jelly. The two outer circles of people are slowly beginning to move in reverse circles. The circle just outside the five stones goes clockwise, and the circle at the outside moves counterclockwise. They carry hot torches. I become disoriented as my will dissipates for the first time here, and I am sucked into an altered state. There is no stopping it now.

The stones are shaking! Quaking and rumbling! It feels like an earthquake because they also move under the soil. The highest density is moving, resonating vibrations deep into middle earth, and sending waves to the stars. The five of us are giving our lives just to hold our position. We are Masters. We are grounding the cosmic power.

But we are human, too. As the pulsating power intensifies, our wills become infinitestimal; we give ourselves up to the magnetism entirely on faith. I am afraid also. As I give in completely I seem to be on the verge of being taken over by a sickening feeling of dread. There is a clutching fuzzy grey form attaching itself to my stone. First it moves in and out of the stone, more adeptly with each pass, and then it begins to clutch at my shoulders. It comes inside me and feels like a jolt. But I don't feel it very much because the five of us have intensified our connection with each other. Next I become light, so light that with this energy I can't hold my position. But I feel totally balanced. We have created a perfect balance with our pentagram, and it is the balance of the gods. Now we seem to be impervious to the forms clutching at us, but I sense that this is not the end of it. The stones are massive resonators of sound from the stars, bringing in the negative force as well as the positive force, and there has to be a resolution. The form causes the temperature to drop; I can see the form in my stone, and the others also see it. I stare into the grey matter, and I see an eye with fire in the iris staring at me out of the clutching plasma.

The greyness becomes a dragon or griffin shape as it focuses on me like a disembodied soul looking for a release or a being to possess. I feel great aloneness and wariness; I wonder what will happen next, and so I force the form to remain in the stone by staring at it and using mind control. The circles moving in opposite directions move faster and faster, the fire is intensifying, and now they are whipping up a frenzy. My will is reduced to the smallest particle in the cosmos, but it still exists. I hold to that tiny particle because my own karma is affected if I fail this ritual.

I sense something coming down the road. I become aware that a group dragging a girl is approaching. She is drugged, she is afraid, she is insane with fear. Her eyes roll in her face like those of a burning dog, and I watch her being sucked into the whirling center like a helpless child drowning in a whirlpool. I move out of my body to enter her essence to see if she is protected. She has protection because she has courage. The other four have also moved their consciousness above the circle to investigate the energies. Inside I feel dread, anger about giving up my will, and energy coming into the stones from the sky. I stand rigidly in my place filling my soul with courage. This ceremony must be completed before the Solstice.

We created this moment with our fire, and these people have come now because the circles of fire have intensified. It is the frenzy point as they bring her, and the circles break to let her pass through with her captors, who prop her up. They take her to the center point of the pentagram, and the minute they put her there she goes rigid. We continue to face out but see her at the same time. We see her the way blind people see. She has long, thick, blonde hair; she is thin and tall and draped in a blue tunic. She is the earth goddess.

She instantly becomes blue-white light, and the eye in the form clutching at the rock intensifies. The form clutches my rock and yet it thrashes everywhere. I stand rigidly as it clutches at my neck. I suck energy out of my aura quickly and form a shining crystalline shield. I am a Master. My shield is round on the outside like an egg, and the inside is lined with hexagonal formations of amethyst crystal. This form cannot touch me. I still feel it wanting to get me, it wants to choke me, but as the power of the evil form intensifies, my shield hums a low sound and vibrates light waves. It can't choke me, but it is trying to get past me and get to her! We can prevent that.

I go even more rigid as the thing pushes at my chest and tries to evacuate my lungs. I feel a rod in my body that almost forces me back, but I stand my ground. The running circles of fire move faster again and the rocks move again! I can see and hear simultaneously now, and a steady deep-toned resonating hum sends out fire-light waves. All five stones are resonating until the low hum synchronizes with the light waves, and then she screams! She screams an unearthly, primal, high-pitched scream combined with an agonizing deep wail from her solar plexus; the stones send our light waves with no fire as the circles move so fast that the fire forms a straight line into a circle from above. Then the light forms a beautiful dome from the circles with the pentagram within to just above the top of her head. Sparks flash out of the top of the dome.

The stones send out light waves as they resonate with the sound. The light waves resonate up and out as the people move like the wind. The dome of light reaches a maximum intensity as the deep sounds quake near destruction level. She screams again, as loudly as she can, just to release the electrical intensity in her body. It is a rippling, inhuman but orgasmic sound of terror, and then everything dissipates. The dome of white light shatters, the resonation ceases, the dense grey forms dissipate. They melt back into the stone like fog clearing when the sun shines.

We turn and take a step forward toward her. She is standing with her palms outstretched to the sky, as if she is grabbing the stars. She is absolutely ecstatic, radiant, as if she has been charged with lightning. She is taller than I, her long wavy hair spills onto her breasts, her low-cut robe is tied at the waist with a weaving of the grain, and she brings her hands down. Her hands are rigid with energy. She moves her hands over her breasts and then down to her side and she puts her head down. Then we all put our arms around her and embrace her. She has won this victory, and we supported her. She has a heart of courage, and the evil forms dissipate in the face of it. And the souls have been passed successfully this year.

She moves out of the center of the circle, the five of us with brown robes follow her, and the outer circles wind behind us like a spiral out of the stone circle. A few hundred yards from the stones, she moves into a tunnel cut in tall hedges. It is a maze cut into a field of ancient hedges. As we move into it, I immediately feel dizzy from geomantic energy. We walk the passages, struggling with dizziness; we seem to be spiraling or making large circles. From the sky, the maze looks like the belly of a gigantic serpent bermed in the soil; the belly is formed from a maze shaped like a figure eight or an infinity symbol. I am overwhelmed with the energy as we move in and through the intersection at the center. We move more slowly as we go around the outside curves and we swing fast through the middle. We are reversing energy by walking this maze, we are causing a backward flowing power that connects the earth with the sky. We do it three times and we are freed of the effects of the release of souls during the ceremony in the stone circle. This maze is like an energy dissipater. When we emerge out of the middle of the figure eight after going around it three times, we are on the edge of St. Michael's stone circle. The circle was made in the Age of the Lion.

We traverse a large causeway around the outside of the stones. The moon is bright and full, and the large stones radiate the soft moonlight. It is almost the Solstice now, and this year it is very powerful because it coincides with the full moon.

Eight priests move into the center where the stones are, and we go into an intense meditation to maximize the Solstice power. Moon light bathes the stones and makes lines on the ancient stone floor of the circle. As we stand we are purified, and we make the connections with the Divine through all the planes. This is how we clear the planet.

It is the exact moment of the Solstice, and the day and night are balanced. Suddenly, like a sylph, like a will-o-the-wisp, like a moon-lit dragonfly, the Goddess of the Grain begins her dance in the circle. Her dress and hair flow in the wind, and her body sweeps gracefully in and out of the stones in the ancient Dance of The Mothers. She is creating a new energy in the circle, and the subtlety is chilling. She is calling the angels and the elementals into this space. She dances with them as they become alert and manifest in this sacred space. She flies with them as we ground the subtle energy by standing in place. We resonate the Solstice power on the earth plane, and she dances it to the winds. This is the time of the maximum divine energy on the earth plane, and we call in the light to our line. We divinize the planet as the Goddess dances the spirits. At the exact maximum point, all the energy lines and planes of convergence become luminous, and she dances where the forces in the lines gather.

Then the moment is past. We all move out of the circle and sleep together in a nearby field that is bathed in moonlight and surrounded by a great forest of ancient oak trees.

Chapter Three

THE DELPHIC ORACLE
AND THE MAGIC CAVE

The storyteller made a home in me when I was four years old, and from that time on, each one of my footsteps was the start of a journey, and each one of my words the beginning of a story. It all began so innocently that now I marvel at a child's ability to connect with the memory in a stone or see the visions in water surfaces and clouds. It happened on a mid-winter day when the air was fresh and moist with crystalline mist rising above the melting snow in the sunlight.

There were always many voices and spirits behind my old brick house and down the long pathways through shiny black leafless tree branches to the frozen river. The snow was deep enough that day to hide the earth ridges filled with Sauk arrowheads and potsherds. And the nearby foundations of the nineteenth-century ice house and blacksmith shop were blanketed in soft whiteness. The remains of past times that adults no longer notice often vibrate with such potency to small children. I wore a fine wool coat with a velvet collar because we'd just returned from Sunday School at the Congregational Church, and on my coat collar was pinned the two jade turtles set in gold given to me by my godfather.

Picking my way through the snow on the pathway made first by my brother, I caught my breath and felt my heart leap when my footfall flushed a pheasant out of a bush on my left side. Even though afraid of the overwhelming power I felt anytime I came close to the river, I walked over to examine the place in the snow where the pheasant had been. Next I was fascinated by her home. My small hands probed carefully into the neat little cave she had made for herself with soft grass and leaves. And I reheard the rustle of her wings in the air and felt the presence of the spirits around my shoulders. Awestruck by her life and the sense of her tiny heart beating within her breast just like mine, I unpinned the precious jade turtles and placed them in her nest as an offering. It

49

was my gift to the unseen power. But when I returned home and faced my mother's wrath, I went back to search for them and take back my gift. I did not find them that day, and I returned many more times that winter. Then I returned to search at each change of season for the next seven years. I never found them, and now there are no longer any people living in that place. But that first offering to the Goddess rebirthed the most powerful female voice in my consciousness. On that cold winter day when I lost my jade turtles, Aspasia, seer and prophetess who loved to ride dolphins in the Aegean, became my guide.

I am tall with a big barrel-chested body and small breasts. My hair is medium-length ringlets like a bunch of grapes, and I wear a heavy decorative headband of copper and semi-precious stones in my hair. My neck is thick and strong, my whole face is large with very prominent cheekbones, and my nose is long and perfectly straight. I am beautiful, a paradigm of Minoan beauty. I wear two or three sinews of coral beads that are woven and intertwined. They feel cool on my neck. I am wearing less clothing than usual, a flimsy gown with straps on my shoulders. I am standing on large stone blocks on an outdoor porch under grape arbor poles supported by stone pillars. I am standing with my hand rested on one of the pillars looking out at the side of a hillside. It is very warm and breezy, and this portico juts out of a steep hillside on the island of Thasos. The hillside is on my left, and the Aegean Sea on my right.

I turn around and my husband, Ahura, is sitting at a round table. He is dark—dark hair and beard. He has profuse dark hair on his chest. He sits with one leg crossed over the other, and the straps of his leather sandals come up to his knees. He wears a leather outfit covering his groin that resembles a small skirt, and he wears a leather collar with metal buttons rivited in it which covers his shoulders. It is military garb, crude and protective. It is strange, actually. I get a very powerful safe feeling from him, but I dislike soldiers.

He is telling me something important as he sits there staring out at the sea. He says, "We may lose the peace, Aspasia. People may come in boats from the west, and they may come to our city. And all the men are talking about how Pelias sent Jason and the Minyae in search of the Golden Fleece. Suddenly, I fear an invasion."

We are not at our house in the city now. We're at our hidden villa where we go to be alone. It is safe here; there is no danger now. This is our retreat, with only one room, and it is very wild out here. But I am

amazed. I am angry. No one can attack our city. It is forbidden! Our city is an oracle! It is a place of peace. We do not even have protective walls. If anyone would ever attack an oracle, it would be a sign of great disorder, great chaos on the earth. This oracle is a connecting link between Delphi and places to the east, to Araxes at the end of the Sea Euxine. The people to the east are very different from us, but I can communicate with them. There is also Dodona to the west, which is very important. We are in between, we are the link to the east from Delphi and Dodona. This is a very important oracle, and I was sent here after being trained on Crete. This oracle has been here for over a thousand years, before anyone can remember.

I am the goddess of the oracle. This is my house. I work here. I take care of it. I take care of all the services, anything that needs to be done. Different times of the year, we have certain things to do, like lighting fires, bringing oil, and anointing people. We burn the herbs, make scents that go into the wind, we purify the vibrations with water, and we vitalize the earth with our rituals. I read the stars. People bring the new crop, the new grapes, the new grains, the new animals, the lambs, the birds. They bring everything new, and we bless it at the oracle. The ryhthm is very, very beautiful. Our rituals balance the energies of the planet, and we are the ones who listen to the gods. We celebrate the newness, the new creation, the beauty, by marking the seasons. We have many pillars out in the front of the building, and we burn oil on the tops of them. Or we put out wooden stakes and burn oil and rags in them. Very, very brilliant fires at certain times of the year. The fires can be seen from the boats or from the forest. Up on the hillside of the city, the burning fires of the oracle signal its message.

We burn the fires at the change of the seasons—and when the emanation comes from the crevice. The emanation is when sulphur or white gas comes from the crevice. The oracle is built into the side of the mountain right next to the crevice, and it is the voice of the underworld. When the crevice is groaning, when the emanation comes, then we burn the fires. And we do that because we're very afraid of earthquakes. And if we burn the fire when the earth is groaning, then we will not be in danger.

We do this because we are in very close contact with the earth mother. We do not fear the groaning, but we feel that we have to respond to her communications. She communicates to us with her mists from the crevice, the sulphur. She communicates with the new life, with the new seasons. So we have many festivals. We have eight festivals.

When the plants are growing in the hot sun
And the people cease their labor,
It is the time of the first festival.

The sweet nectar in the grapes has risen
to a peak like the full noonday sun.
Like blood, life force beats in the grapes.
The priests and priestesses measure the orgiastic fullness
As the people increase their power.

With each seven year cycle,
The priests and priestesses come
Into their own sacred time.
Then the temple virgin and earth god
Fructify the earth together,
and empower the sacred places.
Some of the men and some of the women
Are seized with the sacred force.
They are come together uniting earth and sky
Like the rooted laurel reaching for the stars.
And Dionysius laughs as the people
Eat the fruit, drink the wine, and love in the field.

****

The second festival is the harvest festival.
As the days begin to shorten
And the nights turn cold,
When the women look with slanted eyes,
And the hearth awaits the first fires.

Sadly we gather in the village center,
As we look at our shrine, remembering
The heat in our body passions when
The sweetness was in the grapes, and

The meat sizzled on the spit.

We wait while the slow dirge begins, as
The dancers scrape bones against gourds,
And the people bring bundles of dry grain.
It is seed drying time, reed weaving begins anew.
Like the winter-woven blankets, a long
Story begins in our souls.

Year after year when the light wanes,
We re-weave and re-connect the webs
Of visitations and strange events,
With the sacred gods from far away in the sky,
And the unseen powers in the crevices and caves.

****

When the life forces have completely quieted
Like worms in hard-shelled spit cocoons,
The third festival for the passing
Of souls to the underworld begins as a journey
To the beginning place for each one of us.

The unpassed souls glut our village
And clutch at our throats like desperate
Men drowning, who grasp for a raft,
Like a mother who snuffs the life of her babe
Lest she lose her cock-swollen lover.

We are the ones left here to
Plant, birth, weave, to breathe air for life.
So, as the miasma thickens of the departed ones
Who spy on our nightly rituals and
Wait in the edges of our spaces when we are unaware,
Gently we persuade them, go, go now!

It is bravery we teach in
The ritual of the passage.
We strengthen their hearts and minds

For the long arduous journey back,
Back to the place to choose to return again.

****

At the time of the fourth festival,
The night sky is cold and clear, brilliant and dry.
This is when we become what we are,
We are light beings, just like stars,
The stars where we came from long ago.

Those who are ready—the ones who have
Journeyed through the caves to dark places,
The ones who moved the souls to the next realm—
They come forward like marathon runners,
Strengthened for their journey.

If you were to dream all night of
Falling over a cliff and landing on a
Bottom which is actually false, so that you
Fall throughout eternity, still
You would not have gone far enough.
This journey is beyond the last place of your soul.

No one speaks during this festival, and
No one who journeys speaks when they return.
We know who went, but we never know where they went.
I went once, and I learned how to speak and hear with
    my thoughts;
And, now you do not have to tell me anything, because I
    already know what it is.

We do not know where we went, but
After we return, we know where we are going.
The journey to the stars defines for all of us
Our place in the universe
And the quietest place in our hearts.

****

At the time of the fifth festival,
The light of the night and day
Are equal in the spring.
Like the fall, we balance the planet
so that the eternal cycle can begin again.

We disappear, all the priests and priestesses,
To the inner recesses of our temples.
We await the arrival of the pigeon from Delphi,
With amber burning, we wait in a circle
Around the omphalos, the center of the earth.

The Thasos pigeon sits quietly resting
In her cage of laurel while we meditate.
Suddenly, the air quickens at the equinox.
Every insect, bird, and animal feels it.
The cage is opened as the Thasos pigeon
Flies away to the east.

The messenger from Delphi drops
Exhausted onto a waiting perch, and
We are joyous in our hearts, for the mother
Has not groaned and belched sulphur in the crevice.
Now the planet is balanced, like the birds in flight.

The burning amber becomes a pool of resin,
And we emerge from the temple still
Fused and silent in our hearts, and
The bards slowly begin their stories to the people
Of the beginning of the world, the flood and fires.
Beginning anew, we bless the life cycle.

****

The sixth festival is for the people.
The work of the people feeds the mother.
We are all small against the gods,
But the celebration of our work
Is what gives joy to the gods.

The sixth festival is the blessing festival.
We present our fruits of the long winter nights.
To the gods, we offer our babes, our weaving, and our
  marriages.
We ask the gods to be one with us in our hearts,
So that our acts become divine,
Just like the water, wind, earth and fire.
And then we go to the fields to work after
This May festival of blessing.

****

The seventh festival follows quickly
When the heat of the sun is intense.
All the planting is completed, and
The earth turns so that the
Sun again will move away from the planet.
And the seeds can germinate because
They were planted deep and early.

Like the bursting seeds deep in the earth,
The people are also at the peak of their powers.
The people have their power when the planet
Is in the heat of the sun.
And the priests and priestesses are in their power
When they are nearest to the stars.

****

The eighth festival is the completion festival.
Like the first festival, the people are
Carried away by the life force of the plants.
The sun has done the work of making power in the fruit,
And like the sun, the male organ bursts with force.

The woman is stirred deep within by the force
Coming from the center of her being.
Truly she is the goddess in every way.
And yet, she is not the goddess, she
Still has her life: the baby, the husband, the hearth.

So, the people celebrate the
Favor of the gods. They celebrate
With wine, with feasting, with sloe-eyed
Looks of love—the way the gods
Also look at them.

As priests and priestesses, we
Acknowledge the favor of the gods and goddesses,
But, we retain our human lives.
We center the force, the power, in the temple.
And the temple is the center of us all.

****

I am the one who is in the temple, and all the festivals begin in the temple. I do the timing of the moon and of the stars, and it's up to me to start the fires at the proper time. As soon as people see us light the fires, they know it's time. People prepare for it, but no one quickens the energy until the fires are lit. We light the fires to balance the energy of our city with the cosmic energy, so that whatever we do at our festivals pleases the gods. It's a very happy and beautiful life.

Once the voice of the Goddess was again audible in my brain, a sense of magic was reborn in my consciousness. Like sirens wailing from the sea cliffs, the Goddess called irresistibly to me. For a few months into the spring of my fourth year I was silent as I listened to the voices in the wind, and in my inner ear I heard, "Come back, come back." At night I gazed out of my window over the river, and I heard new sounds which I sensed came from a distant time and place. The power of nature was a source of unspeakable terror to me at that time. There was a tornado nearby that spring, and I was sucked into a vortex of heart palpitations, shuddering, and sweating. I became a small mass of silent, wide-eyed terror. I became the tornado. No one could understand my behavior. "It's typical of children," they said. And then when the power of summer intensified, my inner sight awakened.

Again, I left behind the house of ringing phones, cooking, radio, and cars in the driveway, and I returned to the pathways through the woods to the river that I feared so much. I was not afraid of the little people in my grandmother's house, but I was terrified of the huge spirits in the old trees and the creatures behind the rocks near the river. Still I was drawn by the voices in the winds to return, return, return. My heart pounded in my chest so hard that I was sure I would burst as I rushed by the leering faces in the trees with their long arms and fingers reaching for the bright full-moon sky. The terror rose in my throat like hot acid, and I began to run madly. The faster I ran, just like the dreaded tornado, the greater the swirling fear. I tore my clothes as I neared the black river, and I scrambled up a rise near the crumbling dock, once used for ice-cutting.

I rushed along quickly through the tangled vines choking the way behind a neighbor's barn. She tended her land where the horses and goats grazed, but this was the scariest section because these pathways by the river were walked only by tramps, my brother, and me. As I got nearer to the garden behind the convent of the Catholic Church, the waves of fear finally lessened. I slowed down almost to a standstill as I suddenly felt waves of fusing light and sound. My body felt transported as dancing energy waves of light fused with pulsing humming sounds in my head. I was no longer on this earth as I know it.

I looked to my side into a low cliff of moist rock and tangled tree roots as I felt the presence of the little people. An old green wooden door manifested in front of me, and I passed through it into the cave that I always knew was there into the inner earth. I stepped slowly, careful not to lose my balance.

As I entered, a deep inner glow just like the soft moonlight outside began to light the sides of the cave. The luminescence was similar to the light I'd seen in the swamps at twilight, and a vision rose in the back of my eyes. It was a sight like the glow in a cats' eyes. Then time ceased entirely as the vision before me unfolded. The entire cave, way back into the reaches of the inner earth, was made of millions of precious gemstones, as if the thoughts of angels had materialized in rock. Sapphires, rubies, emeralds, crystals, amethysts, and diamonds all glowed with inner light. And from then on, the sight of Aspasia was mine again. I raced through the woods on the night of the full moon, walked into my cave, and I found the Goddess within.

It is I, Aspasia. I am at Delphoi, standing on a twelve-foot wide stairway of cut and smoothed stone with two huge rectangular stones at the bottom. It's a chilly, breezy, slightly cloudy day. As I look from where I stand on the stairway, I see I am up high in very hilly country. To my left is a great view of rough mountains, forests, and some meadows; to my right, I can see the bright blue sea in the far distance. It's a bay or the sea. It's very rocky here and cold. Behind me stands a small group of very important people connected with this place, plus two of my people, and there is a great crowd of people out in front of me in front of the steps. As I look behind myself, the stairway goes up three broad steps, and then there is a wide stone promenade which is about two hundred feet long.

The stone I'm standing on is light stone. It is very ancient, and the stones are very flat. The stone wall on the sides is four to six feet high all along the way. We're standing in front of the promenade that leads to the sacred mountain. At the end of the promenade, there is a rocky hillside, and then it's steep. It rises about fifteen hundred feet.

I'm standing up on the second step. I turn around, and I walk up the steps very, very slowly. I'm in a trance. I'm not in a trance when I look at the people, but as soon as I turn, I go into a trance. I start to walk up the rectangular block steps, and I raise the energy through my body. My first awareness is the energy—it's in my feet. And I raise it up, right up through my body, through to my inner chest, and I breathe in all the energy round me. More or less, I breathe in the vibrations around me.

I'm breathing in the vibrations of the people. And this is very special, to be able to have their energy. They are here to gift me with energy. The people are all in a state of transcending anticipation. They feel absolutely grounded in the very moment of being here. The very moment of being here is of great significance. It's the spirit of a mass of people, between 3,000 and 10,000 people are out there. I can see 3,000 in the front. But then, there are many more behind, coming up the roads. The roads are very difficult to walk on. They come from great distances, and it is a sacred walk to come here.

So I turn, and then I have the energy of each one individually in the back of my shoulders, up the back of my neck and into the back of my head. And then at the same time, I'm raising the energy from the earth up into my upper chest area. As I raise the energy, it feels thick, dense, and then it becomes electrical. As soon as I raise the energy to my upper chest area and feel a burning in my hands, I raise my hands forward. I raise my hands with the palms open toward the oracle, toward the mountain. I create an electrical force in my hands which I send to the oracle.

The people are behind me, behind those stairs and down the hill, and I'm facing the oracle. There are a few important people on each side of me. They were behind me as I stood at the steps, but as soon as I turned, they all moved to my side. I'm beginning to feel the energy.

I'm feeling it from the people through my shoulders. And it's so powerful it makes me feel thick in the upper part of my body, my shoulders, the back of my neck. It makes my whole head and upper part feel very thick. It's in waves, and it's surging like a heartbeat. I'm in tension between turning to stone versus being electrified. The way I keep from turning to stone, becoming too magnetized and absorbent, is to take my hands, and place the palms toward the oracle. It has to do with the will. As soon as I turn my hands toward the oracle and connect the positive and negative charges, then it's my choice. I accept the energy from all the people, and what they wish from me, but I then discharge it to the oracle. I was taught as a Minoan priestess to take and direct energy in ritual. It is as if I am the first swan in a V formation in flight.

I've come here before. I've had conversations with the Lycoreian guardians, meetings, but this is the first time I've come as the one to lead a ritual. Rituals occur when it's the right time for the energy to come. And that has something to do with the seasons on earth as well as the planets. The oracle is a spring that connects to the power in the earth.

I came here because, as astrologer-seer, I informed them of an astrological event. The guides who are in charge of the care of the oracle know when the oracle itself has energy. So this is a time when the oracle has energy and the planets have energy. I informed the people of the oracle that the right planetary configuration would occur at this time. Many have come to the oracle because the Aegean people fear the future now. I'm the Thracian seer. Jason has departed on the journey for the Golden Fleece, and the oracle of Phoebus was similar to my vision.

As soon as I extend my hands so that I can move forward, I don't feel the heavy weight of the stone-like energy from the people any more. I just feel very energized. I feel light. I walk about five feet, I step very deliberately, I feel great grounding in my feet. My head is raised up, I'm looking forward. I reach a certain point and then stop. At this point, I don't feel the energy.

Now the guides turn and put their hands toward the oracle. They begin to walk forward with the same deliberate steps that ground our feet so well. We walk forward; there are seven including me, three on each side. They come up behind me after they lift their hands. They put a robe or a mantle on my shoulders. And then all the people of the Aegean are contained in the mantle. It's heavy with a hood. It covers my body , and the back of it touches the stone as I walk. The robe is earth-colored with a medium-blue panel covering most of the front, with five gold stars on my breast. The minute they put it on me, there's a strange feeling of them getting their hands off as fast as possible. It's like when you're touching a live electric wire; you want to get your hands off as fast as possible. As they put it on my shoulders and on my body, it becomes electrified. This is not a surprise to them. On each side there are six hands, and they "off" their hands from it. As they do that, it also puts more energy into it. The robe is very old, it's very coarse. It's at least hundreds of years old.

Oh, this is marvelous. What I feel in this robe as soon as they off the energy is like wearing the earth, the dirt. This robe is from the past age when the earth energy was a power that gave people emanations and power. This robe is the same sienna color as the stones, that beautiful orange, earth brown color, and the midnight blue front with the stars is from the days of the five twin kings of Atlantis. The robe doesn't obstruct my hands. I continue to keep my hands facing toward the oracle.

Now the energy is throughout my whole being and not just in the upper part of my body as I go alone. The guides in some way give the people the sense of what's happening, but the people do not see. No one is going to see. Seeing is not it—the people are experiencing what I'm doing, but they don't see it. It's telepathic, in their chest, in their heart chakra. It's like the people have a television in their chests. And they actually can see me walking forward. And my six guides are able to do this with the people. I'm aware that all the people are experiencing it also, as I begin to go to the oracle. But the guides stay with them.

I start to walk forward in stages. I can't go into the next stage until I can feel that the people have been connected to what I'm doing by the guides. I know just when it happens. It is when I get the first experience of the power of the oracle. It is a focalized energy, it's like something that's in place in the oracle. But also, as I begin to walk forward, I myself carry the structure of the planets.

When I'm on the earth, I feel my body is the earth. My consciousness is that the earth is flat and everything is in a sky-bowl with the stars in the bowl. As I move forward, I am the earth in the very top of my head, and I am aware of the structure of the planets, stars, universes, and galaxies. I'm taking it to the oracle in a circular sense because my body is the earth. I'm in the center of it, and everything's around me. I am at the center of being.

But, I carry with me, on the very top of my head, the whole solar system. And I'm going to carry the solar system structure to the focalized point. I have visual awareness of where the stars are and where the planets are. In other words, my tool for carrying the astrological placement to the oracle is geocentric astrology. But in actuality, I exist in a heliocentric universe.

Only those who can understand the use of energy in that way, can do astrology. The temple priests choose and initiate neophytes who live on earth and in the sky simultaneously to be astrologers. On the earth plane, the whole cosmos, the whole consciousness of the cosmos is being lived out as a drama. And only through the astrological analysis can we read the drama in time. We carry the sense of where the earth is going around the sun in relationship to all the other planets, but the actual reading of the drama, the actual focalization of the playing out of this drama through time, is on the earth. The earth is the seat of consciousness of this solar system and of this galaxy. As far as the other galaxies, I don't know.

It's one hundred-fifty feet more, and I've gone thirty feet. And in the last twenty feet, I have organized my logical power consciousness of the placement of things from earth and from the sun. and now I get up to this point, about thirty feet from the oracle to a transition point. It is a dichotomy point.

I'm afraid to walk. I'm afraid to do it. It's a sense of the necessity to step out over to the other side. I'm trying to carry these structures, and the energy is no problem. It just stays with me as I walk. But to carry the structures over to the other side, I let the energy take me. It is the only way to the other side. And so, I start to step, and every step is very, very difficult, and very significant. The whole planet is here. And I have some struggles with will, with the will trying to intrude. I let go and just let the light come. The light is rays of shooting light, and now the whole sky is radiant rainbow energy.

I'm happy to see that light again. It's very beautiful. I'm walking, and behind the mountain and the whole sky, all around, is like shimmering crystals. It's incredible. Every step that I move forward intensifies the light, the energy—electrical energy. I have to keep on walking because the energy has made a tunnel of light. It's pulsating all around, but it has made a tunnel in front of me leading to the oracle.

I have to walk into the tunnel. And I'm not afraid to walk into the tunnel. I will walk into the tunnel of light. The air is turbulent outside the tunnel, and the light pulsations also hum. Sound and light are the same wave lenghth at this point. What I want to do more than anything else is feel it a lot. But if I feel it, it will destroy me.

It's being done to me by the higher forces, and if I stop, I will be atomized. It's like when Persephone is falling through the tunnel, and if she looks back, she's destroyed. This is a key. I'm afraid of this right now. This is why I was so rigorously trained on Crete. It is at this point priestesses fail. Before, Persephone was going away from the light and being sucked through the earth. She was told by her guides that if she looked back once, she would stay in the underworld instead of journeying through the deep.

So at this point, I am very aware that if I do not go forward as I'm told and look back, then I will be destroyed. I'm coming to the transition point. What's on the other side is the total giving in. But when I reach the last point where the evil forces can stop me, this maximum point, that is when the humming seduction, the beautiful light-sound wave fusion is the most alluring. That is when I most want to stop and experience it. I'm going to keep on going.

That seduction, that humming pull is all around me, and there is a tunnel made by some force that I'm supposed to pass through. And if I go forward, and if I do not look back, then the humming and the light vibration cannot destroy me. I'm just about ready to walk through the tunnel. I'm walking all the time.

If I do not continue to proceed, then the tunnel is destroyed. The force protection, the vault, is destroyed. And then all of those forces come in, right to me, and destroy me. Now at that point, I'm coming to the maximum point, and it's all humming and pulsating, and it's pushing on the vault. The vault is like the most intense pounds-per-square-inch pressure on something. It's like being inside the iris of an eye. It's a vault-shaped tunnel from just in front of me all the way to the oracle. And what's important is that every step I take closer to the beginning of this tunnel, the outside forces, vibrations and light, are pushing, pounding, harder and harder and harder.

As I come just to the point where I'm going to go through this barrier, I'm aware again of my guides. And my guides are helping me now. The shape of the vault is rounded, almost like a half of a lemon. It's the ideal shape to keep the evil forces from breaking through, to destroy the light. These forces are disguising themselves as the light and sound fusion energy, but they are low astral forces.

The guides manifest themselves on my side, three on each side. And on the physical plane, this is confusing because they're way back there. But on the causal plane, there's no problem. And they are there because they're going to take the robe away. And they also take all my clothes off. I wonder whether I like this or not. It doesn't matter whether I like it or not. I am nude, and I shiver.

Ahead there is a force field at the passage point. It seems to be a blackish-gray, eight-inch thick glass wall. Now, they put the robe back on, so now I'm wearing only the robe. It goes over my shoulders, and then all the way behind, and the stars are on the front, and I am naked. And they have done this because I have not looked back. They did not know until now whether I would look back, nor did I. What I feel now is great joy, a feeling of celebration, from all of the people and from the gods, because I did not look back.

Now the barrier is gone, and I step forward. The barrier is nothing! As if I had created it in my own mind. The astral light and the humming ceases, and everything on the physical plane is as it was before all that rainbow light energy manifested. I have twenty-five to thirty feet further to go to the oracle. I'm beginning to see it, and it looks like a large alcove, a carving or altar in the rock. But I can't see it very well yet.

I'm walking through two rows of columns. The columns are not really very big, but as I walk between them, they seem very big. They are twenty feet tall. I'm walking through them now, and it's a very regal feeling.

Now I just walk to the oracle. There's a fascia on the oracle that is man-made, made out of tufa stone, which is light and porous. It's crude, Greek. There is an archway. I stop in front of the oracle, and I kneel. And I put my hands in front of my heart and bend my head. Then I put my hands one on each side of the fascia. There's a place for my hands, and I lift myself up. I can't go through! Inside is a red rock shelter around a hole to the center of the earth. I can hear the sounds of the earth from that hole.

I want to put my ear on the hole. My desire is to be as close to the hole as I can be, so I turn my body sideways and get on my knees and bend my shoulders over. I put my right ear as close to the hole as I can, but I can't put it through because the fascia is in front of where the hole is. The oracle is in this hole inside the red stone.

I know the hole is connected to the ancient underground river which also runs through Arcadia and under Dodona. The height of the stone enclosure around the hole is about three feet high, and the fascia in my way is about eight feet tall. but I bend in just the right way to get my ear close enough to the hole. But I cannot say what I hear. It is one of the secrets.

But a voice resonates deep within my consciousness and says,

"Of course, these things are carefully guarded, but it is all right for you to tell me, because I already know."

And so, I hear in my inner ear, "The story is of the ages. and before this age was another age, and before that, was another age. Now is a time when we have to be able to get the energy, get the vision so that we can tell the people that the end of this age, the Third Age, is going to come. Now the sound echoes, it's almost a sense of sound going through the whole cosmos. It's the echoing sound of the hearing of timelessness. It is as if I have moved through the iris and into the labyrinth of the ear canal. I get the vision on the earth plane for a reason. I get the vision that the end of the age comes because the disharmony, the karma, the balances, have been disturbed. Again, the sound echoes.

"The human beings are confused about this problem, but it is not their fault. The humans experience that the vibrations are being disturbed, and when they have those experiences, they think they cause those disturbances. But they are experiencing the disturbances because the last planet outside Pluto has reached its greatest distance away from the earth and is moving closer again. Each time it returns, the orbits and spin of the planets are unbalanced. And this time, Venus is destabilized. The key is Libra, and the Egyptians worship Maat because of this ancient cycle. As the planet moves in, the karmic cycles of humans are accelerated. It is not the fault of the humans that this age is going to end and the next age is going to come. It happens because of the disturbance of the vibrations by the last planet. And when the vibrations are disturbed, they must be reestablished. There is no choice about this.

"So the humans are very confused about whether it's their fault or not. The humans know when the vibrations are disturbed. Lately, the weather has been extreme, and many people have strange illnesses. The beings on the other planets also know that the vibrations are disturbed. So, guilt is not the issue. Responsibility is the issue only in the sense that all humans have the responsibility to try to raise the vibration level as much as possible. That is, they must encounter their karma by raising their spiritual awareness to the point where they no longer fear death. But if they cannot do it, they are not guilty. Karma is only an issue on the human plane. Karma has to do with the emotional plane and with the perfection of the emotional plane. This larger cycle is an issue of the vibrations on the causal plane, and that is another issue. The humans are very confused about the difference. Those few humans who develop their consciousness beyond physical space and linear time are free of fear of this cycle.

"The vibrations on the causal plane are the issue of Saturn, and the vibrations on the human plane, the emotional plane, are ruled by Venus. And the emotions on the earth plane are ruled by the moon. But we're talking about the upper planes, the causal issues. So there's a difference between the human karmic level of vibration, and the causal vibration level of the whole cosmos."

As I hold my ear near the hole to the center of the earth, I see and hear a vision of the end of the world as I know it. And then I am supposed to tell the people my vision, because the oracle tells me that I have to. The human instruction is that certain people among the people who are left on the earth must be given the ultimate opportunity to either survive physically or to survive psychically. If they die physically, they will be able to reincarnate with causal knowledge.

But next I receive some very bad news. I am told that I will fall. I will experience a long series of uneventful lives of low awareness. This is where there is a connection between karma and the vibrations. The connection is that when the age ends and the new age begins, the people who incarnate during that next age have to live through the growing from nothing. They have to re-experience the human plane (the evolution). And this is very hard for them. The soul in people still senses, and in some cases actually finds out, as I am now, that this is the story of the ages. The higher reality remains deep in human memory as the earth plane falls when it goes through the cataclysmic cycle.

I feel very disturbed, sad, to know that I will fall, because I don't want to fall. Who wants to fall? But I am given a very special gift. I am told that I am not alone, that I will always have my daughter, Dacia, one way or the other. In other words, as I go through the fall, she will be with me. This to me is a great gift. As I hear about the coming cataclysm, I think only of her.

Next, a gray fog barrier goes over the hole. I don't see it, I just know. Out there they also know, and I get up and step backwards. I do not want the guides or the people to see my nakedness from the front side. This is not modesty. The real true nakedness should only be seen by the higher forces.

I step backwards about four or five steps, and my guides are behind me again. They take off the robe and put my other robe back on. I feel a great kind of emotion, a communal sort of happiness with them. We don't show it because all the people are coming forward, thousands of them. They all come up from the sides and climb over the rocks. Once the sacred experience is over with, they can climb all over the place. They're all streaming up. But my feeling toward my guides is that I really want to talk to them about this, but we are still in ceremony because the people are all coming up. So they stand there with me, all seven of us, in a concave standing formation.

On my right side is Lucia, a neophyte in my temple. Dacia is 12; she cannot come with me, so Lucia is her stand-in. Dacia needs to know, and when I get the information in the vision, Lucia helps Dacia somehow. It is a great honor for Lucia to be there with me at this ceremony. She is young, she is inexperienced, she does not understand very much, but she knows what to do.

On my left stands Dionysius. He's very dark, looks Moorish, with dark skin. He's all rough and hairy. He seems to be my guard, a soldier, but is also enlightened. Then there are two people from the Delphoi on each side of my people next to me. The Delphic priests wear burgundy cotton robes with gold ties around the waist, Lucia wears a white robe, and Dionysius the guard wears a tunic open on the shoulders. It has leather around the waist almost to the knees, and he wears sandals.

We've done it, really done it well. I was called to Lycoreia because all the Keepers of the Oracles of the Minoan kings of the sea and islands have been told about my vision of red fire in the sky three weeks ago in my temple at Thasos. Just after my vision, the springs at Melos, Delphi, and Dodona ceased to have water. We know the meaning of these signs because our storytellers sing with the cithara and tell of the ancient times. We do not fear the future, we only wish to know the will of the gods.

As I reintegrated Aspasia into my consciousness during my early childhood, many acute sensations were activated. The reality I was born into was very bland, and the people around me seemed to be dedicated to living a "normal" life. Great energy was expended conforming and following the plan of post-World War II America. But the force of Aspasia inside me simply made all that impossible. So, I was a wild little girl which upset just about everybody. And there really was no hope. If only they could have understood how hard I was trying to please them! But I didn't fit. I was in the wrong place. I felt like I'd been dropped out of a tree in the middle of everybody's life. And the dilemma was a serious one. There were things going on around me that drove me crazy. I used to listen for the calls of migrating geese, cranes and swans. When I heard them, I would stop and listen to their messages and watch the way of their flight. But, then, my father would build duck blinds and sit in the early morning with his gun, waiting to shoot the birds! I tried to organize myself according to behavior expected of me that I could not conform to. And gradually I disintegrated inside.

Then something remarkable happened. Almost as if I understood intuitively that I was caught on the wheel of karma and could never escape, I became fascinated by train wheels. When I was five, I would watch the wheels turning round and round and become mesmerized. And at the same time, I was becoming very fearful of death. Almost every day I thought a disaster would come; the house would burn up; the ghosts in my closet and under my bed would get out and get me; or I would fall in the river and be sucked into the deep.

So, one day I began watching the train wheels slowly turning as a freight train moved along the tracks behind my school. We were out for recess that day. I thought nobody was watching me as I moved closer to the approaching train. As if drawn to an irresistible solution that I almost knew better than life, I threw myself in front of the wheels and looked up at the giant metal monster. Something snapped deep inside just as I became aware of my mother on the other side. I shoved with my knees and feet, clutching the metal rail, and catapulted myself forward over the tracks as the train bumped my buttocks.

I didn't remember anything else. But for quite a while I stopped seeking power in the caves and woods. There was something in my attempt to end my young life that made me listen a little bit more to adults and their words of caution. Danger was a condition that I would have to assess.

Chapter Four

THE RAPE OF LYDIA
AND THE LABYRINTH

Awareness of inner power connection came too fast, too soon. I catapulted into spherical time by age five and could not ground myself into my kindergarten reality. I spend the year sleepwalking at night, wandering lost during the day, and sitting under trees waiting for the sky to fall in. My favorite fairy tale was "Chicken Little." I was often found in the middle of the night walking as if lost to all time and place, and I barely remember what I was thinking about. In fact, I remember more about what I was thinking about thousands of years ago than I do then. That is because I was beginning to orient myself in the present for the first time. And because the memories of Lydia were karmic resonances with my own family, it was my pain from Lydia's that lifetime flooded my awareness as I grounded myself into the lifetime as Barbara.

I wear a blue robe with my face covered by a shroud. I am outdoors, and there are people around. They are behind me, talking loudly, and they whisper my name. Lydia, Lydia. I'm 22. It's not that they are talking about me, nor am I respected. I am a fallen woman. I do not like to be here when they are here. I leave because they bother me.

I'm walking up a pathway, and then I come close to an area where people live. There are mud-brick houses, hovels, with one ten-by-twelve-foot room. There are doors in the front, wooden doors, and there are openings—windows, I guess. They have straw on the floors inside. Now I'm moving further into the city. Those hovels were on the outside. And as I get in further, the streets are really narrow, and the buildings are two or three stories tall. As I walk on the sidewalk, sometimes I'm walking under the buildings' overhanging second stories. I am really alone. I have a feeling that I can walk where I want

71

to walk.

I can go where I want unless I am in someone's way. The married women cannot do it. If they do, they will end up like me. I am a prostitute. I have no family, no parents. I feel like I am a dog in the streets, like I have to take care of myself. I wear a big piece of blue fabric over my shoulders and head. My hair is covered. The nicest time of day is the daytime. Then I can walk to the stream unless I am in someone's way. But then I have to go to work. It's what I have to do the rest of the time, and I don't like it at all. But at least when I walk down through the streets or go by the water for a while, I can do what I want to do even though people talk about me.

I stop and go into a shop on the first floor for bread and cheese. The cheese is a ball the size of a baseball, and the bread is thick and heavy. The bread is spherical and flat on the bottom. I pay for it with a round copper coin about as big as a quarter. There is the head of a person on it, and I can see the letters "X" and "I". As I think of it, my city is Lastra in Assyria on the river Lethe. I eat some of my bread and cheese and put the rest of it in a burlap satchel I carry under my robe. My robe is coarse, hot, and scratchy. But I have to be covered up. I do not show my face. I am a pariah. I buy my bread and cheese quickly before they drive me out of the shop.

I am walking up the street again. I have nothing on my feet. My skin is white, my hair is matted and dirty. I don't like that money. That is the way it is. I am miserable. I open a wooden door into a three-storied building. I pass through an empty room in front and go up a flight of narrow stairs to a hallway. It's light in here, even though the window openings are small, because the sun outside is blinding. I go down the hallway and into my small room. There is a small wooden bed about the size of a cot with a woven mat on the bed. There is one simple wooden chair in the room. There is light coming through a window. Outside, I see over the red-tiled roofs of other buildings. This is like a dormitory room, a little space I stay in.

I put the blue robe on the cot, and now I wear a simple white shift with a rope around the waist which goes to my knees. I have hairy legs, my body is sturdy with big breasts. I get my bread and cheese and go down the hall opposite to the way I came into my room. I am going to the back of the building, and there are lots of other doors onto this hallway. There's a courtyard in the back, and other girls are there. We eat lunch, talk, pass bread, cheese, and fruit. We all wear loose clothes. It is hot.

We talk about our families, about kids—not our kids. We don't mention what we have to do.

Soon a man comes, and we have to go with him. He's big, he's wearing a gray robe, and he's fat. He's about fifty with gray hair. He is in control of us, and we go with him. We walk down the street. There are six or seven of us, and he drops us off one by one at different houses. When he drops me off, he stops at a door and rings a bell. He pulls it with a string, and it has a high-pitched sound. He's opening the door as he rings the bell. I have my hood on again. We all wear our hoods as we go down the street. Then I go in.

There is a man waiting for me. He is overweight, drunk, and he smells. He makes me drink some wine. I don't want it; it is sour. He wears a burgundy tunic. The house has some fabric-covered furniture with stone floors instead of straw. He makes me drink more wine, and then he takes my robe off. I don't say anything, and he just screws me. He puts me on this reclining cot, he lays me down, he forces my legs apart, and he pushes his thick meat in. He doesn't take long, and he grunts like a pig. I feel nothing. I am disassociated from my body. I don't know when I learned that. I just want it to be over with as soon as possible. I don't have any choice.

But what I think about is the money. He pays me. I have two pockets in my shift. I put some of the money in one pocket and some in the other. I'm supposed to give it all to that man who came for us. But none of us do that. We all take some. I have to get the money. Otherwise, I'd be in trouble. When he pays me, he pulls it out of his pocket and shoves it in my hand. It is forty . . . It's three coins, one silver, one bronze or copper, and one is very small. The other two are about the same size as the coin I bought the bread and cheese with. I put the copper one in this little sewn-in pocket, and I put the other two in the regular pocket.

I am a commodity, that's all it is. I feel energy in the hand where he put the money. And I feel energy in my heart. I'm really miserable and sad. I am lifeless in the rest of my body. I have no feelings. I just have to do that. But there is another part of me that has a lot of feelings . . .

I remember what caused it all. I was 13 or 14 and was in an alley with my brother who is a little younger than me. Suddenly, there were rushing figures grabbing me. We're behind a building somewhere. My brother tries to help me, but he can't do anything about it. There are three of them. They shove me down, tear off my lower clothes while they shove me in the face. They shove my face so they can't see it. My brother is screaming and pulling at them. They hit him hard; one of them pulls him away while another one wrenches my legs apart. Then the pain—the pain is unbelievable. And I cannot pass out. I have to feel it all, but this is the last time I will feel it.

Later, I came dragging home. My mother is very sad. But my father! He is mad at me! My brother and I were going someplace we weren't suppose to go. My brother is terrified at what they'll do to him. My mother washes me slowly later. She is very sad. And that's the end, the end. My father—my father is mad at me.

My father is mad at me. So that was 600 or 700 AD. But deeply engraved in my body was the sense that a woman has little control over what happens. What a woman's father does determines what happens to a large extent. Women can work hard and make things better, maybe, but in the long run, the controlling factor is men.

But this time the three fates had something quite complex in mind for me. I became increasingly morbid when I was five and six, the oppressiveness with this life intensified, but other inner voices fought to be heard. Psyche searched in the deepest well of my unconscious mind those early years and taught me the way out during sleepwalking. I walked through the hallways, staircases, and rooms of our large house and never once bumped myself. For I was recovering the inner illumination that Aspasia learned from the Masters on Crete when she was initiated in the Labyrinth..

The maze . . . the maze . . .   I remember it as a ritual designed to destroy all fear. The maze was completely dark, so that only the sense of touch and the inner senses were available for getting me through. There were no inherently harmful portions of the maze. The myth of the Minotaur was perpetuated by the priests to make sure that only serious initiates would attempt the education: It was used as a screening process. There were, however, priests present in the maze who would make sounds as they passed by me, would sometimes touch me using various animal parts or masks which would suddenly be illuminated for my awareness of their presence. And, of course, there was a bull stored in one portion of the maze. The bull, which would be sacrificed as a part of the early festivals, was kept in the dark and fed, and his grunting and snorting noises and discomfort would instill fear in the prospective initiates. His quarters were enclosed so that there would be no possibility of making contact, that particular danger not being necessary. The task of getting through the maze was to overcome fear.

The major lesson was that the only enemy of intuitive knowing and of the inner sense guiding one to what one needs, is fear.

The only way I could release myself from the maze was to rely entirely on fear to be released, so that intuition would guide me with an inner light. The maze was tied in with a particularly powerful *coordination point*, or power point in that area. Coordination points have psychic maps contained within them, accessible to an individual who can use altered states of consciousness. These maps are used to provide points of resonance, release, and deflection. The maze was the map of the coordination points on Crete. So, I was forced to develop the capacity to release myself from fear and to open myself to the presentation of the map. With proper awareness, I would have no trouble finding my way out of the maze. Also, my lesson was the deprivation of use of the physical senses in order to stress the importance of developing intuition. And yet, the priests passing by me in the dark would touch me with the stuffed animal parts to allow me to realize that, again, fear accessing through the physical senses, blocks intuition.

Generally, initiates were left in the maze three days. If we did not find our way out, we were removed, and no further training would take place, whereupon we would be tested a second time. If, upon the third testing, we could not be released from the maze, then the training was finished. Through various hypnosis methods, most of what we had learned would be erased from our memory, except those things which would help us in the course of life to be a fulfilled and happy person. I passed through the maze on my second trip.

This was a particularly interesting experience for the individuals who were testing me, because I demonstrated powers which they had not yet taught me and which would have been a part of my training after I had released myself from the maze. I created a sense of illumination which allowed me literally to see my way through the maze. Now, this was not light *per se*, as in a torch, but I did create (through accessing the map of the coordination points) an inner illumination which allowed me literally to see in the total darkness.

The priests who were attempting to frighten me were suddenly surprised by being illuminated by lights other than the torches which they carried to use in presenting the horrifying masks. I was then selected for special education in divination and astrology. As Circe noted when Medea fixed her gaze upon her at Aea, "For all children of the sun were easy to recognize, even from a distance, by their flashing eyes, which shot out rays of golden light."

The island on the river behind my childhood home, Ojibway Island, was a sacred site to the Sauks and those before them, and later to the Pottawatomie and Ojibway. The site of the sacred great white oak tree of the Sauks was in front of my home. When the white men came to this valley in the early 1800s, the great white oak tree well over 500 years old stood on the side of the trail. Every spring, the Sauk, and later the Pottawatomie, would wait for the return of the great white owl who would sit in the tree during the hot summer. In the fall, when it was time to pass the souls of the tribe, the white owl did the service for the Indian nation. The great white owl flew over great Lake Huron with his massive wings and passed the souls into the great deep waters. The Sauks passed their souls with white owl, but by 1700, the Ojibway and Pottawatomie had forgotten the reason for the owl's flight.

White man came and observed this old pagan obsession. The priests disliked it intensely, and now a Catholic Church sits on the site of the tree. White man cut the great oak tree by the side of the trail, and when the great white owl returned to serve the few Indians left in the valley, the white owl had no place to roost. And if too much time lapses when the souls cannot be passed by the living, then the relatives, children who have been trained in the great wisdom of the past, will return to bring the energy of the great white owl.

As I moved out into the larger culture as is natural with most six-year-olds, the inner voices or past lives resonated with my experiences, as is always the case with the inner mind and consciousness. I began experiencing a division in my awareness as the inner voices lending their experiences to everyday living seemed to be one side of myself, and the inner voices responding to mother nature and the power of the ghosts around me from times past were another side. The Victorian Lady, Lydia, the Roman, and Erastus formed much of my inner awareness of what it was like to be a growing girl in the 1940s and 1950s. And Aspasia, Ichor, and the Druid were the source of inner reactions to the voices of the Native Americans of the Saginaw Valley and the profoundly rich swamps and waters of Saginaw Bay. It almost seemed like Lydia, Erastus, the Victorian Lady, and the Roman lived in the house, and the high initiates of ancient times lived with me in nature and in the night. I kept continually searching for experiences in this lifetime that helped me to fit better into my reality. Otherwise, I was obsessed by a sucking fear of being overwhelmed by a dark churning force that reminded me of the dreaded tornadoes.

The Victorian Lady liked to be in church. When I was six, I began sneaking over to the Catholic church two doors away that was built over the roots of the great oak tree. Early in the mornings, I would kneel in the pew close up to the front altar smelling the incense, and one summer morning, I stared into the red sanctuary lamp and found myself walking on a high grassy hillside south of San Francisco.

I am 20 or 21. It's very sunny, the grass is golden and tall, and I sense the ocean pounding on the rocks to the west. My hair is long, light brown and silky, and I wear it on the top of my head. I wear a white cotton Gibson-style summer garden dress with a high neck and a pendant with a large cut ruby set in pearls. I am lovely. I'm walking on a pathway in the hills through yellow grass, and the wind billows my long skirt. I am tall, elegant, strong, and I am striding. I have prominent eyebrows slightly darker than my hair, white and pale skin, and blue eyes. My mouth is soft and turns down slightly.

My dress rustles in the wind, the pathway is narrow, my shoes are tight because that is the fashion, and the only freedom I feel is in the wind. I love nature, it makes me free. But this is a captured image of the Victorian Lady when I was young, and soon thereafter, I even gave it up myself . . .

I sit in a sunny room, the front parlor of my home with a large bay window. The floorboards are soft pine, the woodwork is heavy carved redwood, and the room is crowded with Victorian pieces, oriental rugs and artifacts. But I do not really see all the clutter. I see the sunlight streaming in the bay window and onto the floor next to the rocking chair I sit in. I am leaning back slightly with one leg crossed over the other and gazing out the window with my facial expession set. I am trying to ignore my aunt, who is speaking to me. As she speaks, the ghost of my dead mother floats in the corner up near the ceiling. It is odd, very odd, for I sense I couldn't see my mother at the time. Perhaps if I could have, I would have won against my aunt. Oh, her voice, her voice, it will not go away.

"You will do it. You can't change your mind now because you said you would do it. All the plans are made. You will marry him as you promised."

I got pressured into it, and I agreed to do it, but I never really wanted to. And then I tried to get out of it. But now they're just determined. And it's a really funny situation because before, everything was supposed to be just perfect. Big wedding, everything arranged, and now she doesn't care whether I rearrange for another wedding or anything. Even if I went off and married him that night, that would be acceptable. My aunt is afraid of my energy, but his family is extremely well-to-do.

There's definitely a financial advantage, but I still consider myself to be better than he. And she does, too. I don't like him as a person at all. He's uptight, and he has no sensitivity whatsoever. He's not my romantic ideal at all. The men in my family are adventurous and a lot of fun.

When I make my decision about him, I'm in a church by myself, kneeling at a pew. I'm looking at the altar. The church is very beautiful—beautiful stained glass, beautiful wood. It's Catholic. And I can smell incense. It's a real old Catholic church, and I have a sense of ritual going on there, of depth. I feel like I also have no choice from the Church. There's something in my personality that doesn't really fit very well with this, but it is the only place I feel the past, feel a connection with something secret, intense, and haunting. I'm here because I think that this is the real meaning of life; it's the real truth in here. And physically, in my heart, I almost rebel while I'm here, spirit-wise. And I'm marrying—I'm deciding to marry him because I'm supposed to become really Catholic. And he's a really strict Catholic.

I'm a convert. I became a convert when I was 16 as did my sister. I am in the church praying, and as I make my decision to marry him, I feel a door closing inside. But, I have been thoroughly conditioned to ignore my feelings. In my body I feel this pushing all over my head, a clamping on the back of my head. And I feel all this heaviness in my shoulders and the back of my head.

This means that I'll leave California. He's from Chicago, and I don't like Chicago at all. It's cold and forbidding, and it's his family and his business. Everything is like walking into a jail.

As I kneel in the church in Saginaw, Michigan, I wonder about my heavy, sad shadow. It's almost like I have two bodies in this one body. I feel like she's not dead yet, and I feel too much of her affect. It foreshadows this life, and I come into this church all by myself almost as if I want her to tell me what she wants. Perhaps if I knew, then Aspasia calling from deep within could have her place, too. After all, I am female in this incarnation and therefore finding female power is my true path. Perhaps the Victorian woman even felt Aspasia deep within and now needs Barbara to release her power. I stare into the sanctuary lamp feeling the gray heaviness in my body. And I wonder what happened after she died and before I was born.

I am in the top of the church looking down at my body at my funeral. I'm not really interested in that body, but I am trying very hard to leave, to go up to the blue. I do not manage to leave. My husband, the children, and the nanny are sitting in the front row on the right side. All the people in the church loved me. There are 500 people in that church. A very important church dignitary does the requiem Mass. The casket is in front of the altar but down in the church, right up there by the front of the rows. It's closed now, but they had it open. It's amazing how many people are in that church.

They're there because they love me. There are poor people in the back, way in the back. They're afraid to come up because it's like a wall of armor up there, of clothes and hats and jewelry. And then behind it all, there are all of those poor people. And I touched all those people—really touched them. I did a lot of charity work. I was aware of Hull House, but I couldn't go and do that, because it was radical. I couldn't do that because of my social status. So I did the same thing as much as I could within acceptable channels. I wasn't just a rich woman giving money away. I cooked. I went to the soup kitchens in Chicago.

The only time I felt like I had anything of my own was when I got out of the house and went down and did that.

And in Chicago, everything is just so many people, and it's crowded. I was feeding, cooking and helping care for the immigrants coming in—helping with their children and their old people. I felt good energy in my heart and in my hands.

This was the only way I could make any use whatsoever of the unhappy life I had to live. At least I was rich and I could do this. If I were poor like these other people around me, I couldn't do it. So I'm grateful for the ability and the opportunity to at least do that. It was the only place where I really felt useful at all. And I didn't have the usual cut-off feeling that a lot of wealthy ladies have. I didn't feel cut off from people around me at all, and I don't think they felt cut off from me. They see my eyes or they touch my hands—something about me they can sense right away. That's why all these poeple are here. And it's embarrassing, because what happened was the upper class are there in the front rows, and not really very many considering his family. And there are just teeming masses of people, hordes of people, back in the church.

Rich people don't like those people. They're dirty and unwashed. And my daughter sees it. It's the first chance she has to see all these people. She stares at them with wide blue eyes. She doesn't understand, but it makes an impression.

There is a woman present at the funeral and in the house after I'm dead, who's connected to my husband. I get the feeling he's involved with her. She's a nanny or she's a tutor for the children—she's officially in the house for other purposes. But the possibility that he could have any feelings about another human being just amazes me.

Now I am in the dining room hovering over them while they eat dinner. I died three weeks ago and there they all are. I am very frustrated because I am worried about one of the boys. It is worse to be like this than it was when I was alive, because now I have the Sight and can see his future: He will take his own life. But I can visit him in a dream. He calls me into his dream. I come and tell him not to do it.

It's whimsical, just a quick coming and going. When he was younger, he was always the sensitive one and always the troubled one, always the one who was afraid. I check them all out, and I've given him the message in a dream, not to do it, and I just leave.

Now I just get images of light. There are black lights mixed with purple and sapphire-blue light. I have a feeling of a little bit of blackness pulling in, which could be kind of scary maybe, but it doesn't scare me particularly. I have the feeling that maybe I've gone up to a place above the earth, but I don't go beyond that. I still feel tied, but it's not frightening. I've still gotten away. Physically, I'm not captured like the way when you're a spirit or something. So it's all right.

In the place I'm going to, everything's just gray with black spots. And then, it's just a lot of visual images. They're somewhat earth-oriented images. Not trees and water or hills or anything like that. Just kind of . . . nothing remarkable.

A whole bunch of people are with me at this time. They're spirit people; they're not earth people, they're equals. They don't do things. They're energy fields. I'm getting a lot of dark colors, disturbing colors. The times are very bad and the people around me are reacting to that. I'm aware of real misery and war and death and strife on earth at this time.

I feel like I don't have any choice about returning to earth, which surprises me. I pause for a few moments longer and make a pact with my higher self—to have children and really free them up this time, keep myself healthy and strong so that I don't have to leave them when they need me.

I do have a desire to get back on the earth plane because of all the trouble—to act and not just observe. I feel like when we're on this plane, the astral plane, we can't get free of what's happening down on earth. We can feel it. And so the more time goes by the more I feel like getting in there and acting, rather than just feeling it.

It's really bad, really terrible. But then at that point I lose my sense of where I'm going to go. I have this funny feeling there's no sense choosing where I'm going to go because I'd make a bad choice anyway. I'm so concerned about the trouble on the planet that I just let it happen. I make the wish to be incarnated again, but not in the sense of direction about where in particular I'm going to go. I want to get out of the astral plane because it's so uncomfortable. I am still passive even after my own death.

I am going down, zooming down! Now I know why people like to speed. I am atomizing down, zoom! And then I land. It is soft. I feel inside the womb. I'm in the kitchen of the house where I grew up. Strange . . . I am inside her womb and aware of the room where she exists now.

It is the kitchen they never changed, the room with white metal cabinets with stainless steel handles. The wall paper is of recipes and spices, spaghetti with bay leaves and oregano, and the salt and pepper shakers are a red and white rooster and hen. Everything is at waist height as I'm carried by her. I am tiny, and inside and outside at the same time. She moves heavily, slowly, and everything feels very hard for everybody. He's not around; she is by herself but seems content. He's away because it is the War. She's in her own house which makes it easier. There isn't much anybody can do about it all; people just live from day to day waiting for the horror to cease.

Yes, it is very odd. I have a vision that I couldn't waken again until years later: I am inside and outside her body at the same time! I can feel her feelings, and now I know the pain of her heart.

But time moves along . . . I feel pushed, pressed, and now I am fully inside her body. Yes, I am trapped and all is dark. My curiosity wanes as panic builds. It's so tight! I can't breathe. I hear her heart beating next to my skull for the last time from within as I begin to let go of her body. Everything is pressing, pulsing and pushing. I feel my leaving like a plug pushed down a tube, but my separation is drugged. I come out like a drunken fish gasping for outside air.

The experience of my own birth in regression was the beginning of the opening of a more embodied awareness. In a sense, I became sure that I was really here for the first time. And once I knew that, it became possible to perceive with all my senses, and I began to take risks. But I also was beaten by my foster father when I was very small, and I was molested by a group of neighborhood boys when I was four. And every place in me of past life pain and trauma was reactivated in my body by these experiences. Until I could confront those inner wounds and heal them, I was very much out of my body. And reexperiencing my birth was a courageous and conscious choice which enabled me to dive deeply into my early childhood trauma. My early life really was very much a chamber of horrors, a labyrinth of challenges that caused me to reaccess intuition, the Sight, because I was forced to let go of fear or die. But the initiates of the Minoan culture were trained to stay in their bodies while they learned courage. Since I was adept at jumping out of my body in this incarnation whenever anybody hurt me, I was always going to be limited in my growth toward wholeness. My rebirthing session was the beginning of an incredibly difficult healing process. It was like turning around and walking back through a chamber of tormenting monsters. And Aspasia was the voice in me that prodded me on, because Aspasia knew all the pleasures and powers of being a woman and being free of inner fears.

Chapter Five

THE RENAISSANCE ASTRONOMER, THE MEDIEVAL MERCHANT, AND THE ROMAN

The turmoil of all the inner voices began to quiet when I became really engaged in school. And when I began to evidence a great love of knowledge, my grandfather began to teach me about myth and ancient cultures and gave me many books as soon as I could read. The intense power of Aspasia found an outlet in Jason and the Argonauts, in Euripides, in the myths of Ariadne, of the Minotaur, and Persephone. Ichor rested more easily inside as I poured over Egyptian temple inscriptions and stories of Osiris and Horus. And the Druid was satiated for a while by long walks in the swamps and searching with my grandmother in the pantry for traces of the little people.

Reading history and hours spent pouring over my grandfather's globe in his study awakened new inner voices. As my analytical mind developed rapidly, the inner memories from the right brain broadened my perception.

I'm sitting at a large table in the library of the Count's house holding a pen in my hand. I'm muscular and very well built, and my body still feels excited and energetic as it did when I was the jester, but now I am a student under the Count's tutors. This library is very large with many shelves of books, and scholars come from a great distance to study here because there are few university libraries. At this time, private libraries are the best ones. I like it here. I wear a brown shift to my knees with a rope around my waist. I feel all this energy in my body, but I sit quietly. I am tonsured, and my hair is black. My head is shaved, and the tonsure suits me.

I'm drawing the earth with the moon going around it. I am looking at a picture in a book. It's a picture of the world, a picture of the world if you're standing on it. And it's not round. It's just flat. It shows the circular horizon, like a bowl. The top half is just a bowl upside down, which contains the stars. The flat part is where we are, and we see the inside of the bowl. It's blue and black. There's a dragon under the flat part, a really ornate dragon that breathes fire. But I don't agree with that. I feel that's wrong, and I'm not the only one who knows it. There's no dragon under us. There are other people who already know that the earth is round, and that is the big controversy of the sixteenth century.

It's not any kind of insight for me to think that the world is a sphere and the moon is going around it. It's not a new insight. But on the other hand, I'm trying to understand the orbit of things. Because all the books teach that everything is flat as in the picture. In this drawing, the world is flat, and then the planets are inside the bowl. I see Saturn, Jupiter, Mars, Venus and Mercury, and a large quarter-moon.

So what I'm doing is I'm doodling on this piece of paper trying to make things circular. Past where I'm drawing, the moon is going around the earth, and it's short of my vision now of Saturn's orbit. I'm interested in the idea that as something orbits something, it seems to be flat. I'm trying to visualize an orbital plane. And inside, where the earth is with the moon going around it, is the sun.

And I'm really trying to understand, to understand where things are. But it's nothing new. I'm just trying to understand it myself.

Later, when I'm older, I'm teaching something like physics. I keep on having images of planets. I'm teaching about the solar system with the sun in the center instead of the earth. And I've now reached the point where it's all right to teach that. And I believe in it, and I'm just filled with the excitement over being able to study and explore it. The students are very interested in what I'm teaching them. What I'm teaching them is new and exciting, controversial to them.

When I say it's like physics, I mean I have this amazing, intense physical feeling of gravity and balances and weight, this physical sensation of balance and the placement of things. When I try to explain to them about the sun and the planets and the orbits, I feel it physically myself. I'm so involved with the ideas I'm communicating.

I am thirty-five or forty years old. I'm tall, and I still haven't gained any weight. I'm physically fit, active, and I study so much that I forget to eat. I have good muscles, though, because I work hard and I'm active, just like when I was dancing in the court; I've got a strong sense of physical integration. When I talk about the balance in the solar system, I can feel that balance in myself. When I explain it, it's something I already know about because I feel it in my body. I communicate that to the university students. They're fourteen to twenty years old.

I'm a young genius, a young scientific discoverer, and I believe in the work of Kepler, Galileo, and Giordano Bruno. But it isn't hard for me to understand it at all. Whenever I find some sort of physical equation or whenever I come to a formula, it seems I already knew about the relationship before I came to the formula. Learning is like rediscovery to me. So I communicate a great excitement to the students because it's not boring to do all this hard work.

The work is catching up with the ideas. I'm studying the laws of the universe. The universe, the orbits are the way they are because of gravity and weight. It's not Newtonian physics, but I'm involved with equations and formulas and scientific study that explain all of this.

There are tall windows on the whole side of this room, and they have glass in them. It's not stained glass, it's clear glass. It's bubbly and extremely distorted and thick. It lets the light in. This is the University of Leipzig. I'm looking out of a window over the tops of some buildings, and I see lots of tall spires on buildings and churches. It seems as if whenever people get hold of a piece of wood, they have to carve it.

I don't see a river, but I know it's there. It's down below or off to another part. It's lush, very green here, with rolling hills. There are no mountains, but many rivers. the land is really beautiful. The fields are yellow and gold, and the trees are an intense medium green.

The reawakening of Erastus Hummell in my consciousness has had a potent balancing effect. Erastus chose to incarnate at the early stages of the development of rationalism in Western culture. Yet, much of the reason Erastus was in the forefront of his culture was because of the inner knowledge, especially from Aspasia as astrologer/seer and from Ichor, Egyptian priest and astrologer. But, on an emotional level, the life of Erastus was also a breakthrough. Erastus hated "superstition," felt oppressed by centuries of suppression of mental freedom by his culture and religion. He literally ran into the light and the library when the opportunity was presented to him. There was also a driven quality in Erastus, a part of his soul that was also escaping. For, buried deep in the subconscious mind of this jester was a memory of a close shadow lifetime in earlier medieval Europe when forbidden new ideas caused death by burning at the stake. For Erastus, to be able to be free to move with the new culture against the old was a profound accomplishment. Erastus overcame his shadow.

But shadows are very hard to grab hold of. So, at this point I sense that balance between the polarities—in this case scientific progress and the mysteries—is a revealing solution.

As I gradually woke up and took a good look at my culture when I was seven, I was horrified at what I saw, absolutely horrified. Because of my unusually clear past-life memories, I knew intuitively that something around me was gravely wrong in comparison to what I had often lived with before. After all, in Aspasia's culture, to even kill a spider was a wound to the great mother. And all I saw around me was death of frogs, butterflies, foxes, wolves, fish, and birds. It was like a holocaust in slow motion that nobody could see! All the time I was saying, "Don't you SEE, don't you SEE?" and they said I was "rambunctious" or "hyperactive." It was like seeing a fire burning up hundreds of people and crying out to the people walking by and being ignored.

But much worse for me inside was the strong knowledge in me on all levels that I, too, was the killer, the rapist, the castrator. Deep, deep inside, because I saw so clearly so early, deep inside me were all the voices of past lives who had participated in the sins which were now culminating all around me. And this inner awareness manifested in the early stages as odd memories of nomadism, odd memories of the lives lived during times when human roots where torn from the earth, from our mother. It caused me to be very fixed, when I was little, in any support around me that was anti-nomadic, any support that was a protection of the women. So I resonated with the centered home, the ideal of the fifties, while I was haunted with deep inner disease. I was beginning my first stages of the ability to find the sources of that deep disease within myself, so that perhaps I could someday understand it in the culture. And my lifetime as merchant in medieval Europe was a lifetime as a nomad, with all the levels of estrangement from the land and the inner self.

I am in the body of the medieval merchant, and I experience a feeling of density similar to the feeling of the earlier lifetime in Rome. I am a male; my body is slightly heavy, and I have coarse and slightly curly black hair. I have a short beard and mustache, and my nose is large with a bump on it. I am wearing a tunic; I am bare-chested, and I have hair on my chest and stomach. Leather straps hold the coarse cotton tunic, and there is a leather strap about five inches wide around the waist. The leather belt around my waist is thick with rivets in it, and a scabbard hangs from it. It holds a sword which is 18 inches long, wide and sharp. I hold the leather waistband when I pull it out, and I grab it hard and yank it out. I am a soldier.

My arms and legs are strong, my hands delicate with white skin and hair on the backside. I have leather bands on my wrists with rivets in them. My hands are smooth but strong. My shoes are odd; they are narrow and tight.

The room is large with a wooden planked floor and plastered ceiling. It is a meeting place or workroom. It is octagonal in shape and all shut up. It is lighted by torches on the walls, and there are other men dressed like me in the room. They are soldiers too, bare to the waist, and they wear hats with a round top and a boat-shaped fat rim around them. I do not wear my hat. I'm giving instructions.

The men are walking around making quite a bit of noise. I tell them to listen. They're not really paying very much attention, but they have to listen to me when I say that. This is a stone castle which has eight or ten sides and is four stories tall.

It is early spring when the leaves are first coming out, so it's very light green. There are lots of trees, and there are rolling hills that go on for a long distance. The castle is up on a rise, and I can see a great distance from there in many directions. The castle is Iranian or Greek Orthodox or Russian Orthodox, Eastern. We're going to go toward the west from here.

We're going to go over the hill and down to the valley to the river, and we're going to make a big fire. That's the first day's journey. After the sun sets, we're going to use the star to find the way. We're going in the direction of the evening star. We have a long way to go, which will take at least two weeks. We're walking.

They have to listen to me because I'm in charge of them. I was called into the village court a few weeks ago and given instructions. I was called to the central administrative office. There was a bearded man in the office wearing a cloak. He sat at this desk with pen and rough pieces of paper. He told me there wasn't enough food. And now we're to go out on a journey to find out where we can get more food. I'm a soldier, but I'm not going out in military capacity. We can travel quite easily, there isn't danger. We don't have to worry about being attacked. We're not setting out on a war mission. I need to go back to see how I got here . . .

I was called in for orders. The official's office was fairly small and quite simple. The desk was crude, made of plain wood. He was a bureaucrat, not a military officer. There were benches and chairs with banks on them. There was a small window on the back wall behind where he was sitting, and it had iron bars. There was light coming in, no glass, and a wooden shutter outside. It didn't get cold very much then.

We're just supposed to go and find a good way we can get food. Find out where the food is, find out how far away it is, that there is food because we don't have enough. We haven't had enough rain, the crops aren't growing, everything is dry. In fact, in the building we're in, everything's dry now.

On the day I received my orders, I ate my evening meal with my parents at my father's house. There were quite a few people in the house, with a large round table. I had bread and a wooden bowl of stew—vegetables and meat, broth in it, all together. And we drank red wine out of pewter goblets. The food tasted good, the stew was warm and tasted really good. The bread was coarse but good, with a lot of flavor. I just had a hunk of it. It was a fairly flat round loaf.

The people who lived in the house, my brothers and sisters, and guests sat at the table. My father was jovial and liked to eat and drink. My mother was slightly overweight with dark hair and white skin. She didn't say much, and my father talked a lot. He wore leather and wool clothes. He had a fur pelt on his collar, and there were fur decorations on the edges of his pockets and on the front of his jacket.

My best friend sat at the table. He was quiet but very, very intelligent. When he wanted to say something, he talked a lot. He's been my friend since we were young boys, and my family liked him a lot. He was often a guest, but neither one of us stayed here.

After dinner, my friend and I left together. We came out a thick wooden door, round at the top. We watched our heads. The street was a narrow dirt lane with small, primitive houses close on each side. They were connected in some cases. The houses were wood with stucco between the logs. The roofs were thatched with heavy grass, just like layers of straw.

In front of the house, the road started to descend, and we walked down the lane. We laughed and joked a lot and walked in the middle of the road. We walked a quarter to a half a mile. We came down the road, and then we went into a door that was eight or ten feet wide. We opened it, and it creaked. We pushed it hard, just like going into a barn. It was really squalid there. It was a barn-like place made into a barracks for people to sleep. There were old animal stalls inside, and we slept in bunkbeds or lofts on the wall or we just rolled out a bedroll in the straw around the room. We went to our stall with a few cots in it, but I really would have rather been at home.

There were people getting ready to go to sleep, and it smelled like hay in there; it smelled like urine, and it smelled like candle wax and fire. It didn't smell too bad, but it didn't smell too good. We were all soldiers in service to the village.

It was a pretty town, and the other streets were like the street my parents' house was on. There were some houses that were bigger, and there were churches. Churches had bell towers. The church in the center of town on the hill was bigger than the rest of the churches. It was medium sized, made out of reddish stone, but it was bigger than the other ones. I had to go there, but I didn't like it. Everybody had to go. There was a bishop in this church.

I was in the church. It had very simple stained glass windows. We sat in rough, very crude wooden pews, and light was coming in through the stained glass windows. The glass was mostly red. The ceiling was high, quite simple with wooden beams. But it was very mystical in here. It was very quiet, and they burned incense. I should have taken it more seriously than I did, but I couldn't.

The bishop had an elaborate miter on, and the robe he wore had lots of embroidery and color. He was always bending over; he bowed and scraped a lot. He bowed very low. He was bending at the waist, and he got down on his knees. Sometimes he got down right on the floor in front of the altar. He took the headdress off and put it to the side. It was really a big thing, almost two feet tall. It had two peaks on the side and a rounded part in the center. It was white or cream colored, and it had gold on it.

His voice echoed throughout the church as he chanted. He didn't speak, he chanted. The church was filled. There was a cross, Jesus on the cross. It was very grotesque, very graphic. His skin was white, His face looked green, and His eyes . . . He was in such pain, He was bleeding. It was a wooden cross, a carved wooden crucifix. It was almost as big as the size of a man. It was up above the altar. I was supposed to go to church almost every day. Everybody went, even soldiers.

It was a village, a large village. And the villages were not close together, so we had a town organization place, an administrative office, and each village was important in its area. The village was on a hill, and there was a river down below. It was fifteen to twenty feet wide, ran fast, and you couldn't put a boat in it. We walked, and if we were moving something heavy, we had carts with wheels. If they wanted to move something, a man was between the two handles of the cart, and he hauled it around. They had some donkeys which they used sometimes.

The village was in Poland or Yugoslavia, and we had to go tremendous distances to get to another culture. We went west for food, for land. And I had to help my village.

It is time . . . The men quiet down to listen to me, and as I begin to speak, I feel intense energy course through my body. I have never felt this before, and I am afraid I will have no words. But next, a hot beam of white light strikes my forehead, and I speak to my soldiers.

"We are hungry, tired, and confused. We came here to sleep and eat from the stores of the way station, but others before us have eaten all the food, and so there is no food for us. Now we know the hordes are moving west from places even further east than our village. We all endured the terrible winters when it seemed the sky would never stop snowing, and we all watched as the crops and plants died in the searing dry heat of summers with no rain. We left because even the trees died, and the rivers are nearly dry, and the children began dying. We may never see our families again, and we may starve. but we must hold together because we are the only hope for us now. We cannot just stop and rot."

The next few weeks were a living nightmare as one by one the men died. I realized we would never report back to the village. But my friend and I survived. And when I crossed the Rhine into the land that was not desiccated, I was a different man. I was going to survive no matter what I had to do. As if in a dream, soon thereafter I found myself in the beautiful cathedral of Rheims. I am amazed that it could even have been built because there was nothing like it in the village. The building is vaulted, and even I feel mystical inside. I don't want to return to the village.

Everything is changing. In the cities, there's business, commerce. People come and go, people from many places come and go everywhere. I can't stay in the little village any more. It's such a time of change. I'm thirty-two now, and I could become a merchant. I could work in a trade. I didn't marry, and I'm free. I have a little bit of money. I didn't like it in the village, didn't like it at all. I didn't like that church, I didn't like living and working in the village. Now I feel like I have a

chance to make a choice.

I walk out of the church, and I'm wearing a short leather tunic with a loose cotton, finely woven, blousy shirt underneath. I wear leather boots that come up over my calf, and they are well made. I walk out into a large square central plaza that is filled with people wearing brightly colored wool clothing. There are three to four-storied buildings all around the plaza, and there are merchants with booths. It's very exciting. The weather today is beautiful, very sunny and breezy and about fifty-five degrees.

There's all kinds of trade going around from one country to another, one village to another. I think I'm going to get involved in trade. My friend came too, and we are going to work together in some kind of small merchant-type business. I walk across the square and look at all the people, and then I go down a narrow stone street. The buildings are close, with doors opening right out on the street. I walk maybe a quarter of a mile. The street curves this way and that way, and other streets come into it. The buildings are three stories tall, and they are closer together at the upper stories. Some have balconies, which make it even more crowded up above. In some cases, it's only twelve feet, fourteen feet from the balconies across to the other side, even though the street is sixteen feet wide. The roofs are red tile, and you can only see the sky if you look straight up.

I come to my apartment. The door is right off the street. I open my slatted wooden door, and the stairway goes right up. It's a very narrow stone stairway. I go up past the second floor and up the stairs again. I keep going up to the door on the third floor, and that's my apartment up there.

It's two rooms. The first thing I see is the front room. It's fairly light and clean, almost monastic. There's a small round table with two chairs, and there's a couch against the wall. There's a relatively big window in the front. The light comes in. There's no balcony. There's another room behind this one: a cold, crude kitchen with a beehive oven where I can make a fire. It's a rounded oven with a hole in it, and it's in the corner of the wall at the back of the building. I can make a fire, and I can stick bread in it and cook meat. There's no running water. There's a stone sink with a pitcher, and there's a little window in back there with no glass. In the front room, the window has small panes which are bubbly, thick and hard to see through. If I want to see anything, I have to open the window.

My landlord lives down on the first floor. I don't like him, and I go down there to pay him rent. I hand him a silver coin about as big as the Liberty half dollar. There's a geometrical circular marking on it like a mandala. It says 10 drachma in Arabic numerals. The other side of the coin has a bird, a flying bird, a griffin. It would take the average working person a month to get one of these coins. This is my rent for six months. My landlord is a tanner. He doesn't tan here, but this is his shop where he sells his goods.

Eventually I become a successful merchant and end up with a house in the city when I'm forty years old. I never get married, and I'm very bourgeois and middle class. The house I live in is a city house, connected on both sides. It's two stories tall instead of three, and I own it. There's a door right on the street as usual, and then I go up four or five steps into a hallway. Right in front, there's a great room, a hall. It goes up two stories, and stairs go up to the second floor. The second floor overlooks the first floor; it's a loft. In the back of the first floor, there's an eating room and a kitchen. I live alone. I have a couple of servants who cook, clean the house, make fires if they're needed. I don't have to do that kind of work.

I am a merchant, and I travel and mostly trade. I buy things in one place and make arrangements to have them go to another place. That's the way to make money right now. Those people who were smart enough to get into that make a lot of money. Every time I buy something and sell it, I can charge a lot more.

And so I travel a lot. Sometimes I travel by riding a horse, and sometimes I go in a carriage. I ride around in a crude form of carriage in town, but usually when I go a distance, I ride my horse. My friend goes with me a lot to facilitate trading. We're important merchants, beginning capitalists. We will entertain any possible propositions.

It's 1208, and we sit at a table talking while the servant girls bring us beer and wine. We're talking about the crusades in the south part of France. These are unsettled times, and we're trying to think of ways to profit from the situation.

Before I go into my experience during the crusades in southern France, what is significant about the medieval merchant's lifetime up to this point needs to be explained. Lurking close behind the memory of the medieval merchant was the life as a Roman small landowner, and close behind that memory lies the germinating force in the body of the Egyptian, Ichor. And the shadow of Erastus was all of them.

As medieval merchant living at the dawn of the market economy, the beginning of consumerism and free trade, I was concerned only with survival. Historically, the droughts combined with a mini-Ice Age caused the death of all but the survivalists. And being a survivor is not always a virtue, a growth in consciousness, at all. But my role as survivor this time was a response to the passivity I evidenced as Roman landowner. Why is it that we are sometimes passive or sometimes we are determined to survive even if it means selling our souls? The Victorian woman and the Roman were the most passive experiences I remember. And in both cases, the larger reality was so huge and oppressive that the spirit only wished to leave as soon as possible. But by giving up, subsequent karma that needed to be dealt with was just more immense.

Our villa is west of Rome on the way to the sea. I am twenty years old, I wear a short white toga, and I am standing on the edge of a low hill. I can see the ocean far away, and I have a view over much of the land. Down below me, I stare at the land which used to be swamps. The Romans have drained the swamps. The large-scale projects they do, like the aqueducts in the city, are marvelous, but I still remember the swamps. We have farmed this land for over a hundred years. But things are different now; it has just begun changing lately. For many years, our family farmed the grain for the goddess Ceres in peace and tranquility. I look over the hills to the blue water, and I wonder if I will ever feel tranquility again. We once had a natural rhythm, a slow pace of life, but now we have constant pressure from Rome. The Roman authorities give land to the slaves and rabble in the city, and no one seems to care about the farming, the growing of the grain for the goddess.

Hmmm . . . I am in a courtyard on the side of the hill. We come here to eat. I see the water, and it is a beautiful blue. I see many green trees in the distance. The soil is clay-colored and sandy, and close by, I see jade trees and dogwood. I am young, I have tremendous energy in my body, fire energy. But I feel danger, like being caught in the eye of a hurricane; it is dreamlike, caught in time. It is an inner sense of panic. I move through the trees and go up to the villa. The house is . . . like a tunnel. Horses . . . riding horses, riding a horse. I am riding fast . . . I am riding a horse down a wooded pathway. I feel danger, but I can't see anything. I stop my horse and get off, and they grab me! I can't see because I'm afraid, and I know something is about to happen. I see a large Roman building, a lot of people, and somebody grabs me by the shoulders from behind. I knew before I even got here it was going to happen. They grab my horse, they take me, hit me in the face. It is unjust. It isn't fair. They are going to put me in prison.

They accuse me of not paying my taxes, but there has been no money for a long time. The ones who grab me are Roman soldiers who wear helmets with crests, armor on their shoulders, arms and legs They take me into a room with a man sitting behind a table. It is not fair, no one can pay the taxes, they are taking everyone's land. The most incredible thing is that no one seems to understand that the land is for growing the grain for the goddess. Their only understanding of the land is to buy it and sell it so they can be rich. For years we have farmed the land and provided food for the people and the nobles in Rome, and it is as if we have done nothing!

The man behind the desk is fat and wears red robes. Now there is one man in power in Rome—Caesar; it has never been this way until now. They grabbed me because I come from the middle class, and we once had money. Now all we have is land outside of Rome. Now he wants me to sign over my land as payment of the debt, and I can't. I already sense what they are going to do to me, but I can't sign over the land. That would be sure death for me and my family.

Somehow we have to get through this time and make the grains grow every season again. These people will go away someday, and the land will bear fruit again. But even I am not sure any more. There is no value any more in the money, only value in being lazy, so maybe the land will just lose its power to grow the seed. The country is in bad shape. There is chaos and hungry people everywhere, as the land is being dessicated and no one seems to care. It is 52 BC in Rome.

The man accuses me of being of the old value system of producing crops and bringing them in for the people. He says the people must have the land and produce their own crops. I hated coming into the city. Everything is breaking down, here and in the country. I was a fool to come here. All commerce is breaking down because of the rioting, all the money goes for war, and the people do not work in Rome. The people in Rome come from all over the world, and they just do not work. I should have stayed out. It hasn't broken down this badly out in the country yet. I came in to plead our case, to get them off our backs, but I knew from the beginning I would lose. Everybody loses these days. They take me out and start leading me down a long hallway. I feel helpless, sick with hopelessness, and gradually I begin to know what they are going to do to me . . .

The experience of the lifetime as the Roman farmer had a very strong impact on my life as Barbara because there are quite a few similarities between the Roman Empire and America. The most critical one for me has been an almost obsessive fear of debt and inflation, and the destruction of arable land. I have watched the farmers in this country lose their farms one after another, and I know from experience that famine and hopelessness will be the result. Lately in the farm country, I can feel the elements rebelling and striking out against the human oppression. This lifetime has been especially gripping because much of what we live with today is a repeat in so many ways. Yet, we should be able to learn from the past. But just when I have felt like there was no solution, that is when the culture sees another solution that has not been considered before.

That solution lies in a new awareness of human consciousness and the ability of the human mind to create new realities. If enough people see a new way and practice it, a new reality will emerge. And the proof of the nearness of a new reality can be found in the state of decay of the old reality. Whenever any culture is as energyless as this one, the old one is dying and the new one is coming.

Chapter Six

THE VISION IN THE TEMPLE
AND THE SCARAB

It was one of those cold November days before my seventh birthday when the family was deep within our house. I pushed the back door and then the storm door quietly because I wanted no questions. It was one of those times when I was called to go someplace but could not explain why or where. I crept down the back stairs closely, moved out of the vibrational shadow of the house and waited for direction. I was pulled to my left, moved with it, and in moments I climbed over the tall stone wall between our house and the neighbor's driveway. I moved into the center of the driveway, looked up, and saw that all the elms, chestnuts and thick underbrush were encased in a thin layer of ice. Next the wind blew like a quick whoosh, and the universe became a loud roar of thousands of snappings and cracklings.

Now I had to hurry, and I rushed down the driveway toward the closed high iron gate between the stone and brick walls. I stopped at the gate and put my hands on it as if I wished to open it—impossible—and I felt my mittens stick to the damp cold metal. Hurry, hurry! whispered my inner brain, and I turned quickly to my right, leaving my mitten stuck on the gate. I began to climb the ten-foot-tall right portal. My knees scraped on the ancient bricks as I sought toeholds and gripped with my bare hands. At last I got hold of the stone top which was square, flat, and with enough surface to hold me. I raised myself up on it and sat on the top with my legs gripping round the carved stone ball, the decoration on top of the square topping.

I rested my elbows on top of the ball once I was secure. I looked west down the pathway to the river through shiny black iced trees, and I was sucked quickly into an airless womb-like envelope. My head jerked back quickly, and then the deafening, rippling church bells in the tall cathedral tower began ringing. A huge spiral of water energy began whirling around my tower, and the last thing I remembered was feeling weightless, powerless, and unconnected. Next, each ringing bell caused magnetic light impulsion, like a rocket was igniting in my head. I felt like I had grinding ball bearings in my head, as I felt pulsations and heat in parts of my brain I'd never felt before.

I was knocked unconscious, my body fell from the six-foot tower, and I lay on the ground.

> *"Go back, go back to the moment before you fell from the tower. You must remember; you must remember your journey into the light. Otherwise you are barred again and again from your ability to touch your most powerful part—your life as a Hebrew prophet."*

I was perched on my tower with my head snapped back, and a purple beam like a laser shot into my head. And a part of me that was always there but I never feel consciously ascended out of my body just before I fell. This part left me because it was magnetically drawn to go for movement somewhere. It was my light body. It went up, into the sky.

I go up very high to a place that seems to be clouds. Lots of light, lots of clouds, and there is a circle of angels. I'm trying to see how many there are. It's all like a Blake painting, like a Blake drawing with cloud substance similar to the angelic substance. There are four archangels, and there is a being in the center who is not human. The being is sitting on a throne and holding a ball of light similar to a crystal ball. I'm going there to be healed. I go in front of the being with the ball of light.

I am just light, a hot, contained center of light. I'm a sphere of light, a body of light, *I am* my higher self. I go into the center of the ball of crystaline light. It's like the earth; it is a sphere. I go to the very center of it, and I radiate out of it. The archangels around the being are healing me as I exist in the center of the ball of light. The archangels radiate love into the fusion of my light body into the ball held by the sky being, and I am balanced. I feel a subtle shifting in my spine, in my shoulders, in my head centers, then an indescribably hot fusion of sound and light. The last thing I feel is a magnetic heaviness in my body which stimulates every cell in my being. And then I am lying on the ground.

But then people around me changed. It was almost as if some people couldn't see me. In fact, my favorite TV show was "Topper," a show about a ghost that only some could see. My little brother changed towards me. It was a miracle. He was three and spoke to very few people himself, except he talked to furniture all the time. But he studied me carefully with his large, blue, unfocused eyes, and then he began to show me his secrets. He took me into the woods with him and taught me to walk the paths of the Sauk silence. And the little creatures gathered around me. I was no longer afraid of the trees, the wind, only afraid still of the deep water.

And my grandfather looked at me soon after my vision as if he'd never seen me before. He taught me more about ancient cultures as if it was his chosen mission. I was only happy with my grandparents and my brother. After this experience, I felt like I was "marked" by another reality. No one else knew me! I was very unhappy in school, very unhappy at home, very disconnected with everyone around me. There were no other energies that matched that few moments of ascension. Later, I found many, but childhood was very difficult from then on because my body was altered by the infusion of my higher self.

Once my vision shifted, I groped outside myself for the Temple. My search was so intense, so driven, that I began a peculiar habit of "walking intuitively." Everywhere I went was the opportunity to see it again. My right hand and arm were often extended as if my staff would manifest again. I was attuned to great distances, almost as if I could feel the beginning of the wind. My eyes could see great distances because I was always waiting. And my heart began to expand out to everyone around me. I did not understand yet, but I had become the shepherd.

But also, I "walked intuitively" because I remembered the time when I walked into the Temple and saw the vision before.

I'm in the city, and I am walking swiftly, but with second sight. I am sore afraid, for the father, my king, is dead and my people are lost. The dust blows in the empty streets as the people hide away, already fearing invasion. My heart is heavy with their fear. I come to the Temple steps, ten to the entry door, and I stare upwards at the dark, swirling sky. The fig tree on the door seems menacing, and I can feel the two pillars shake as if an earthquake is beginning. I walk up to the heavy doors and push them open. Even though this is consecrated by them to Yahweh, I seek Elohim.

There is a black cube in the back where the sacred object is. But in the space of the Temple, in the air, I see a vision. I see a massive woman, a Queen of Heaven figure, an angelic female goddess figure. She keeps on changing form as if she is the ancient goddess and then the beautiful young goddess. She is a radiating goddess in the center, and as I bathe in her glow, I feel my chest cavity fill with hot searing liquid, and

I cannot breathe.

I look above her, and I see arches. Angels fill the sky around her as if the air is pulsating with life, and she continues to change form as the angels fill the air with light and doves swoop in and out. Then, above the arches where this queen of heaven is, there is a male figure with brown robes, a great staff, and enormous wings. There is incredible light radiating from this figure. He is like a patriarch to me—just amazing light, radiating out, and as the light radiates from him, it forms into enormous beings, enormous angels around him.

As I gaze upon him, I feel amazing power in my shoulder blades where my wings would be if I were an angel. I feel a hot coal in my heart that seems to draw me forward. But as I move a step, gryphons— no, seraphim—manifest in front of my vision, and I stop. I feel the hot coal in my heart move out of my body and into the hands of one of the seraphim. He holds it between his index finger and thumb, stands in front of me, and he holds it in front of my third eye, then in front of my throat. Then with both his hands, he passes it back into my heart.

The two seraphim move back into their guarding position, and I know I am not supposed to move forward. Instead, I quiet my heart and vibration for the first time in many weeks, and I raise my eyes. The goddess continues to change form from virgin to hag, as the angels swirl about her. I raise my eyes to the great patriarch.

He thunders, "I am Enoch. I tell you now that you must speak to the people. You must get rid of all your inhibitions. You must see the vision and hear the sound." Now there is a resonating sound. "And you must not hold back any more. You must speak to the people. You must preach to the people, telling the truth. You must . . . " He is not really speaking words, but what he is communicating is that I must connect up all these higher planes with the earth plane.

"You must speak to the people in relationship to the higher planes. Soon there will be great destruction upon the land, and few will survive. and just when you think it is over, can never happen again, that is when it will happen again. The only hope that humans have at these times is offered by Archangel Michael. If the people will learn to hear and see, they will be healed. People will be taught now that they are the sacred seed of the earth. The Hebrew people will act out a drama for the human race. The land of the Twelve Tribes will cease to be located in the homeland of the fathers. Out of your pain, you will disperse to all the lands of the earth. You are the sacred seed. You are to learn that your God is in your heart and not in any country or temple. But if they persist in the ways of men, the cycle of fire will continue for them. You are to tell them they can escape the fire merely by choosing life. Some see as you do now with the Goddess that manifestation exists in time and space, and beyond this place is nothingness. Archangel Michael always offers courage, and there are a few who accept. But with Michael's gift, the heart is a feather."

I stand before Enoch emptied and in a state of desolation as the coal burns in my heart. It is as if the inner fire is searing the inside of my body, so loathesome to me is my physical link with the eternal cycles of destruction.

"No, chosen one, you do not quite see. All is illusion presented for your pleasure, and contained in the illusion is the path to the light." The hot coal in my heart suddenly expands and explodes and shakes me to the very fiber of my being. I am timelessness and formlessness now, as he speaks to me again.

"Always, at any given time in the consciousness of man, the truth is heard, seen and known by all. Otherwise, your free will would be absurd. You are chosen to tell them the truth so that I know it has been done. You now know timelessness, which means your consciousness is infinite if you heal. Just like a feather, or a moment of a child's laughter; all of this pain is just that, light, when healed. What one man thinks about could heal the Cosmos instantaneously. If just one man lived with his soul in his body, then he could place his feather on his hand and blow it to us."

I turn and walk out of the temple. As I come out the door, I feel like I'm getting pummeled by the air. I'm disoriented, and I just walk. As I walk forward, it is as if all I've seen and heard becomes not real. And yet I am forever changed.

The only house that made sense then was my grandfather's house. I could do anything I wanted there. I could wander in the garden amongst the vegetables or flowers, I could walk down Fifth Street all the way to my uncle's house. And I could go into the attic under the second story eaves and peruse the Latin and Greek books. The house felt timeless to me as the sunlight filtered through the lace curtains while a fire burned in the first floor hall to keep out the draft.

My grandparents were always lost in some timeless pursuit downstairs in the library, and one day I went into their bedroom and inspected all the objects I could reach. On top of Grandpa's dresser I found a gold ring with a large ruby set in it. I stared into the stone as I became aware of rays of light

shooting into the facets that seemed to flicker like the tongues of fire or the sun-
light in the glass. I shifted inside, almost like little bones clicked, as I felt grey
fuzziness in my head, and I was gone again.

I stare at my initiation ring. It is large, made of gold, the front part
is oval, and there is a lapis serpent on the sides and around the oval
part. There is a scarab set in the ring, but it is translucent, and I see
through it down to the marking beneath. The serpent is my initiation
into the rite of Osiris, and the scarab is my initiation into Horus. I had
to earn the Horus initiation to have the scarab, but I can still see the
ring as it was under Osiris with the inscriptions in the gold under the
scarab. I still wear my Osirian bracelets.

Today is very sunny. The light is very white, so light I can hardly
think. This is the place of many temples. I am in front of my temple. It is
a rather small pyramid with two tall columns in the front with a wide
triangular top set on the columns. The columns are in front of the
entrance of the temple, and they are about thirty feet tall. They are fat,
and the temple is not much taller than the columns. the pediment on
top has a lot of writing on it. The actual entrance is much smaller than
the columns; it is human-sized. The columns and the pediment dwarf
me, but the pyramid does not.

I turn and begin walking toward the temple, and as I move, I am
infused with energy in my upper chest. I begin to pull energy in a
special way into my legs as I begin stepping up the steps. It is some
kind of technique we learned so we are magnetized before entering
the temple.

Stepping up is different. Stepping up is lifting my weight and
bringing energy into my heart. Stepping forward is moving like a trajectory forward through time. And as I do that, I'm moving forward,
pulling with my legs forward, and my heart energy is contained. It's
holding. but the energy from the sides is pulling at me from each side.
It is like walking through water up to my neck. I am pulling it, and it's
pulling me. It's like pushing on a string and having it pull on each side.
The heart energy is what keeps me going forward. And the steps are
designed so that this process can occur. In other words, the number of
steps I have to take in between each step is planned to be like that.

There seems to be an energy field that is present in this walk to
the temple. I bring it from the sides as I step forward with the energy in
my heart, I bring the energy that I carry on the Nile once a year to the
temple. When I carry the energy on the Nile to the pharaoh and to the

seven gods, I do not feel it in my heart. I feel it in my third eye. Now I come to bring the energy to the heart.

In other words, when I bring the energy on the Nile each year to the pharaoh, I carry the energy forward for the people, and I leave it there. After that circuit is complete, my heart is great with power—I can barely lift my legs to bring it. And I lift it here—my own energy—to my temple.

I am fresh like the morning dew. I am free of the pharaoh, and the energy that I have is my own energy. And coming to my temple, it's my privilege and my gift. It's not all mine, but it's my way to have the energy of the heart. So as I walk forward after stepping up and taking the heart energy, I feel resistance from the energy that I carried from the Nile. I feel the pull of the need of the people and of the country. Now it's time to find my own energy, but I feel some energy from the Nile to be taken to my temple.

I step forward further, and the pulling from the sides feels like restraint. It feels like restraint on my arms, restraint through my shoulders. It feels chaotic and undifferentiated on the sides. And so I am trained to move forward. So I step forward. What I'm anxious for is what is inside. But I can't get there yet. I step up again, so anxious to go inside that I keep wanting to be further ahead than I'm supposed to be. There are seven steps up.

The first step was lapis. The second step that I step on now is homunculus, a green stone, anchorite. As I step up, the light intensifies in the front. The pull is hard on the hands, on the arms and shoulders, and the light begins to flood my head and heart. It's strange, because the energy that seems to be stopping me is a kind of spherical barrier. It's all around me, in front of me, and then it's pulling on my arms. I feel like I'm breaking out of an egg, but it's a strange egg. It's not an egg that hurts or pulls or restrains. As I've stepped up over the anchorite, and the energy and light in the egg is the same size of my body, I look up ahead. There are five more steps, and everything is on my scale except for the tall columns and the pediment on the top. I'm not supposed to let the size of the columns and the pediment disturb me. They are the kingdom. So much of what we have to go through is structures and impediments that people put there. So I ignore them.

The light energy that I feel is very small in proportion, but much stronger and brighter. And it's a light intensity and a color that is like titanium. It's not a light energy that I see with my normal sight. So as I step forward, now I walk forward with my legs again, and I feel that pulling. It's a different pull, though. It's not like a string now. It's egg-like, a shield in front of me, and the strange titanium light. I walk forward, and suddenly the titanium light dissipates. It's like the dissipation of water droplets—it atomizes.

I'm still walking forward, and the energy pulling from the side is gone now. And I step on the third step. The third step is red, carnelian. And I feel heat in my hands, in my arms, up into my shoulders, and into the back of my head. It is the heat of free will. And this is the only time I feel this. Now I feel floating, I feel dreamlike, I feel the power of something else. Now as I step forward, I do not pull any more; I float forward. But in my body, I still feel my feet. I'm very aware of my feet.

But the feeling of floating is very pleasurable. It's very definite. I'm walking, and I know I'm walking in my conscious mind, but I feel like I'm floating. And it's a little difficult to stay down, but I do stay down.

I come to the fourth step. I feel like I float up to it. It is yellow; it is berylium, it is the third eye. It also is white; it's mostly white and chalky, but it has yellow in it.

Now as I walk forward, I do not feel like I am floating. I feel like I am being carried. It's very confusing because it doesn't feel like when I've been carried. Sometimes, I'm carried in this chair they hold on both sides. This is a different kind of being carried. I am being carried by the mind, the mind of Mena. The mind of Mena is a mind that is larger than mine, a mind that passes to me what it knows.

Now I am ready to go up the fifth step. And I feel like Mena goes with me, but that's not the way it is. I have to walk up the steps myself. The fifth step is amethyst. Now, the reeling is multifaceted. It is my amethyst turned toward the door of the temple, the feeling of the light going into the back of the stone and then radiating out through the facets.

I feel like the back of my neck from the back of my brain through my head is like the gem, the amethyst, with light going into the center of it and going out through the facets. My being is preparing itself to listen to Mena. I walk forward. Mena carried me up the fifth step. Now I walk forward myself. I have a feeling of being very high now, like being on a plateau, as I walk toward the sixth step. I see ahead of myself, and I have passed between the two large columns and under the pediment. On the pediment, I can see the hieroglyphs, and I can read them!

This is the temple where the words of Horus are spoken through the ages.

The temple was built by Ptah, and Ptah is the energy that existed in Egypt, ancient Egypt.

Ptah was the grand initiator, the grand teacher, and the maker from clay, the cosmic potter.

It is from him that we are given the light, and through the words of the cult of Horus.

Anubis sits at the gates of the temple. Anubis is the symbol by which Mena and Ichor can read the message from ancient Egypt that is there for them if they ask.

Only the beings who can communicate with the Guardians can read the temple inscriptions.

Only the beings who can hold the serpent have the power to enter this temple.

All those who do not hold the serpent may not come in.

That is the end. I will step to the sixth step. I am past the gates, past the pediment on the top. The top of the temple is the unlocking of the key. It is the key only for those who have been given the key by initiation. I am now going into the entrance of the temple. The sixth step is going into the entrance. It's not the entrance just yet, but it's going into the entrance.

Something is on each side of me. It is two temple guards. They are here in case someone tries to go in who cannot go in. They will kill anyone who cannot go in it. They, of course, do not bother me. If you cannot go in, they will grab you on each arm as you step up to the sixth step. They are beings from Atlantis. To those who see them in the physical form, they appear to be gryphons. They each have an evil eye. The evil eye in the being is like a laser beam. It has no problem with people who cannot come in. They simply disappear at that point. On the physical plane, the beings appear to be stone statues of gryphons. On the astral plane, they appear to be temple guards, and I see them in my head.

I see a bird with a small hooked beak, with a blue and gold striped headdress. The guard's eyes are very powerful, like birds' eyes, and the rest of them is human. They're male, and very beautiful in physical form. They still exist on the walls of temples throughout the world.

I step up to the sixth step, the step of the crystal light that pulsates, light that troubles me in my third eye. It is the light that takes away my free will, as when I go to the small pyramid for the energy to carry to the pharaoh. I'm very tired of it. That's what I have to do, and I don't like it. The reason I come here now is to be regenerated. I come here because I'm very sick of my Osirian ritual duties.

The crystal light is exhausting, and my work with it is most of the work of this incarnation. But because of my service, I can pass by the astral guards. The one on my left is Acanza, and Dion is on my right. They are the same, but the controlling one, Dion, is always on my right, and the one on the left is the one of the light. I step up to the sixth step, and I'm very tired of carrying the energy. But it's the cock number again. At this point, I stand on the sixth step with an erect phallus. Acanza and Dion send a rod of energy through me, and I am in control. They raise their hands over my shoulder in the healing position, with their palms out.

They say together, "Ichor is the carrier of the energy of the Atlantean light. We are just as sick of carrying the energy forward as you are, maybe more so. But the gods command us to make you do this. We know that you do not like it, and we give you the power to carry the energy without being tired. You will do it because we tell you to do it. We are in control, because we have to be in control. If we do not maintain the control, all is lost. But we are tired of it, too."

I feel a release, an acceptance, an ability to go to the seventh step, and the seventh step is the step of the Seventh Seal. It is no color, no vibration, it is formlessness. It is formlessness in the sense of stepping onto it and then falling over into a void. This is confusing to me, because I know that even though I might sense a void, Mena is in there.

I step up to the seventh step. Up ahead is an energy point. It is pulsating inside the temple. The pulsating vibrations have a center, and the vibrations going out from there are very strong. The center is three interlocking circles of light—blue, blue to purple, pulsating back and forth. The light radiates out, and I am becoming fascinated.

The darkness around the entry into the temple is behind me. I am inside, and the circles with the light are pulsating, throbbing. I go, and now I stand, just stand there. The inside of the temple is about thirty feet with six corner points. I am drawn into the center where I saw the three circles of interlocking light. I can't see them anymore.

I walk to that place and stand. Mena is everywhere around, but I'm not sure where. From somewhere, he flashes his right hand to the center, and a stone chair materializes right where I stand. I sit in the chair. Then I can hear a clinking sound, and a door has opened.

I am extremely spaced out, drugged, and I am aware of an alteration in the air flow. There are six altars which are like grottoes back in the six points. The feeling is like two interlocking triangles with six points. In the grottoes there are stone bowls with fire in them, and that is where the light comes from.

Oh, I see. As I took my place in the center, Dion and Acanza manifested Mena between themselves, and now he has passed in also. The door closes behind him. Mena stands in front of me, and he has the scarab in his fist. I am totally spaced out and numbed by humming vibrations because that scarab is the transmutation of the energy of Atlantis.

Mena has many different levels of manifestation, so on the physical plane it burns his hand. On the astral plane, it is pulsating so much that he's trying to hold it tight. And on the causal plane, Mena's heart and mine communicate with complete understanding. Mena has problems with the will power, the will control of the Atlanteans, also. The scarab is something of theirs, and he doesn't want this stuff any more than I want this stuff. They have brought him here today.

He was four or five hundred miles away in the upper kingdom. He was sitting in his room, his library, reading a scroll, and then he was sucked away and transported through time and space. He doesn't like it very much at all. He found himself between those two beings, Acanza and Dion. I don't like them. I don't like to remember them. He found himself between them, and then they said, hold out your hand, and they put the scarab in his hand. and he is angry, very angry. But his heart is the same as my heart.

We love each other unconditionally. He doesn't want to give it to me any more than he wants to hold it. It burns Mena's hand because it is the energy of the Atlanteans.

He says to me, "I am very tired of transmuting the energy of the Atlanteans to the Egyptians. They have power over my being. Whenever they want to break in and make me do something, they do it. Do you know how bad it is? I could be taking a shit, and they interrupt me. That's how rude they are. They are very, very rude. And that's one of their problems."

There are still Atlanteans using those powers here in the Egyptian time because they did not maintain the flow of energy from the positive to the negative, the polarity energy. And the way the polarity energy is contained on the physical plane is at the base of the pyramid. The base of the pyramid—the four points—are the four points of the polarity. The center is the fixation of the energy level.

The Atlanteans had great powers in the manipulation of energy, ability to manipulate energy. They could fly, they could crystalize. I was once an Atlantean. We could split the energy in water. In other words, we were able to split the hydrogen atom in water. So we learned how to do that, and then we built our cities, our temples, and our ways of conveyance. And we got lazy. Because all we had to do was just take the energy and just do it. We became obsessed with our power. And then we committed the great sins.

There were other beings on other levels of mentality. Some of them were savages and primitives on the earth. They lived in Africa, Brazil, China, in modern-day language. We bothered them, which was really not fair. We didn't do that to help them. We discovered we could take a whole forest away if we needed wood. It's disgusting. We also started communicating with beings on higher levels than ours with our powers. And that is where we made the mistake. I don't know exactly how it happened; I don't know what triggered it. I just know the causes.

There were good Atlanteans and there were Atlanteans who misused the power. And toward the end of the Atlantis phase, the beings of Atlantis found ways to make sure they still had contact on the earth plane. They built a pyramid, but more importantly, they built the Sphinx so that they would have ways to get through to the Egyptians. In other words, if the Atlanteans could not figure out a way to have places on the planet, temples and places of transmutation of energy, they could not manifest themselves on the physical plane. When all the ancient temples have lost their power, then the Atlantean hold will cease to exist.

When Atlantis was destroyed, many people understood that the end was coming, as is always the case at the end of a cycle. And so they made sure they could get through in the future if they wanted to. Since they had attained total control over their astral bodies during their civilization, then as long as they could establish a place to tie into if they wanted it, they could influence world order.

Like all beings, the Atlanteans were adept at experiencing many levels besides the physical. They became fascinated with the many planes of manifestation. They let go of their original physical balance and enjoyment of the body, and they began to value the other planes more than the physical. Like Icarus, they tried to become gods themselves. They tried to take the power of the gods. So, all that is left of their influence is that they participate in earth balancing by means of the pyramid and the Sphinx, and they are very involved in initiatory rites such as were practiced in Egypt.

Mena is holding the scarab given to him by the Atlanteans for Ichor, and Mena says, "You have mastered the carrying of the energy forces to the power source. You have caused the dissemination of the energy out into the vegetative land. You have gathered back the energy from the vegetative state into your heart, and now you are ready to speak from the heart."

Ichor says: "I receive my ka. My ka has been in a jar in the lower kingdom." We are in the upper kingdom, in Thebes. We are in the temple in Thebes, the temple of light. And my heart was in a jar in the lower kingdom, Heliopolis. What has happened is Mena has just passed me my heart, which means that because of my work and my obedience, I now get my high self, which is my ka. My ka has been fed, nurtured by many beings.

We had various techniques for keeping the high self alive and energized so that it could return to the self, the spiritual self of the being. The key to this is to be found in the Book of the Dead, and Ichor has much to teach of his experience over time. But the fusion of the higher self in Ichor's life was completed when he was initiated to the cult of Horus. So let us return to the scarab. The dung beetle goes through many turnings . . . and Anubis is in sympathetic relationship to the scarab.

Mena initiated Ichor at Giza when Ichor was fourteen and never expected to see him again. Now Ichor is twenty-seven years old. And then while he was reading a scroll, he was brought to Ichor's temple to give him the higher initiation of Horus. He stands between Acanza and Dion, and Dion puts the scarab in his hand. He walks into the temple, and he is amazed, really amazed. Because sitting in the chair in the center is Ichor.

Mena is shocked, he doesn't know what to do. He stops dead in his tracks, then he walks over to Ichor. Ichor has his hands out together. Mena becomes as disoriented as Ichor is. He takes the scarab like it's a hot potato, and he puts it into Ichor's hands. He normally would never do this, not in a million years.

He is afraid. He is Ichor's teacher, and he has not seen him since the initiation. He says, "I initiated Ichor according to the command of Ptah. I felt in Ichor something special. I always follow the word of Ptah, and I did as I was told. I am the temple priest of Ptah. I did the initiation, and Ichor became a priest of the cult of Osiris. And now, I'm going to destroy him if I put this scarab from the Atlanteans in his hand."

But he looks at Ichor. Ichor speaks through the uraeus and tells him to put the scarab in his hands. So he does it. Mena stands and watches. Ichor has become Horus with the Golden Headdress. His face is the face of the Hawk. He is transfigured. This being knows something that Mena does not know.

Ichor says, "You are resisting the energy from Atlantis. You are ready to get that now. But you have to understand the scarab. You should have known that you could not hurt me if you gave me the scarab. Now you are ready. Mena, you are ready. Our third eye connection is so intense that . . . this light is just amazing."

Then the light in my uraeus lights up the temple inscriptions, and I read:

The fish swims down many streams,
The fish continues to swim down the streams of death.
The fish has swum down so many streams of death and
    annihilation,
That the fish will die.

— the porpoise

The water bearer carries
The water to the hearts of the people,
And pours it from the jar.

— the water bearer

Ptah is the maker of the jar
That carries the water of the
Streams where the fish swim down
And the people drink water from the
Teachers of Ptah.

— Ptah

Over the ages
The teachers of Ptah will
Fill the vessels of the earth
With the waters of life.

— Horus

Now in my moment of enlightenment, I turn to my teacher, for never again will I see so clearly. I say quietly, "You are making the mistake of all teachers. You will always have more wisdom than me, but you are not listening to me. You will never know what I have unless you can listen. You have underestimated me, you have projected your fear on me when I had none of my own."

I put the scarab on his third eye, and we hear the message together.

"We work together from the plane of light. My sight is obscured by my confusion over the layers. The layers are being removed, but they are not all gone. Those are the layers of the ego, the layers of control of the energy. The scarab carries the secret of the divine wisdom. The scarab dies, and then the scarab is reborn into another essence. When the scarab dies, and the new essence is born, you are not to be afraid of having the same energies in the new essence. You will not be destroyed by the energy, and you have people working with you. You have been chosen for a very special purpose. If we just let the layers go and let it happen, there is nothing to fear."

Mena removes the scarab from Ichor's uraeus, and he places it into Ichor's initiation ring. And Mena and Ichor become equals as initiates of the cult of Horus. Like dung beetles, we are all parasites of the earth which we can decide to deny or nurture.

Chapter Seven

THE DARK NIGHT OF THE SOUL
INTO MAGIC

My chronological age ceases to be a factor now because I am embodied. My head in the clouds of the higher realms is connected to my body, and next my feet had to connect into the dung. My initiations with my highest self threatened to burn my body, leaving nothing in the heart of the furnace, and so the pull into connection with the cosmos forced me into my feet. The journey into the darkest night of the soul began with total compulsion because I needed to shine a searchlight into my deepest recesses or cease to be. And whatever I would find would be my teacher.

It is 1208, and we sit in an eating house on the edge of the Seine. I see torches across the river to the island in the city where they are tearing down and burning the ancient hovels for some alterations in the back of Notre Dame Cathedral, which we can see looking over the river. The Cathedral is very beautiful; it is so large inside that I feel very small. But, in spite of the power and majesty of the Church, these are troubled times.

These are crazy, crazy times. I sit with the other merchants planning trade along the routes of the crusades, and I feel this driven, crazy force that I felt when I left my village many years ago. That magnificent church was built early in my lifetime, yet I cannot forget the hunger and fear I saw in the eyes of my people before I left. Life seems unfair, and of course I do not care about that at all, but I just think of it. Here in Paris the Church was building this magnificent structure to capture the angels in the air, and back home the deep snows came and froze the hearts of the people as if ice was the tool of the devil himself. The ice and snows were so fierce that the people died of the plagues just to escape, as if anything were better than freezing. I stare into my burgundy in a thick, green-seedy goblet, and I know that it killed my soul to watch all the vines die and even the great trees. Even the boars were driven out into the open as the village wise women could no longer search for herbs. And yes, it was the death of my mother that seared the deepest into my heart. After I left, she froze next to the fireplace of cold coals when she could not get up to close the window, blown open by the vicious winds.

But these are different times, crazy times, and the Church has decided to stop the cancer growing in the south of France. And I am carried along with the force of the times. I was just on a trip down there, and nothing has happened yet. But it will. The people force it upon themselves.

The people are fascinated by witchcraft and strange ideas about mysticism from Spain and Arabia. And as I look over at Notre Dame, one of the merchants says that even the Church is infected from within, that the alchemists supervised the building of the Cathedral! And everybody all the time talks about the next thing that's happening. Just rumors all the time about strange things coming to pass. The times are just charged with mysticism and fear and occult practices. And we think they're all really crazy. But we're going to make money off it any way we can. People are coming and going from across Spain, from Africa, from Italy. And the Catholic Church is trying to make people stop doing what they're doing. They're afraid of mysticism, occult rituals, and they want to stop it.

I'm not interested in mysticism because I am smart. I am amazed people can take such chances against the Church. It is because they are crazed, crazed from hunger or something. The Dominicans are right in the middle of it all. They are the busybodies, the manipulators, they are the politicians of the Church. And we're just interested in making money from the situation because a lot of money was made by merchants in the crusades to the Holy Land. The people are wild all the time because they don't know what is coming next. And I hear rumors that they are burning people in southern France, burning women because they have strange ideas.

The women are mad, their eyes are wild, and I have seen this same crazy look in the eyes of my people when they were starving. To me nothing matters except getting money. But it is really strange now; whatever it is, I can almost feel it in the air. The women have had power, and the people have followed the women. The women have been preaching, they have the herbs and oils, they have their own power, and the Church does not like it. These women hate the Church; they are in touch with the earth magic, with the wind and the plants. And I don't know what will happen if the Church burns them, because in my village these women were the healers. There was nothing wrong with the healers in my village, they healed the sick. But the women in southern France are very powerful with the earth magic.

The people say these women control the crops, the plants, the animals, even the rain and water. And we can't sell anything when these women are in control because they take care of the needs of the people. And now we control the needs, and it is better that way. The women didn't prevent the starvation in my village. I agree with the Dominicans, these women are evil.

And you have to watch out for these people, because they sing and do poetry. That is dangerous because it makes the people feel too much. A few weeks ago, I was at a noble house and they had "Chretien de Troyes," the mystery play. And the mysteries are very dangerous. People get crazy when they have the mysteries. It is better to have the Church just control them, we can organize things better that way. Some people think that the Church is doing the wrong thing, but I agree with the Church. They should kill all of them if that's what it takes to clean them out. They are like a cancer, they will destroy us all unless we kill them.

But I stop myself and think a little more, because there is something about this that bothers me. Somewhere deep inside I know I am advocating killing a part of myself.

But that is okay, to kill a part of myself, because then I escape the boredom. I love the products I find and sell, I love traveling everywhere and being in the center of things. Then I am alive, there is always something new. After all, this is the first time ever a person could be this rich and not be royalty.

Now my friend is different from me. He is troubled. He was fine with everything until they started burning people. But I don't agree. I am not burning anybody after all. But he made me really angry. He will not trade any more because he says that our energy is killing the people, killing ourselves. He says he will stay out of it and that I am a murderer. I do feel bad about the women and children, I admit it. But I can't do anything about that, so I don't care.

So I never think about not being a merchant, in fact I work harder, but I do feel disturbed about what is going on. It is very ominous. The madness spreads like the plague. The people get involved in mass rituals to build their own power. The people run through the towns whipping themselves and carrying fire, and we hear about more and more burnings at the stake. The people go to watch the burnings, but I do not. I do not do that. I will admit that I feel fear in my heart, that a part of me knows better, and I admit that now I feel thickness in my throat as I see fire all around and smell the stench of burning flesh. But I will not look, I will not look.

I am here, down in southern France, with a large trade to sell, and this woman comes to me because I am rich. She is crying, and I want her out, away! My valet shoves her and she almost hits her head, and she throws the door open in my trade office and she screams as my people grab her. They tear at her hair, at her dress, and I stop them and say, "No, let her go! Don't grab her!" She screams, a piercing scream, and she falls forward and lands on my desk, her arms are clutching my desk. She is a mess, she is crying, and she screams, "You can stop them, all you have to do is pay, pay the Dominicans. If you don't, they will burn her. She is my little girl, she is only twelve! You have the money, you can pay the Church. If you don't pay, they will burn my little girl."

I feel nothing. As if my heart is a burned coal lying in the hearth where my mother died, frozen for days. I feel nothing. My men grab her shoulders, pull her away, and throw her out the door. It is twenty florins she wants. I make that in an hour. But there are too many of them. Imagine, if I did that, I would be flooded with filthy ragged women begging for their daughters.

But suddenly a ray of white light pierces my head between my eyebrows, and I stand up clutching my head and stagger as if I am having a stroke. My muscles lose their tone as I fall against my desk and my men do not move. The laser beam of white light stabs the previous awareness into my consciousnes as Hebrew prophet. As Hebrew prophet I told the people how to live, and I left behind my own wife and children as soon as the light of my mission took over my soul. And now I am here again as medieval merchant with another chance. But I do nothing. I collapse in my chair and ask for brandy because I am afraid I am having a heart attack. My heart is racing and pounding, and I do not want to go any further. I am afraid.

But I will never go to my center, find my ground of being unless I go to that fire, unless I go to that burning girl inside. I will be condemned to refuse the heart throughout eternity.

I am an old man now. I am the merchant, but now that I am old, I have feelings. I begin to think about the different things that have happened in my life, and I go back to that time when she was being burned. It is odd because I watched it happen then and didn't feel anything, but now I watch it again and I can feel the hot coal in my heart. It is so unearthly hot that it tears through the flesh of time. It becomes two coals, and now I see her eyes.

I remained a while in my office worrying about my heart as I sorted brocades from Florence, and then I was drawn to the square. They have a tree-like stake piled with faggots ready to light. People are screaming, and there is something terrifying in the sound of them. They sound like animals, they have no soul here. I hear a small scream above the crowd, a screaming small sound like a wounded bird, and they are bringing in this little girl. They're pulling on her shoulders, and rags are coming off exposing her flesh. I realize that this is the little girl when I see her mother behind. Five or six men are holding her and laughing as she screams the most unearthly sound I have ever heard. It still tears at my soul as I live the Laws of Karma.

They are bringing her through, this raggy, mangy little girl, and as she comes close to me she turns and I see her face. Time is caught momentarily, as I stare with horror into this unearthly beautiful little face, beautiful eyes, skin, white skin. The eyes are the hot coals and I am staring into the face of my own soul, my own daughter. (It is my only daughter in *this* life, Elizabeth, and it is my own soul.) And I have allowed my own soul to be burned by killing it with indifference, killing it with the fear of keeping my fire in my heart.

I know I've seen this face before, and I am terror struck. I fish in my pocket desperately for twenty florins, but I have brought no money in case the beggars would try to get it. I look up again at the face and I know it is also the face of my daughter in Thrace, but now I am a male merchant and I don't understand. But she knows me better than I know her. That is why she is my healer. So, then I run toward her and grab for the men who are carrying her along. They see my good clothes and they seem to be ready to stop, but a Dominican shoves one of them hard and they move on. He whispers in a raspy voice, "It is the devil, it is the devil."

Then there is the crowd of crazy peasants. They see my good clothes, and they become angry at me. One of them pulls the gem ring off my finger and almost breaks my knuckle, and then I am more afraid for myself than I am for the little girl. One of them grabs me by the throat and starts to strangle me. I can feel it in my throat, and the pain is unbearable. Somebody stabs me in the heart, I think I feel somebody stab me in the heart, but it is the sound of that little bird stabbing me in my heart. I have my own dagger, I hear her cry again as the flames sear her flesh, and I stab myself in the heart. I never want to have life again. Then I'm lying on the ground and I feel flames and the heat. Somebody kicks me in the side of my head and that is all I remember.

And that was the last straw as far as energy in my body that has life. Later we will return to the actual physical death of the medieval merchant, but what is seminal here is that a decision was made to not be fully alive as a human again. Full living is not possible without the full energy of the woman within/the daughter within. This karmic wound, and everyone bears such wounds, was so monumental that only a return to the astral state, the experience of the emotional body taking on full density could open the door to healing. The burning at the stake of the little girl is the killing of the heart that can only be healed with many tears.

The emotional body, the astral body, is the most potent part of our being to others. It radiates all around us, attracting people and situations to us that give us the opportunity to learn in each incarnation. This incarnation is the time for the return of the daughter within, for me and for all women of my times. And the calling to myself of the experience that would be my teacher occurred at the very early time in this lifetime.

I feel very dense, so dense as I call in this awareness of the body that I feel like I am being turned to stone. I am afraid, very afraid, because now it is the time to pass through the experience in this lifetime which reaccessed all the old traumas: the Roman castration, the burning of the daughter within, the rape of Lydia which was the death of the trust of father, and the apathetic puerile life of the Victorian woman. All of these lifetimes felt like my body was stone, yet my throat choked for breath. I am back there again, back there in early childhood in this life, and I am being thrown against a wall. As he throws me, my foster father during the Second War, against the wall, I fall to the floor with a thud. I feel nothing. My body feels light, like grey fog, and I feel nothing. And when I was molested at age five, I felt nothing. I cannot feel at all.

But all you have is a body, it is the seat of consciousness and the spark of the soul. Whether you feel it or not and become whole again depends on what you desire. And please be aware that you, as medieval merchant, would not have burned the daughter within if your soul was in your body.

The density intensifies. Now my body feels like lead, and the light around me is deep vibrant purple. It is time. I see the daughter within and she is very small, only about two inches tall.

Perhaps if she gives me a gift she will grow bigger. She gives me a brown horse with garlands of spring flowers in his mane. Then she grows larger until she is the size of my daughter now, and she cradles herself in my lap. I wish to give her a gift. I give her a cornucopia of fruit, of grapes, pears, apples, and oranges which she takes with her hands. The brown horse now is doused in spring flowers, and he grows an eighteen karat gold horn on his head. My daughter within rides him bareback, and she is now as large as a girl.

Next I see my father, and he is an ogre with brown fur, warts, and glinting eyes. I hold out my hands to him, and in my hands is a beautiful tiny white unicorn with spring flowers in her mane and a horn of shining gold. He takes my gift into his being, and he offers me a bicycle. Now my daughter is me, and we ride the brown horse together as my father smiles at his shining white unicorn. And in my heart resides a pearl.

Now my body becomes charged with power and energy, and it also feels dense. Now I know that my body is too light, there is too much that I keep out because of fear, and pain, and anger. Every time I think I am going to get hurt again, I shift the energy out and I become less dense, but also powerless. I cannot have my horse to ride if I am this way. I cannot feel if I am this way, I do not care about anything. And always in the past, when I did not care was when I failed.

And worse than that was when I did not care and had no free will. Apathy is the worst because I was used by others for their needs. I understood those Dominicans being used by the Papacy because I was used often when I was a priest. It will always be that way unless each person is autonomous. Aspasia is autonomous, she is courageous and filled with her power.

And what is it about Aspasia that offers the secret of wholeness? We will experience more of her powers soon, but identification is needed now as I explore levels of integration after so much experience up to this point. For the secret to full living is interconnectivity and inter-dependence. If I had possessed that secret in the thirteenth century, I would not have burned the daughter within. The secret is that if I alter any one of the holographic memory patterns lying in all my cells in this incarnation, then the holographic memory pattern is altered *throughout eternity. That is what freedom is, and when understood, it is easy as blowing a feather off your hand. Then all the heavy stone places within the cells can be bathed in the healing tears of true sorrow, and the cells become emptied to nothingness as the force, the creative cosmic force, fills the cells with white light. If I can find love with just one person, take healing in just one instance, and trust just one teacher, then all the cells of the body are altered throughout eternity. Then my essence is diffused into the All.*

Before we move on to more adventures of the movement of the white light from the high self through the many incarnations that are me, let us return to the medieval merchant as he lies wounded on the pavement in front of the pyre of his daughter within. Otherwise, if we leave him now, then he is lost and so am I.

I'm in bed and my two men are caring for me. So, somebody got me out of the crowd. I did't die then, but I wanted to. It reminds me of my life in Rome; it is the same kind of not wanting to live any more. I don't care about gold and silver any more, that cry took away my desire, it sucked it out of me. I want to blame it on the times, like in Rome, it is the awful times that suck my life out of me. I lie there and I know that I don't really believe that. I made my reality, I was the cause of my castration and the death of my male force then, and I am the cause of the killing of the daughter within. Later, a time of historical chaos will come, and I will heal it instead of being a victim to it. I learned a lot from my death when I was a merchant.

I'm riding in a wagon with two large wheels which resembles the old Roman chariots. I stand in it. The wheels are wooden. The horse starts to go too fast. I am about seventy and rather weak. Normally I don't drive it, and so I can't control the horse. The right wheel hits the side of a wall and the cart shakes violently. It's all very quick. I am thrown very hard, I hit my head very hard as the horse can't run and kicks back on his haunches. I am killed instantly, and I rise about six to eight feet above my body lying in the road. At the impact, I had this feeling of being engulfed by fluid. I'm lying on my side, and my body is all broken. As I look at it, I realize I am dead, and I am not at all disturbed. The people in the street are shocked, and they all become obsessed with the fear of their own deaths. I don't mind in the least.

Then next I take one last look and I ZOOM! Fly sideways and up like I am an airplane. I have a sensation of the flight as I just go straight up—ZOOM! I leave the planet, then the earth's atmosphere. The light is white and then it is blue.

Something up ahead is pulsating, vibrating, and as I get closer it vibrates faster and faster. I go into the center, and as I enter it I lose all of my physical being. It is an essence, and in the center it is vibrating so fast that it has no vibration. It is an essence, and I went to the essence also after my lifetime as a Roman.

Now I evaluate this lifetime as merchant. It was necessary for me to live this life in order to experience all levels of karma, to know that I hurt myself when I hurt another. It was my turn to learn that part of being human is to know all levels of humanity. I learned for the first time to never let things on the human causal plane, the experience level, to take total control of my consciousness. And I learned what it is like to be that way so I can understand humans in the future who are controlled by things, and not feelings and soul. Now I see how someone could kill someone, how one can be controlled by greed, how we cause pain for others by our apathetic response to life.

Now I know how to reach people who are locked into that consciousness. I can only reach a person in that space by appealing to their higher selves, and I learned that it is a matter of timing. People are only open some of the time, even though they would like to be open all the time. This life was a blow to my ego. I would have thought I would have been studying with St. Thomas Aquinas, and instead I was out in the marketplace selling skins and trinkets! And it is interesting that I was such a eunuch, that was certainly an appropriate response to my experience as a Roman. But I also learned to cover my ass in this lifetime, where the Roman threw caution to the winds. And I certainly had some interesting dealings with the Roman hierarchy.

But my basic soul pattern has been to work with the light, and after the incarnation as a medieval merchant, I was given a reprieve in the angelic realms. And what I found in these celestial realms was most curious, because the time had arrived after this life of dense pain to experience time and space as spherical. There is no path in the universe that is linear, it only seems to be so.

I am in a place of golden light. It is a temple. But I also see golden clouds. But I am at the same time also on the physical plane as an angel. And I am in two places at once. I live in this golden light, very warm, it's like the sun. And everything is just very different. And then

I come down, like right now I am down in the top, in the air space in the top of a cathedral, and it is about the 6th or 7th century in Gaul. I see black slate walls with drawings on them. I have some very special information as my gift because I was present very, very often on the earth plane, but as a spirit, as an angel.

As an angel, I am a mental being, and my consciousness can affect people's minds. This church is very old for a Christian church, and the energy up here is very divine. There are places on earth where the energy is very fine, and one of these places in the Age of Pisces is in the Christian churches. Many angels come here. We come here because we like it here. Often we come when the people start to sing. I love humans, and I can feel what it is like to be human since I am human at times, also.

We can do quite a few things to humans if we want to. We can go into their minds and change their thoughts. I can go into their bodies and make them feel good. I am like a cloud, I can go right into them. But only if they want me. If they don't want me, I can't do it. Humans have these powers potentially while they are on earth because they can remember being angels too, but it is hard for them to develop these powers and easy for me. I've tried to go into the humans who don't want me, and I can't, because their bodies are like stone. But sometimes I rearrange the cells in their bodies to make them feel better, to make them fill with light, to make them feel good and be happy. I am radiant and they are dense. If I use my radiance with their density, if I shine in them, they feel a spirit. They feel they are shifted and changed. There are lots of us here, and some people here have more angels around them than others.

The spiritual people have the most angels around them. Regular people just think about their houses, their children, or food. But spiritual people have learned how to not think. They feel the angelic presence so strongly that they don't think any more. For example, as I look down into the body of the church, there are a few down there who are all white light. We can pass in and out of them like the wind. They turned into white light by stopping thinking and magnetically drawing in the spiritual essences. They have gone through a lot of stages in their incarnations, and they've become adept at shifting into higher levels of awareness. Then we gravitate to them. It is a gravitational issue. It is also magnetic, because we are naturally drawn to the light, and then we try to magnetize those who are not so light.

We can tell about someone's light because we can see their

emotional state. For example, see down there in the church? There is a man down there, and there is a black cloud all around him. He is angry. And he is red too, black and red, and it is also cold around him. We can't reach him and we don't try. Only an earth healer can reach a person who is red and black. Our work is only to magnetize those who can be drawn. But there are more people receptive here in the church than outside, because they come here to make this contact. They don't know that is why they are here, but that is why they come. When they're in the marketplace or whatever, they're not thinking about spiritual things. The ones who always have the most light are the children. We visit them the most often, especially the little children, the babies. Some babies are so shining that they even almost blind us. At age seven, all children begin to have less light, because the child must then learn to use the will, the real use of the will. This lesson temporarily clouds the inner vision. When they are old enough to have true choice, then they can reject the light. Because of this age factor, we work very hard with the children to fill them with our light so they will recognize it more easily after they have gone through the crises of the will. We do what we can whenever we can because the human will limits our force.

It is a complex issue, and I would like to show you how it works because some humans are not aware of the greatest ally and force they have at their disposal, the angelic force. I am above a gray rock wall on the side of a grey stone church with crude buttresses holding it on the side. These are stone braces about twelve feet tall. There is a ledge or bench at the bottom of the wall, and a person sits there wearing a grey robe.

I can see the robe and the body sitting there with the knees crossed, but l can't see the head. I am up very, very high. And I have been magnetically drawn to this place. What it's like is, it's like I'm kind of whirling, swirling around up high. The person stands up. He wears a robe, and then he has a hat on his head that seems to be—it's hard to see—like a fur or something strange. Looks like a crown, but it's not a crown, it's a hat. What I have to do is, I have to key in to what he's thinking about. I will read his mind for you, if you like.

"Should I go to the crystal cave? If I go to the crystal cave, I will have the power and when I have the power, I may be in danger of being contacted by strong forces that are very dangerous. I ask for light so that when I go to the crystal cave I am safe."

Now that is why I am magnetically attracted. He needs my light to do something. I have to go with, I have to . . . I come down, and I hover over his right shoulder like a guardian angel. And his hat is . . . I'm next to his hat. His hat is quite finely made. It's velvet, and it's in three parts. And then his robe goes all the way down to the ground. Now he feels—I am fused with his mind. So I am with him.

He walks, turns away from the foundation of the old church, and he walks around the front of the church. This is an old ruined church, very old. And he walks down a pathway in front of where the church was. All that's there now is just a lot of rubble. He walks by a gate, and he stops. He looks around, looks over his shoulder and he looks into the distance. He suddenly jumps over the gate. The gate leads into very overgrown, very thick, brambles, with rocks on the side, almost like a tunnel but not exactly. He shuts the gate behind him. He goes down this path for about thirty or forty feet. I get the sense that it's along the side of the church, the other side of the church. We walked in front of it, went on the other side. The church is on the edge of a hillside or a cliff of some kind. He comes out of this tunnel-like thing where all the brambles are, and he starts climbing down the side of the hill, holding on with his left hand. And he's using his right hand to hold the roots so he doesn't fall. He goes along the side of this wall for about twenty or thirty feet, and then there is the entrance to the cave. I feel I am protecting him, and I like it. It's like someone gave me a job after I've been unemployed for a long time. So I like to go with him.

Nothing can hurt me. It's like being able to go on a trip with some-body because I can't be harmed. He goes in through rocks into a cave entrance, and goes in a little way, rocks and stone, and then it changes. It is moist with some water trickling. and there are reflections, there are crystals. All of a sudden I see lots of crystals on the top, on the sides. The crystals are black crystals, purple, white and yellow. And something smells funny. It's sulphur, a stuffy kind of smell.

He goes and sits down on the floor of the cave, and on the floor of the cave it's sandy, very fine sand. The water—it's a spring, and in front of where he's sitting there is a little pool in the rocks with crystals growing behind the pool. And the water trickles off to the right-hand side and goes someplace in the cave. Now I am wondering what he wants. He is very upset. He knows that he's safe, he knows that it was

Comme un gryphon viendra le Roy d'Europe
Accompagné de ceux d'Aquilon,
De rouges & blancs conduira grande trouppe.
Et iront contre le Roy de Babylon.

MCMXCVI

the time to come. But he is upset about something. He crosses his legs and puts his cape over his legs. He starts to stare into the black wall behind the pool at the wall of crystals. There are white crystals in the center, fanning out and becoming purple and amethyst on the sides. It's like a fan.

Something happens in his mind. I am in his mind, and something shifts. He can see the pool in front of himself and the crystals on the back that fan out, he takes them into his mind and his mind becomes an image of the pool. He merges with the crystalline form. He is staring ahead while he has this image in his brain. He's staring ahead, and the pool begins to become misty. Steam and mist begin to rise off the pool. And then he begins to see images in the mist.

The first one was . . . it's gone already. It was a green, red and white creature, like a griffin. He sees a griffin.

The next one is . . . the body of a griffin from the side, not the face of it. It's not green any more, it's a white griffin. Then he sees a woman with blond hair, and someone cuts her head off. Then he sees the man who cut her head off. He sees, there is an image of his hand, and he cuts the head off with a—it's like a scimitar or something like that. It's a weird blade, like a half-moon blade on a stick.

She has her head on a block, a stone or something. People are holding her. As he cuts her head off, she looks at him, the man cutting her head off. Then they bring another person, a young boy, and they put him down there. And then he cuts his head off again, and they just keep on bringing people one after another, and the heads just roll off everywhere, to the side.

He is Nostradamus. He had something strange happen to his brain, a little click in his brain. It's like a camera recording what he just saw. He records what he saw. He records it in great detail. He records the clothes, the picture that he sees is the 15th century and he . . . That's important to him. He makes a mental click of the time, who the people are, everything, for some reason.

Next thing I see is a wide river. It's moonlight. The moonlight is shining on the water. And there are people in boats. They are very quiet. They're sneaking someplace, sneaking into the river. The boats are wooden, large boats that hold about fifty or sixty men. They have oars. And the boats are filled with men who go across the river and get out on the other side as quickly as they can.

He's watching, he's watching, getting the details, trying to get the date. It's very curious. He's an historian. It's very strange the way he wants to know where it is, when it is, what it is. He's watching—it's like he's watching a movie screen, and he's trying to get as much information as he can. He just watches.

I see a Bible. And right after I see the Bible, I see lots of armies, soldiers. Lots and lots of armies, soldiers, horses, big battle scene. What's important is this image of the Bible. It's a religious war. And I, as I see the image, I don't like it. I make a mental note to myself that it's typical, having a war over the Bible. I don't like it at all.

The horses and soldiers are . . . I think they're French, French or German. It's on the Continent. And they look later than the time of Nostradamus. They look 17th century. Red, they all have red puffed-out shirts and black armor over their bodies. The horses have leather with brass decorations on them. They have shields and swords. War again. I always see war. They fly flags in the front. There's one with a flag. It's a red flag with a lion on it, a golden lion. And two fish on the bottom. Two silver fish. The next flag is blue with diagonal cross lines on it. That's all I can see. It's blue, and above the two crossed lines, diagonally crossed lines, there is a crown.

It is 1592, and these armies I see are in Holland or Belgium, the Netherlands. I came here to see because it has something to do with the English throne, with the pressure of Philip of Spain. He married Mary Stuart, she is dead, but he is still pressuring England. I have come to see into the future of Philip of Spain.

I was asked by a secret society, the Knights Templar, for information. I belong to them, and I often give them information. They want to know what is going to happen so they can take political and financial action. They get as much information as they can so they can put their energies and money in the service of the light. They have a lot of gold, and they will shift it to the French crown. They have alchemists who make gold, and they will use their power if they have to.

Now I leave the mind of Nostradamus, and I return to my angelic consciousness. As you can see, the angelic vibration moves totally into the awareness of the mental apparatus of any being that it enters. The awareness of Nostradamus is very visual, very prophetic, very historical, and so that is what I saw in his mind when I entered it. His mind was very open to my awareness, and so I experienced him fully.

I am diaphanous, and if you can let yourself go into my vibration, you will feel me in your brain. Eventually, as many mystics have done, you can feel my presence by how I affect your brain, and you can cultivate my existence. And if you do that, you will begin to function beyond time and space, and you will react differently about the pain of being human.

My divine awareness will give you awareness of meaning, of the purpose of suffering, it will be in perspective and you will be wise. And if all this seems very dreamy and unreal, turn to the Dolphins. The Dolphins are the angels of the animal kingdom.

Chapter Eight

THE ARGO PASSES THROUGH
THE SYMPLEGADES

As I matured into adolescence and then into my twenties, a painful dualism between my generation and the older generation began to predominate. I was just busy growing up and exploring being human, but expectations about how I was to live my life were being projected upon me that were meaningless. For years it was not a defined awareness to me, but the older generation, the ones who were supposed to guide me, had lost their credibility: They had created a massive absurdity—the means to destroy the planet. And the evidence in my small reality was even more damning to me. It is simple from a child's perspective: Nearly every species of fish, frog, bird and wood creature that I loved as a child was virtually extinct by the time I was twenty. There was simply no way out; my generation would have to develop new survival tools. And we would do it in secret, because the whole culture was determined to destroy the child within. And I am the child.

How can one grow in the middle of a genetic holocaust? As I matured and took on more power by working with my own generation and reaccessing the inner powers from previous lives, the only way out became apparent to me. The only way out now is to transmute the situation by means of initiation which is a holographic alteration of the fundamental cellular structures. And with that understanding, I became ready to tolerate re-experiencing and reaccessing past life initiation.

I am at Giza. I am fourteen, I am tall and very thin, my thick curly hair is covered with a tight cap as if I am bald, and I wear a white skirt with a thick gold belt. My head, chest, wrists are bare. This is my initiation as a Priest of Osiris, and I am in the temple with Mena. I am lying in a basalt sarcophagus which looks like a crypt, so that my crown chakra is the same height as Mena's waist. Mena wears a tall head-dress. I can't see him because I am in the box, but I sense exactly where he is. The top of the stone box fits perfectly. They have just closed the top.

It is completely dark, but I am radiating light. It is dark in here but it doesn't seem like it to me. Next I begin to feel powerful energy, it is absolutely overwhelming. It's coming in from all sides, and it is very strong. It is overwhelming, like being plugged into a power generator, but I have been physically trained to tolerate it. When I am sufficiently ready, which is determined by Mena and seems to take about four hours, then I begin to feel like I'm floating. Mena makes sure the air that I require goes right through the stone to me. That is what he does out there. But I wonder if I die in some way. I'm not sure, but a part of me has to die so that I am capable of a new level of living. I am being initiated as Priest of Osiris, and this initiation is the recharging of the root chakra so that I can manifest the earth force. My body is altered so that I can absorb greater magnetism than is usually possible. Also, I must now become a channel of the higher forces to the earth, that will be my role. And on the personal level, Mena is altering my astral body for my work. He is working throughout the whole fabric of my being, through all the internal organs of my body with rays to alter the essential fabric of my being. I am not sure whether I am in my body in the box as he works on it. I think my Ka, my higher self, goes somewhere. But, the place cannot even be revealed now. For I am to be an instrument of the Pharoah to balance the Kingdom. Since Mena is my teacher, he is making new connections in my physical apparatus because it is the focus of my awareness. None of the higher planes can function within my awareness, my body, unless the actual holographic imprint of my being is altered for this work. What it feels like is difficult to explain. There seems to be a membrane around my brain and spine that separates my physical body from my higher self. This membrane, the arachnoid membrane, is filthy, with specks of bluish white light. It is radiation, my physical body is being irradiated!

I am not well connected with the root chakra, I lack sufficient sensation in order to hold all my levels of awareness on the earth plane. My Ka, my double, cannot find a place in me. I am very highly developed on higher levels of awareness, but the fundamental link to the earth plane must be connected up. When this is accomplished, then I will be able to manifest reality which is the highest potential skill of humans. When everything is connected up, then we can cause events and make good work simply from what we think about. We are not initiated until we have been trained on what to think about. We are taught that humans, unlike other creatures, can alter the earth reality with our thoughts, we can change the physical plane by generating thought from the etheric level. For example, the Atlanteans built the Sphinx by using their minds to lighten and transport rock, and now we use this technique to build the pyramids.

We demonstrate our skills with matter for two reasons. One reason is that it makes our work much easier. I can't imagine, myself, building a pyramid any other way. But the second reason is much more important, and that is occult verification. Humans are capable of many magical powers on the physical plane, but they do not know it unless they experience it themselves in the physical. Our training as Egyptian priests is mainly work with occult verification. If you study the messages we left for you on temple walls, especially at Abydos, you will see that humans can become and manifest any force. You will learn that you create your reality by your own thoughts. We are taught, for example, to communicate at a distance with another person, and then the message is verified. We are taught to move stone, and the power is verified by the movement of the stone. This is reserved for the priesthood, however, because these powers can be used for good or evil. We take the utmost precautions to use these skills only for the good. As we progress in our training in occult verification, then finally the knowledge is embodied in us during initiation. And then, if the higher beings see that one of us is a fit instrument, we are also given the power to manifest mentally. Very few are given this power. That is the Horus initiation.

At this time, Mena is working with my physical and energy body to empower me for the work of the Gods through the Pharoah. Any human being is capable of this level of power, but few ever know it because deep inside they are afraid of this level of awareness. For most people, it is impossible to believe that anything is possible in our reality. For then, they would have to take full responsibility for what we have created. So, my body, like any human body, carries faults in it. They are little pockets of resistance that keep me from becoming clear and manifesting my divinity as an earth creature.

And I think it is about time to reveal the riddle of the Sphinx. It is obvious. The very existence of the Sphinx and the size of the rock it was carved out of proves my point about occult verification. And for humans of any age, knowing how the Sphinx was created will be the key to recovering full human potential. Just stand in front of the Sphinx and allow your total being to embrace its existence. If you can take it in without judgment, then you will be a seer. Paradox and riddles will fade into the Egyptian night, and you will find the lion in your soul. The key is the body position of the Sphinx, the direction it faces, and in the fact that it is half lion/half human, like the Centaur, Cheiron.

But let us proceed with the initiation. I lie flat for a long, long time as Mena moves throughout my body, in and out of organs, reorganizing them back to their natural state, which is perfection. Then I receive an incredible jolt throughout the whole spine. It started out by firing off in the upper part of the root chakra, it moves up my spine and out the top of my head. This goes on for days, or possibly for seconds! The energy comes in from the outside from 360 degrees to my center which causes a continual jolting. I have been prepared for a long time for this because the energy could destroy me otherwise. It seems to be electrical energy but it resonates deep in my bones, vibrating my body at a low frequency. They do something out there that causes a continual jolting. They finally finish sending the energy up my spine, and what I feel next is very pleasant. There are waves of undulating warmth going from the top of my head all the way down my spine to below my feet. If you could see the waves, they would be about six inches from peak to peak. It feels wonderful.

Mena is very sad throughout the whole initiation because he would rather initiate me into a higher level of serving. But he has to follow his instructions. To be a priest is to be obedient. He was told to initiate to the level of the rite of Osiris. This is a lifetime initiation which aligns me with Osiris for this lifetime. But then later I will be initiated into the rite of Horus by Mena. I am aware that I will serve the cult of Osiris all of my life, but I will receive the scarab later from Mena as a symbol of our connection with higher beings. But, Mena does not know I will work also with Horus.

Actually, the reason Mena is sad is because he is aware of the priestly conspiracy that is determining my training. And just as I was able to move into the mind of Nostradamus or enter humans as an angel, so can I now rise above the sarcophagus in the pyramid of Egypt and travel into the Akashic Records in order to find out about the conspiracy against me during my lifetime as Ichor. The records read:

"In that lifetime you were the second child of Amenhotep II and his queen, and your elder brother was Horus who reigned for about 37 years after the death of Tuthmosis III. There was about eight years difference between the two of you, and you two shared the same psychic fabric. He insisted that you be trained as he was although it was not usual at that time for the other sons of the Pharaoh to be trained in the same way. He feared the powers of the priesthood of Amun. Ichor means "blood of the Gods" in Greek; that is why you bear that name, and it is only one of your names. We cannot yet reveal your other names.

"Horus was skilled in clairvoyance and divination, he knew he would have no children, and his intention was that you might take over some time. His wish was to take advantage of various temple manipulations if necesssary, but upon his ascendancy to the throne, you were seen as his Achilles heel. A revolt in the temple resulted which was squelched by leaders in the temple, but a curse was put upon you by the priests of Amun in Thebes, which rendered you physically ill, almost to the point of death. Horus, a Master, was capable of removing that curse, and he did so to signal superiority over temple manipulations. And then he executed the priests who participated and disassembled their temple for all time. Their cult died because they overreacted to the battle between Horus and Seth. They caused imbalances by becoming obsessed with good and evil, dark and light. They tried to deny the face of chaos: Seth.

"But, they had also rendered you impotent and sterile, so you were initiated into a celibate sect which dealt with transforming sexual energy into fertility rituals. These battles in the temple would later result in the takeover and corruption of the Pharonic line by Amenhotep IV, who would even alter his name to Akhenaton and move the temple sites to other places. The earth energy of Amun-Min would be blocked by moving the temple. That is why you were selected to carry the energy for the harvest for forty-nine years, and that is why you resented this task.

"You died six years before your brother to make sure you would not come into power during that lifetime, for

you would have been ineffectual. But, as Priest essence during that incarnation you channeled in a great amount of
transformational energy to the kingdom, and hence you
possess that power throughout time. And whether one
reaccesses a curse from a previous lifetime depends on
whether you choose it or not. If you allow yourself to repeat
Karma, to be drawn into the old lessons again, then you
could reaccess such a curse. We create these kinds of realities
for ourselves by what is in our mind."

*Ichor as me—that incarnation was not a very happy one. So much
of me was pulled into temple service that I disliked, and I suppose I
sensed the Pharonic line was doomed. But, as I surveyed reality before
I incarnated as Ichor, I could not imagine being anything but a priest
then. The twentieth century is actually radically different from these
earlier times because now all people, men and women, can aspire to
the priestly level of awareness. And few of us have any idea how far
back and deep the priestly roots are. There was a time long before
Ichor when the orders of priest and priestess were in charge of the well-
being of our planet. It was a time when many of the priests were also
Masters. It is so far back, but we will go far back in time in order to understand the many ways we attain our highest aspiration—to be co-
creators with the higher forces.*

*This is very interesting . . . As I travel back this time I first end up
in a very strange place. Actually, I end up first on the tip of the horn of a
Unicorn! At first I am a tiny speck of matter and then I begin to form, as
if I am creating myself, and creating myself on a Unicorn's horn! I
manifest as a priest of Enoch.*

I am large and barrel chested and my feet shine. I wear a helmet of
silver metal with a cone on the top of folding layers that sits on a broad
brim. The ancient Sumerians wore similar helmets. Underneath, my
hair is brown and kinky, curly and not very long. I am bald on the back
of my skull, and my features are large and fleshy. My nose is prominent and hooked. I have thick lips and full teeth, and I wear a long full
cape that gathers at the shoulders. My cape is white and fastened by a
gold chain, and it is nicely woven of linen. I wear a light silky tunic, the
bottom is pantaloons, and a heavy belt around my waist holds a
weapon. I pull it out of the holster, and it's a 6" disk. It is light, it is not a
weapon, it is used for something else . . .

I am up on the top of a hill by myself, and I have it in front of me. It floats in my hands and radiates out ultraviolet rays. It has a life of its own! I hold it to keep it from spinning out of my hands. The reason we began on the Unicorn's horn is because a Unicorn made this object with me. It is flat to my chest, perpendicular to the ground, like a heart. I feel a lot of energy and power. Next I want to put my hands underneath it and hold it in my hands, out in front of myself. It's very powerful. I have to really hold my position with the power in my knees, standing firm on top of the hill. Otherwise, it will spin out of control.

So, I am continually jolted as I struggle to control this wild being, as if she were a Unicorn herself, and then it moves forward into my hands in front of me. This is a sacred act. It is still hard to hold onto, it has a will of its own. No, that is not it. The key is I control it with my will . . . Okay, so I get it into position and I don't feel so much energy in myself, and now it speaks. It takes in something and brings it back in sound. No, it doesn't speak words, it hums. The sound means that it is bringing other minds, other thoughts, from other places here to me in my hands. It is my instrument because I live here on earth, and it brings thoughts from outer space, from stars, not planets. As it brings in energy which goes out the back of my neck, it is bringing in a transmission that I don't know how to translate. It could kill me if I weren't in a position to take it, because this is how we receive word from the gods. What I receive is the humming light. It goes right to the center of my disk, and then it radiates everywhere. The light is white and it is the size of a big egg, like a cosmic egg.

My disk is somehow a translator, more like a transformer, a transformer that changes the electrical energy. But it is not electrical, it is magnetic because it hums. Again, it is jumping all over the place and I am trying to control it. It is like balls of lightning. It is like a fight, as if ball lightning was trying to drive me off my hill. But the way my will is involved is I accept the situation, I do not try to control it.

So, I am trying to get the light of the Gods to connect with my disk. I hold my hands with the disk just above as the light shoots around. It does not touch the disk. This is like being right next to a short circuit between two high voltage wires. I continue to be jolted by the force. It goes into my heart, through my feet, up and down my spine, and back out the top of my head. I am just handling it and doing what I'm supposed to do. I just have to hold enough space for it and stay conscious, otherwise I lose my place on the tip of the Unicorn's horn.

The light connects with the disk finally, and the energy is reversed through my crown chakra, through my third eye, and into my body. What an incredible shock! It is the involution of energy of Elohim, the Gods. And finally I feel the energy in my hands, in my hands as if I could form the cosmic egg or heal a soul. It is wonderful. Now the light and the disk cannot destroy me, for the light of the Gods is in my hands. This is what it means to be fully human.

So I stand with the energy flowing into me, into my heart, and flowing back out to the Gods through my hands. The waves I feel later in the pyramid in Egypt are now in my hands. The energy of the light is now in a larger field. The disk is gone, but somehow it is connected with the ball of light. The ball of light is somehow diffused into radiation going out from my hands, going outward, but it is still connected to the Gods.

So, now it is possible to make the connection verbal. I don't know how to do it yet, but I know it is now possible to express the reality of the energy of the gods for humans. But I can say what it is. It is the ineffable.

> "We are the same, we are one. There are no barriers or transmitters. We are in the heart, we are always in the heart, and we can be reached only if the energy is connected and radiates outward. We are in the heart, and we can speak to other hearts. We are timeless, we can speak to hearts back to the beginning or to hearts now who know the ineffable.
>
> "You, that is you as your higher self of every body, you don't even know that I don't know who I am yet. I will know my self only when you know me. I only have existence when humans know me in the heart.
>
> "You, wherever you are, you can see with your third eye those who also know the beings in the heart. You can see them with your third eye. You can hear them in your mind with the humming deep within the center, and where you hear them in your mind is where you can speak to them. Listen to them deep within and feel their vibration. That is where they are within you."

I return to reality holding nothing, and I now stand on the Mount of Transfiguration. It is there that I go for the energy of the Gods. So, now I am open to the awareness of the ineffable, but I need to go to the mountain to find it. But it was difficult to do that, I had to force myself to go that far. But now as I stand, the power of the force continues. It goes right into the spinal column in reverse, and finally goes into the heart and melts. It is hot, and as it goes into the heart, the connection is made in my hands. The light energy is coming in from the Gods through both hands, and the hands transmit with the heart like a triangle, a trinity. It is received in me in triangular form, but as one-ness. It is just out there radiating, and this is how one can receive it. The oneness goes into my heart. My third eye speaks of the ineffable:

> "The level is nine, the level of the divine is nine. If you receive the energies as the one, the gods do not fight in your heart. You have made your eight, your way to receive after you have the energies in the seven chakras, and you receive with your eight in order to be at the level of the nine, the ineffable. I am Enoch. I am priest of Enoch."

I am one with the divine energy because I am transmitter of the divine will to the people. I made this disk, I was told by my third eye, and the messages come to me on the mountain. The day I made my eight was the first time I knew the ineffable.

I had walked up my mountain on that day feeling anxiety in my hands after failing at a healing. In my work as priest, I heal with my hands. I move energy through the body to heal, and I just finished working on blocks I could not move through. I was burning in the heart over my helplessness when up ahead I saw a beautiful Unicorn. I walked slowly toward her as she stood on the pathway waiting for me. When I came close, first she drew me into her eye. Time and space were altered as I swirled into her eye, as if I traveled on a mythical spiral. And next thing I knew, I was at the base of her golden horn and spiraling up to the tip. As I spiraled up, I felt magnetic energy in my whole body, and I looked to the top of the spiral, just like the spiral in the priestly cone hat, and I saw my eight. I saw through the eye of the Unicorn that I could not heal alone, I could only heal with my eight as the base of my triangle, from my heart to my hands. Then My Lady teacher was gone.

Possibly the most confusing aspect about becoming empowered comes from the body's inability to cope with the rising energetic; to re-balance as new levels of depth are encountered within the body cells, and to find ways to live fully in the current reality as the inner depth unfolds. The greater the differential between what is felt inside and what is outside, the greater the stress the organism encounters. Obviously, the stress is overwhelming at times, and retreat occurs. But for me, retreat was never an option. I found myself driven into a new vortex of deep energy each time I went through a new barrier.

It is difficult to say it right, but as I ingested my inner awareness of my Giza initiation into the rite of Osiris and regained my healing energy in my hands from taking in my unicorn again, I felt like I was spiraling into a bottomless pit within my own being. The further I fell, the deeper was the inner pool. We are all infinite inside, but we can only find it if we freefall, spiraling into the unknown.

Often my struggle for breakthrough was in a male body, but the revelation that came after I gave in to the force, was always female. And the final integration was androgynous. As soon as I made my eight and traveled through the inner body blocks, the goddess was waiting with her corn . . .

It is I . . . Aspasia. I am large with medium length curly hair like bunches of grapes. My body is thick, I am barrel chested, my lips are prominent and my nose is aquiline and straight. I wear a loosely draped linen shift with sandals, and I feel my feet firmly on the earth. My stomach is large, and I like my bigness. I am standing on a stone stairway in the courtyard behind my house. It is almost time, but I linger for a moment longer so that I can get my power. It is early evening, the sky over the ocean is still rosy and glowing from the setting sun, and only the evening star has appeared. I stretch my arms out as far as possible to accept the energy from the Goddess. I close my eyes as my head becomes numb instantly, and I stand with my arms out as the wind rustles my tunic and chills my bare inner thighs. I hear a faraway voice in the wind calling me to Crete, to the inner sanctum, to my teacher. I go in my mind to my guide as I fold my hands and arms to my bosom. I close my awareness into my heart and the image forms in the front of my brain that sends tentacles into my inner brain. At last I see it, the eye of the Golden Hawk, glowing into my being . . . and I am ready.

I turn to pass into the hallway, into the inner courtyard where the people wait for me, as Jupiter and Saturn glow in the early night sky near Venus. Many more people have come at this time than usual. The inner courtyard of my temple has a shallow pool of water with an opening above it to the night sky, and all the thick wooden columns around the inner circle are lit with burning amber. The people sit on the floor in front of my stone bench waiting for me.

I . . . I don't know what is happening . . . I have never been so swept by awareness . . . and I raise my hand to my handmaiden to remove Dacia, Lucia and my son from the temple. I see Ahura look at me with confused eyes, and I move my hand down to indicate he must stay. I am carried away like a dolphin in the high tide, swimming under the Pleiades, and I let go into my need.

I become very dizzy and confused, and so I pace around in front of the people in front of my bench. Quickly a white light comes into my head and chest, and it is a hard energy to take. I'm clenching my fists hard as the light focuses into my third eye like a cutting laser beam, and I am intensely jolted. I have never felt it like this before, and I am overwhelmed. Now I know why I was so well-trained for this very moment, and I have to accept it all.

There are about thirty people sitting on the floor watching me, and they are all very different and wear very crude clothing. It is hard to see them, because I perceive them as a group and not as individuals. They are mostly men with long facial hair. They wear leather and animal skins, and most of the men wear headbands because they are tribal chieftans. Quite a few of them have military power, and Ahura knows them all. They come from far away places, mostly from the north up to Heligoland and east to the River Pharis, and they are all different colors, some very dark and many olive.

I ground the light with my third eye as my whole body seems to be magnetized, and I immediately go into a deep trance. You see, it is not me who speaks. The voices flow through me like the wind. I am only an instrument.

"This message comes to you from the Kabieroi because it is time to give the sacred warning again from the tablets of Orichalcum. The sacred revelation of Enoch is given throughout the ages so that you may know service to the people. For always in times like these that are to come, unless you resort to your own angelic resources, you will remain the victim of the forces of chaos. So, listen now, that you may know the myth of the ages.

"You will first notice the changes with Basilea. And then Venus will tremble at the time you sense the pulsations

from the Pleiades, the daughters of Atlantis banished to the skies ages long ago. The great Cheiron left you with the true story about the origins of the stars. And Cheiron is now in the heavens with Cronos and Uranus as the guardian of this cycle. Listen and beware! The time is coming soon when a comet will appear in the sky and send light to earth. Remember the most sacred teaching at this time: The volcano is one who births, and the comet is the fertilizing force. The volcano is the container of the cosmic seed brought into it by the comet. Remember also, that like the ripe womb of the young female waiting to be fertilized which draws the phallus irresistably to its home, so the volcano draws the sky force into the realms of Pluto. Otherwise the earth is barren, but woe to the man who is on the earth when the earth is fertilized by the sky.

"People on earth must prepare because the tides will be altered, there will be terrible winds, and the body in the sky will become the great monster, which is already known to you in the ancient myths. It will begin with the eruption of a great volcano which will collapse into the ocean, making the ocean rise and inundate the land.

"Great fissures will open in the earth, swallowing man and beast alike, and the land will heave and roll so that even the gods will not know what is sea and what is land. Civilization will become like storm litter on the beach. Few will survive, and the writing and art of the Gods will be destroyed. For thousands of years, the world will believe that the Minoans did not have a written language. The animals will cry in death as little babes are thrown to the ground, and the suffering of the mothers over the death of their babes will be worse than the pain of the children. The fish will come out of the sea and be thrown on land, the animals will be thrown into the waters, and the skies will rain fire that will destroy all that remains. The islands will be inundated, the rivers will run backwards, and the sea will wash back and forth as if it were soup in a giant's bowl. Even the Triton will reverse its flow. You, Aspasia, you are to watch the dark side of Basilea, the dark side of the moon.

"When you first see the comet, which will be soon, you will know the time is close. Then you watch Basilea. and as the comet comes in, the dark side of the moon will light up from the light of the comet. When Basilea lights up, the prophet Mopses, who is with Jason and the Argonauts, will be bitten by a snake. There is great danger of planetary collisions, it is likely to hit a planet or the moon. This is a terrible extraterrestrial event. Everything is going to be chaotic, everyone will be afraid, and the hordes will be very dangerous."

My vision is finished, and I am exhausted. It all drains out of me, and I raise my head and look at the people as they sit frozen in horror. Our civilization is highly developed, even though we live very simply. We are very advanced in our thought rituals, and we cannot imagine such a happening. We are all shocked because I have never had a vision like this before. Normally I work as an astrologer for my people. I cast charts for the rising star in order to help the leaders make decisions. Often we just meet and discuss events and predictions. Always when the white light comes, I feel agitated, like I am going to have a fit or convulsion. The power is an alien force. In the past I have been correct when I had a vision, and so the people are stunned. I am as surprised as they are.

So, I initiate a group discussion to determine if anybody else has heard of a prophecy like this one. Has anyone seen or heard any signs of an event like this? A man comes forward who has come from the north woods to tell me about signs he has seen. He says the swans did not return to the lakes in March or April, the eagles are not nesting, the sheep are barren this year, and horrible snakes never seen before are coming to the villages from the caves. The priest from Araxes who came here because he heard Jason and the Argonauts were coming from the west says that he wondered if the message of the secret oracle of Phoebus was of a cataclysm. A woman from Adrino wearing a grey robe comes forward who seems to be abnormally agitated and says that she has seen too many stillborn infants and babies with birth defects this year, and she took a baby to the high cliffs born wih three eyes. She tells me she is afraid to look at the moon now. Then four or five men start talking among themselves about strange things that have happened with their animals this year. They have found dead animals in the fields, and stillborn animals with birth defects.

A very disturbing picture begins to emerge as we talk, and I realize I will have to contact somebody in Greece immediately. None of us knows what to make of this, it is so bizarre. So, we end the meeting agreeing that no one will repeat what we have heard, and we will watch for signs.

What I have said is accepted as the future. What I have told them in the past while in a trance has already happened, and we are in a state of shock. They all leave.

Then I go get my daughter, Dacia, and we go out into the back courtyard together. The sky is filled with stars. I tell her that we're going to start watching for a comet, a star with a tail. As I look up into the sky, I feel fear. The sky is a place of ominous warnings. The ancient seers taught that a great light was seen in the heavens before the great flood. The ancient myths say that Thetis lives under the sea because the sky was burning up. It is where I look for signs of the future. We can't see a comet. Dacia and I always watch the moon together, and I don't tell her very much, but as always, I teach her about the sky.

Later, when I'm alone, I think about what I feel. I am not afraid, but I'm curious about what will happen because the news reminds me of something I know about inside. I'm worried about the people, mostly because if this comet comes, it will bring out their worst form of behavior. First they will think they did something to cause it, then they will think it is the failure of the temple, that we have not sacrificed enough to the Gods. We have a lot of tension right now in the Minoan culture. The male priests are trying to control the power of the Goddess. The priests will blame the comet on the Goddess. Then the people will run in mobs and pillage instead of helping each other.

I leave the temple and go to my casting room where I draw sky charts. I unroll my parchments with the maps of the rising stars, and I think about where the planets will be in the near future. Every night I watch the position of the planets we can see, and I also tune into the positions of the planets we cannot see—Chiron, Uranus, Neptune, Pluto, and Nibiru. We do not know where they are, but we were taught to feel these qualities and orbits in the temple initiation. That which cannot be seen has more energy from the gods, for if we could see it, it would influence humans more. Also, we know much about the unseen bodies because of our experiences in our yearly star journeys. When we travel out, we pass by them all in our inner mind.

Now it is time to journey deep within myself, for what I have heard agitates me greatly. Since everything that is without also exists within, by journeying inside, I can learn what this comet is. Just as I am highly aware of the cycles of Uranus unseen, so I can know the story of this invader. Deep within a voice resounds:

> From the first age, heat gave life to creatures—fire
> From the second age, breath gave life to creatures—air
> From the third age, blood gave life to creatures—water
> From the fourth age, flesh gave life to creatures—earth

Thus creatures are made from everything that comes from nothing, and so it is that new life comes from chaos, the opposite of form. The ultimate ecstasy comes from chaos and escape from form, and thus you now feel the great allurement from your creator.

Hmmm. Then next I remember all the ancient stories of the dragon, the destroyer, the teacher of humanity's smallness. I feel an inner stirring, an inner memory, and then I begin to feel a knowing take shape. A new space is being created within me for a new force.

Chapter Nine

ENOCHIAN, DRUIDIC, AND THRACIAN DIVINATION

It is late afternoon. Did you know you go to find God in the late afternoon? As I move in time through a tunnel to find the deepest pool in myself, I'm not sure whether I go forward or backwards. I just let myself fall softly and move farther because I've gone so far that I can't turn back.

As I walk along the pathway, I become aware that I am the priest of Enoch. He wishes to reveal himself to me again. Today it is rather chilly and damp, about 65 degrees; it is usually warmer here. I am coming down from the Mountain of Transfiguration, and I have left the sacred disk behind. The mountaintop is untouched by human hands, but the steps down the side are steep and there is a round arch down below. I walk down and through the arch, and then I can see the city. Only the priests of Enoch can go down these stairs. As I come down, no one is around and there is a long pathway in front of me. There are buildings on both sides of the pathway that are two stories tall and made of grey and white stone. The people live on the first floor, and the second stories are high rounded towers in the center. I can also see temples, and they are very beautiful. I can see a long distance, the terrain is rolling hills, and the buildings are close together. The buildings undulate with the terrain, and occasionally a rocky hilltop with a few trees emerges in the middle of the stone structures. Far in the distance, I can see the sea, but past many buildings.

The city where I live is densely populated. As I walk I can see in the distance a four-sided step pyramid which has stairs going up the middle of the faces. It is worn, very ancient; it looks like its once sharp edges have been worn away by water. Way beyond this pyramid I can see a huge tidal zone, a beautiful salt marsh to the sea. There are

wonderful large-winged birds flying out there. This place is Atlantis after the first flood. More floods come later. As I walk along the pathway, which is elevated about eight feet off the ground, I look at the buildings. They are very classical with columns and pediments, and they are very thick and strong. The smaller buildings are round huts with small domes. I walk on the pathway of the gods; the people do not walk here, only the priests. The pathway is very long and eventually leads to the sacred mountain, the ancient temple from before the flood. This path I walk on is fascinating because it is an elevated causeway from the Mountain of Transfiguration to the sacred pyramid: as the priests of Enoch walk the pathway, the people can see them. The people meditate with us as we walk because we maintain their energy. The people worship the gods in their work, and we connect the energy of the people to the gods by walking the pathway. This is synchronicity.

The pathway winds and goes on for a while and then comes to the pyramid. The pyramid is thousands of years old, and our temple is located next to it. As I come to the end of my path, I begin to feel energy in the back of my neck and in my hands. I will go to place this energy in the temple. I will put it there for balance. The temple has straight thick Doric columns in the front with a large pediment across the top. It is dark and cavernous inside with a rounded ceiling in the center section. It is five-sided, and I go inside and stand in the center under the dome. I realign my chakras and shoot my energy up my spine and out my crown chakra.

When I am finished, I go back to my cell. I walk out of the temple through a small back door, and as I pass the ancient pyramid again, I bow deeply and do the heart blessing. I enter a small courtyard where the cells and small cubicles are located, and each cubicle is small but has four columns in the front. The space inside is small and square, and the light comes in through a round window up high above the columns and through two lights behind the columns. The light from the high window shines on the stone floor. This is like a monastery. The front room has uncomfortable stone benches and an eternally burning fire in a small hole at the center of the floor. My sleeping room is behind this room, and it opens to the garden in the back.

I am thirty-seven, and I have chosen to be celibate. Most of the priests had wives and children once, but some of them have taken the priestly vows after age forty. It is 5000 B.C., and this city is near the North Sea. Our temple is one of the few structures remaining after the flood.

I want to return to the time when the pyramid was newly built, so I will now go through a time warp back to this place before the flood . . .

I shoot through a time tunnel. The temple is now unmarred by time and weathering. It is stepped, it has four openings two-thirds of the way up the four sides at the top of the steps. I am disoriented. I just shot back far in time. The pyramid is an initiation place, but an initiation is not occurring now. I look around and there are not so many buildings around as there were in 5000 B.C. Many people live in small huts, and the climate is milder. This is a seafaring land, and I ride around in a little vehicle. It's like a sportscar that flies; it moves like a jet plane with tubes in the bottom. The airflow goes through the tubes which propel it from behind. There is no fuel for it, and I am not a technical person so I can't explain that, but we can only ride on certain lines in the sky because it runs on magnetic force. I can tell you how I drive it. The steering wheel is like a half-moon, and I grip it on each side as if driving a space ship. It is made of a metal like silver, it has twelve-foot-long wings on each side, and I can make it go fast or slow.

I am alone in my machine, and others are flying around in the sky. I wear a tunic tied at the shoulder. I am a male merchant. We are at a high point of development in this culture; we trade with many places, and we are very civilized. Sometimes we travel on water in a small speedboat, and it is powered the same way this ship is. I will travel to the largest city now. I move fast and level above the ocean, and we approach the city.

As I approach the city, it is surrounded by a huge wall. It is like a fortress. As it comes into view I see that it is ruined! I don't know why I came here! This is my colony, this is Calceon at 41 degrees latitude. It has been destroyed. It is chaotic here. There are a few people here trying to survive, and some others got out. They went to Central America, to Africa, to Italy, to Ireland, and to places that no longer exist on this planet. This was the main colony, but now the main one is where the pyramid is located at Heligoland. This was the largest city. There were eleven cities in Central America where the people went after this place was destroyed. The largest one was Quetzlcoatl named after a god. The pyramids there look like the pyramids in my city and the step pyramids in Egypt are similar. That is because we manifest energy on the physical plane with pyramids. The alchemy pyramids are flat on the top, and the initiation pyramids are pointed at the top. People do not live in the pyramids. They would atomize if they did. But we can store food in them.

I came here to get minerals, the metals. We don't have any on the main island. They smelt here, and they manufacture finished products, sometimes with metals. That is what the flat part of the pyramids is for. Priests send the metals from there. They move them on the astral plane, and we use them in the physical. As I travel and think about moving metals, I feel light. I am not very dense, and I may be in another dimension. I'm not sure I'm really here: I may be time traveling.

I'm curious about these metals. There is something interesting about the density of the metals. But my body vibrates faster than these metals, so they are hard to comprehend. I can manipulate them and shape them, however. I do it with my brain. This metal is Pleiadean, and we also use gold, silver, zirconium, titanium, astronium, and lithium which is also a gas. We do not alloy the metals because we don't want to mix up the vibrations. That causes bad energy. I cannot use my brain to move an alloy, only a pure metal. Maybe we alloy them after we get them moved. I don't know.

The strange thing about this reality is the density levels all seem peculiar to me. I'm not as dense myself as usual. In fact, if I bring my hands together, they move through each other! And all the other humanoid beings here are on different density levels. The ones less dense are energy beings, divine beings, and they balance energies, work to protect the planet against chaos and negation. My work, however, is more difficult than theirs. My work is manipulating metals and moving them long distances. I am an alchemist, and my training was long and arduous. I had to learn to focus my mind so I could alter vibration levels. The dense beings around here are very peculiar. Some of them are fully human; the best humans are beautiful women, and they can't see me. We do not interact with them, but we play many tricks on them. We like to watch them, especially when they take their clothes off. The beings who are denser than the humans are a mixture of animal and human forms. Some of them are gross with deformed limbs and faces, and they can be very strong and violent. Some are part goat, or with dog bodies, or lizard bodies, and some are half sea creatures. Some are very beautiful like unicorns and mermaids. We never underestimate them. I wonder if they are mutations?

No, that is not all it is. It is more like when I go to cocktail parties today, and I see people as their animal nature when I'm bored. I've looked around a formal table and seen pigs, chickens, lizards, and cows, and what I was seeing was a facet of their personalities. I have great energy right now, and I feel a stabbing fusion between my left and right brain. My brain is operating on one channel, and that is what I see when I'm seeing in one channel. This is actually what things look like when the left and right brain fuse. It is actually possible to see a physical manifestation of a person's emotional character. Before I move into my density, I become aware that this strange reality I have just visited can teach me a great lesson. I learn that we are not essentially physical at all, we just think we are.

Children who play with mudpies are not wasting time; they are learning to lose themselves in doing something for no reason. Then they move into another dimension. When I was little I think I knew nothing was fixed in space and time. I used to stare at a lamp on a table and see lines radiating off it, then geometrical forms of light would manifest on the surfaces of the object, and I would be someplace else for hours. And we all know that modern physics has established that there is more "nothingness" than "beingness." Come with me and travel on a plane that cannot yet be explained, a plane that takes us into nothingness. I have found trips into other realities are facilitated by using crystals.

I sensed a connection with the Druids even when I was small. But I was only able to access that material again after my father died . . . . . . yes then.

This time the dynamic of the room I find myself in is like the inside of a human skull; the energy dynamic is like the dynamic of brain operation. We worship the human skull. Everything is made of gold, and the whole world here is set up to facilitate my presence. Everything in this room is chosen to energize the higher centers. The gold is shining, the floor is purple granite; this is a place of the earth memory. The floor is made of energy lines that all go to the center, and the stones feel like people have been walking on them for thousands of years.

Lucca and I enter, and the people take notice. Lucca and I always work together for channeling and ritual. I am the receiver and he is the sender. This is the time of the winter solstice. We are late; there are thirty or forty earth priests in here, and everything is made of shining soft gold. It feels heavy. Lucca is on my left, and the others are in positions around the edge. They wear robes of many colors and are projecting energy into the center. Lucca and I enter, and we walk around the center circle until we stand opposite each other, about thirty feet apart. The altar is in the center between us. There is a hallway all around the circle outside the columns, and the priests are moving around in the hallway. We are surrounded, and we are bare headed because we removed our headdresses. We are both nude except for a heavy robe from the god at the center of the earth.

I am confused; I am afflicted by double seeing . . . as if images are being projected on the floor of many colors and move in and out of other dimensions. It is like a movie is being projected into the space in the center of the circle, and the screen is the surface of the molecules in the air. Also, that is the way I visualize my dreams. It is extremely distracting, so I focus into the center with Lucca. I raise my arms, slowly pulling the earth power with my hands; I aim my palms to the center, and the force shoots across the center to Lucca. His power meets mine simultaneously, and the fire in the altar extinguishes. A blue figure of light manifests where the fire was. It radiates light out from itself, increases in intensity, and quickly fills the whole cavern of the temple with pulsating, shooting blue-white light. I feel the power of the manifestation in my higher head centers as if my brain was filled with gnashing ball bearings, feel the blue-white light energy above my eyes and throughout the top of my head, radiating back into the back of my skull. The light is hard to contain in my head; it wants to shoot out.

Next I raise my hands slightly so that they are exactly aimed at the blue figure of light in the center, and Lucca does the same. He is also focusing the energy in his head into the form, and an arc of white light manifests from my head to Lucca's head over the center of the blue figure of light.

Now the double seeing dissipates like a dream slipping away upon waking. There actually was no fire in the center; there is only an opening in the stone to the earth and no colors are radiating all over the floor; we were merely seeing our own energies. There is no gold on the walls in this room, only cold grey stone. In the center of the room where the opening to the earth exists is a beautiful and perfect quartz crystal ball giving off an inner light. The light in the crystal is an inner glow caused by refraction from the arc of magnetic light between our higher centers. We are intensifying that light arc; it moves in long waves like the waves I feel in my spinal column. I now have a connection into Lucca's higher centers, but we are a polarity and we must walk to the center. I am negative and Lucca is positive; I am a receiver and he is a sender.

As we walk into the center, the priests on the outside move in also. We walk with stiff-kneed steps; each step is taken with absolute concentration. My energy is so pure, so directly powerful, that I do not have to hold it in my body. At other times this has been so different. Now what we are doing is like walking right into an electrical generating power grid fully connected to the energy of it, but we are so grounded that we are not shocked.

Our movements are slow, simultaneous, and automatic as we approach the center, and I feel a rush of joy because the priestly caste has not changed this altar. It is simply the earth, there is nothing in the way. The rocks form concentric circles to the center with the lines between getting closer and closer together in the center. There is a circle of rocks about fourteen inches in diameter around the opening in the earth. The crystal ball, which is six inches in diameter, rests on the earth in the center. It is clear and perfectly round. Lucca and I move to the hole and sit down opposite each other. We cross our legs with our cloaks over our knees, and all the other priests move in and sit close to us.

Now we have wings! We are angels! The angelic being that exists in all of us manifests as we sit opposite the simple hole of earth containing nature's greatest creation, the quartz crystal ball. We are humans and we are priests, and I feel my heavy wings attached to my shoulder blades. Again, the gold seems to bathe the room, the swirling colored images sweep the room, and the gold columns shimmer. The etheric plane is manifesting in the physical each time we move deeper into sacred space. Ah, I see now! As an angelic being, I see all reality on the etheric plane. Everything is bathed in gold, it is lovely. Gold is the purest vibration level, and it is the container of light on the metallic plane. There are many dimensions in this room. It is like being in the inside of the human skull. This is why we make cups of gold in the sacred skulls of the Masters.

In the back halls, the priests begin burning incense on all sides; it fills the room and we begin going into a trance. As I breathe it in, I feel density increasing in my body, especially in my arms. Lucca and I are about to begin channeling together. There is no ritual, no mumbo-jumbo, we are simply getting ready to begin. The density builds in my hands and arms as I breathe the incense deep into my lungs. My third eye tingles. There seems to be something in the incense itself which moves me into a trance. I'm becoming heavier and heavier, denser and denser, and a grey sphere is building from my hands to my third eye and down to my feet. We are building up magnetic force so we can channel.

It takes a long time, or at least it seems to take a long time. Now I have built a sphere of magnetic energy from the deep recesses in the earth under this ancient temple, and I hold it in and breathe it deeper. I feel like it will crush my chest, suck the air out of my lungs, but it doesn't. Then the idea forms deep in my medulla oblongata that I am going to travel into the center of the crystal ball.

Lucca whispers to me, "The passages are between the lines, and the lines are between the flat planes. We are ready. We are ready to go through the passages. The edges of the passages are broken on their natural planes, and the way to go inside is between the planes. We are ready."

That is a signal to me that he has magnetized himself and that the channeling energy is present. It is to be found by meditating on the natural edges of the crystals, the edges that break on planes according to natural growth. That is how I can key into the energy inside. Lucca has said we are sufficiently magnetized to move along the planes. The edges of the planes of the crystal are the location of no polarization, and that is exactly where they fracture in nature.

Then he says: "Move into the crystal by traveling along the lines where the planes of the two surfaces intersect. Along that line, it is not polarized, it is magnetized, and that is where the passage into the etheric plane exists. The lines of intersection are where a new crystalline plane has formed in a space that was a potential void. But instead of a fracture in nature, a new crystal was born. Those places are new creation places."

We can move freely in the crystal along the intersection planes where I am magnetized. Having magnetization is the prerequisite for me to move in the planes while I exist in the physical. Getting away from polarity, getting out of dualism, is the key to the center. Magnetic energy is heavy yet fuzzy grey. It hums, and I just keep going into that essence.

The arc no longer exists between Lucca and me. Next we make an arc connection between our third eyes. All the other connections in our brains that were in the original arc now project into the crystal, and we form an isoceles triangle from third eye to third eye, the crystal ball to my brain, and the crystal to Lucca's brain. Lastly we look into each other's eyes deeply, and then we shut our eyes.

We are sitting with our legs crossed, our palms turned up resting on our knees, and we are ready to focus all the magnetic energy out of the inner head centers and into the center of the crystal. We do it. All the magnetic density lifts out of my body, and I become pure white light. I am journeying into the crystal! The part of me that goes in is the intense light in my pineal gland. But all of me goes inside, and what I find is a vision I have carried deep inside that I always wanted to see again. What I see is an inner beehive of hexagons of pulsating white light like the cones which transmit color and light waves in the back of the human eye to the brain. The forms are six-sided, and like atoms in matter, they are the form of light.

A man with a long grey beard and a purple robe walks up to us from behind and sits at my right-hand side. He carries a lantern of incense, is very reverential, and sits very quietly. Nothing could break our concentration.

He says quietly, "Are you ready, Masters?"

Then Lucca puts his right hand over the crystal ball about four inches above it, and he seems to be jolted by energy in the ball as he passes his hand over it. I don't really know what he is doing because I am inside the crystal now. I am in a faraway land of geometrical, prismatic light forms. But as he passes his hand over the ball, the molecules in the crystal begin to spin. He has energized the crystal so it can transmit for me from the higher planes. As it happens, I want to strike my head hard right in the center above my eyes to block a blinding headache, but I feel no pain. This is why I was so thoroughly trained for twenty years by the brotherhood. I am the one who will channel the voice. I am in a deep trance state now, deeper than I've ever gone before.

The man says, "Masters, we have called you here today to ask you a question about the Roman Church. The Roman Church has polluted our lands with Mithra. North of the Rhineland we are oppressed by the cult of Mithra. The Romans got it from tribes from the east. They pollute our land with hatred and a love of negativity. They rape our women, burn our houses, steal our food, and they steal the hearts of our children. The Roman church itself has been oppressive, but this Mithra is even worse.

My head hurts. It is hard to listen to him because I breathe his pain with him as he tells his story.

He continues. "We need to know if we should attack them. We are the people of nature, the people of the tree spirits, but we will kill for protection. This is not an issue of whether we should kill or not, it is a question of whether we will win or not if we attack them. Will they destroy us? Should we attack them immediately before they establish even more camps?"

The date at this time is 560 A.D. He has asked me a very heavy question. He knows he is not supposed to ask me this unless there is a very good reason.

He goes on: "I want to know the right answer because if you tell us to attack, we will. We will attack them now."

Lucca puts his hand back into his lap and looks at me gravely. I've had my eyes open and I've been watching and listening. Now I close them, and I see many visions in the planes, the molecular planes in the crystal. I see the Roman camp, and I look to see how many soldiers there are and how many horses they have. Oh! This is incredible! I can see anything in the world right now, It's very easy. I look at the various camps in the Rhineland, where we are now, and I look at their headquarters in Rome. I know how many men we have, of course. But, to get an answer, I move into the future. I move twenty years into the future, and I see such terrible pestilence, famine and suffering that I can barely stand to look at it. I do not tell them what I see. We never tell people the future. Knowing the future is privileged information given to the brothers so they can help mankind. The way to recognize a faker is to be aware when the future is foretold. I see that soon the whole army, all the Romans, will be felled by a terrible plague. It is already rampant in the south. They all get so sick that they cannot oppress people any more, and they shrink back to their homeland. What I see is that we should just wait, because the Romans will get sick and go away.

So my answer to him is, "No, do not attack at this time." My vision clears, and then he says, "Yes, Master, we will not attack at this time. Next I need to know if we will lose our gods if we follow the Roman religion in order to avoid persecution. Some make us worship Mithra in caves, and the Roman soldiers and priests make us be Christian. We worship nature, we worship God in the trees. Our priests, the Druids, are great Masters of the ancient ones. We were here first, and we have spread into many lands, into the east, into Gaul, into the Islands, and here. When we have our ceremonies, they invade us and break up our rituals. They want us to go to their priests and pay them to forgive us our sins, but we do not agree with that. Will we lose our religion if we just do what they say but think our own way?"

I look into the crystal and everywhere I look into the future I see destruction of the ancient practice. I see chaos, disease and confusion. So I reply, "In times of trouble, you must remain strong. You must not give up your beliefs and religious practices no matter what happens. It does not matter what they make you do if your inner strength is clear."

But I am very confused by his question because I am playing a double role myself during these chaotic times. I am officially a Roman priest, and then I am a Druid brother in secret. I do that to stay in the center of the conflict so I can bring in as much light as possible in any given situation. I am a brother, and I serve the esoteric order of the Druids. I serve the Liber Frater. The brothers are always above politics or religious affiliation. It is hard for me to answer him and not tell him what I do in order to cope with these difficult times. But I must protect my identity at all costs. If I weren't doing this work, the times would be even worse. So it is in times of danger.

The ability to prophesy the future is a very heavy burden and responsibility. Above all else, prophets are required to inform the people of danger, as Aspasia did when she saw her vision of the comet, yet we cannot tell them of the future. We are now moving out of the Age of Pisces and into Aquarius, as we were moving out of the Age of Aries and into Pisces during the period Christ was on earth. During the ends of the ages which I have lived through during other historical periods by doing regressions, the cultural prism is always keyed up into a frenzy of fear about the end times, the apocalypse, the eschaton. People are very aware that religions, economic bases, political organizations, and heroes are about to fall. The times are exciting but threatening, and fanaticism seems to flare up like fire triggered by lightning in a dry forest. As we move rapidly through the end of the Age of Pisces, most of us feel the powerful current of the Aquarian energy, but we are afraid of the future because we don't understand it. It is at times like this that we need the true prophecy which teaches us that it is at times like this that we need to flow with the river, to move in the current without fear. There is much to be learned from the Druid because he moves so effortlessly, he can flow with a channel without fear no matter what he sees. The Druids understood spiral energy, and we are now in the tight curve of the spiral. But, great channeling power is traditionally a receptive power, a power that comes from the feminine part of our being. We can see this as we move deeper and deeper into the self, and we can ask how this Druid acquired such a great talent for moving on the magnetized inner planes of the crystalline ball. The Druid's source is the Goddess, and he'd be the first to acknowledge it. His own power came from Aspasia, and all of us have the Goddess within to help us divine the meaning of the Age of Aquarius . . .

I am the priestess of the Oracle of Thasos, Thracia, and this oracle connects to the west. East of Thasos is Dodona and Delphi. and west lies Araxes by the Euxine Sea. This oracle is an outpost between the main ones, and it has been here for more than a thousand years. No one can remember any more when it was first built. It is 1555 B.C. I am thirty-seven years old; I have cared for the oracle for eight years, and there was another Priestess here before me. I am very disturbed right now because my husband, Ahura, says someone is about to attack this place from the sea. He says bodies are washing on shore, he says the minor priestesses say the birds and trees cry of danger, but nothing can happen to the oracle. It is the place of the Goddess, it is sacred. This time is before I yet experienced my vision of the comet. Ahura says he is a soldier and not a religious maniac, and he says he was born in Pelasgia and knows the danger signs. He says he does not live on faith, he is a soldier. The boats are washing on shore, and the bodies are in them. It is my job to find out whether he is right or wrong.

So, I am in my private room in my temple, and I have heated a large iron pot on my fire that contains sheep organs, sheep intestines. When they boil, I watch the steam coming out of the pot as images form in the steam. Now, in the steam I see a mask with black-and-white marks, it is like a cat or lion, it is a warrior mask of the soul, the astral body of the person my husband says will attack us. I have conjured it up.

As I do this, I do not assume they will or will not attack. But I conjure up their astral body to see what they intend to do, what they will do. So, I have conjured up the being of Assan, from the East, and he is very surprised to be here. He has to be in my presence, in the steam, until I find out what is going on.

I say to him, "Assan, will you attack Thasos? Or Stagira?"

And he says, "No, I would never attack Thasos or Stagira."

I dissipate him. It is not my place to ask anything more of him. I immediately inform my husband and the people that we will not be attacked, and Ahura informs his soldiers. The oracle is sacred space, and I have the right to conjure up anyone's astral body and ask questions regarding the oracle. Because I am the keeper of the oracle, they have to answer me.

This is how I communicate over a distance, by the way. For example, if I want to communicate with Delphi, I just conjure up the priestess in my steam, ask questions, and she replies. Often I check to see if we are all getting similar messages. My grandmother taught me how to do this, and men can't do it. The person I conjure up experiences it like a dream, and that is why I am only allowed to get certain kinds of information, ask certain kinds of questions. When I conjure someone up, I enter their mind. Dreaming and conjuring a person's astral body are a similar experience for the person contacted, and that is why dreams often contain accurate messages. This is a skill only to be used ethically, for when I go into the deepest recesses of someone's mind, they have no free will. They cannot stop me, and this is only used as a last resort. The person I contacted does not even know I did it, usually, so they don't even know I know something. This is similar to when one knows what someone else is doing even though they haven't told you. Some people are experts at this skill, and they ruin their lives with it. But, it is a great power, and I can use it to heal someone who is physically or mentally ill.

I can also travel in time by staring into the mist of the sheep intestines. This is a great and wonderful power. I can't travel myself, move my body, that is, but I can move into someone's mind in another time. But today I am disturbed. I have received a message in my steam from a priest named Dionysius at Delphi that I am to come immediately to Delphi. I keep getting this face in the mist of this priest, and his eyes are black and intense, a heavy and prominent brow, a rough face with a beard, and he looks angry. There are trees, rocky ground, and white clouds in the sky behind this face. He seems to be on a hill, and he looks part human and part animal, It is a strong feeling of a mix of astral and physical. He is goat-like with little horns on his head, and he wears a leopard skin.

He says, "You must come to Delphi because the water in the ancient spring has stopped flowing. The spring at the Delphic Oracle has flowed since the beginning of time! The water flows over the rocks, and the people heal themselves there. Always the water stopped flowing while the oracle was being read by the seers, but now it has stopped altogether."

"Why do you ask me to come?" I ask. "Why not someone else?"

"You are the one to come. I have imagined you every day, and the water has ceased to flow for weeks now," he replied.

"But why am I being asked to come?" I persist.

"Your husband did not get the right messages when he said Thasos would be attacked. But, your husband knows something is wrong. He is aware, he has a sense of balance, he is in touch with the people, the animals, the earth, and with the Goddess. He knows something is amiss; he just can't figure out what it is. And now you think it is all right because Assan told you he wouldn't attack. Well, Assan is nothing. Something is very wrong now, something between the earth and sky god, and you are the only one who can help in a matter like this. Soon you will have your own vision of this reality. You can read the mind of the sky god if you come to the center of the earth power, Delphi. I sent the message out to someone who could contact the sky god, and you are the one who appeared for weeks."

Now I realize I do have to listen to him. His incursion is acceptable, and now my curiosity wins out. He is in the steam, and I ask him, "Who are you? I am also one of the guardians of the earth spirit at Delphi, and we are only women. I'm not going to come unless you tell me why you are there."

"This is a great secret," he replies. "I have come through the veil of time now because an issue of grave danger has called me."

"I do not understand at all. You have to tell me more than that," I respond.

He shouts, "I, Dionysius, tell you right now that you have to obey me whether you like it or not. You have to come here if I call you, right now."

I shout back, "I not only do not have to do that, but I am conjuring you now to find out what is on your mind. You can't give me an order when I am seeing you!"

You are wrong," he says. "This is different. You know very well what happens when you use the black arts as you have done this time. Free will cannot exist when power is utilized. You can't control the result when you do this, Aspasia."

Well, I stop short and consider that one. He is saying he has power over me because I used black magic. And I am certain he may be right because I always knew that was a risk. So I reach into a little bag I wear on my left hip for a quartz crystal. I hold it in my left hand and activate it quickly with my natural magnetism, and then I put it to my third eye and say, "Master Horus, do I have your protection?"

Master Horus replies, "You have my protection. You did well. If you had not asked for me at this time, grave harm could have resulted. You have done the right thing because of what comes later. This is a case of Sethian destruction."

And Dionysius crowds into the steam saying, "All right. Now you know you have to deal with me, Aspasia, Horus is with me."

Then something very strange occurs. Suddenly I am not where I was any more. I am someplace with Dionysius, but it is not physical because Horus is there too. I am in the mental plane! I am so light. and I see images of Horus and Dionysius. There is no will here, my will is Horus. We are outside of time, out of the physical, and we can see things we normally cannot see. Messages come to me, but I do not understand because I cannot access anything as usual. I am sure, however, that we are in grave danger. It is a grave omen that the spring has dried at Delphi, it is a sign that the mother is wounded. The importance of the time now is to help people move through as much Karma as possible quickly. I must give as much service and awareness as is possible. And so I return to my temple and make plans to travel to Delphi immediately.

Chapter Ten

EXISTENCE AS
FORM

*Scientists have now confirmed the most essential knowledge of
the soul: all matter, organic and inorganic, exists in our own bodies
going back to the dawn of the planet. We are one in the cosmos, and we
move with the ocean tides, with the wind, with the planets, and with the
rays of the sun. When the solar winds carry cosmic rays to the earth,
when a quark falls deep within a high rock mesa, we know it in our consciousness. Deep within the right brain, all is known at all times.*

*But the journey we take through time and place during an incarna-
tion in a human body is our only way to know God, because God knows
him/herself in us as we journey. And so, ultimately, in the embrace of a
loved one, in our feelings when we lose our mother, in our knowledge of
ourselves when we experience death and birth, that is where God is.*

*This incarnation for me was one heavily laden with trauma until I
was over thirty years old. And each trauma in this lifetime reaccessed
past life traumas so that my higher self could enter more fully into
incarnation than was possible in other lifetimes. Our tormentors are
our teachers, and now, even the age we live in seems to be our tormen-
tor. Over and over again as I traveled through many lives, I found that
the pain and suffering of others hurt me much more than my own. It is
the sins of omission and the pain we have inflicted on others that torture
us throughout eternity. And that old karmic pain will appear and reap-
pear in our children, parents, mates, friends, and enemies until the soul
has learned all its lessons.*

*Throughout my whole life, many people have not understood why
I am the person that I am, given where I came from. Only my soul history explains it. If we try to believe that each baby is a clean slate, nothing makes sense.*

So, where is the hope? The hope lies in all the experiences offered to us which offer wisdom, experiences which heal us and will ultimately make each one of us divine. Before I go into the deepest issues in this investigation of the divine in the human person, I will enter the human realm into the depths. The really human experiences I had before coming to this time and during my life are the final teachers. If you go deep within yourself and try to move through the knots of resistance, the little hard pockets of past life injuries that hold you back now, that is where your teacher waits for you.

Erastus is waiting inside, offering us more enlightenment, because Erastus was the one who taught me that I wanted to live in this time . . .

It's me, Erastus Hummel again . . . The room I sleep in is very beautiful. It is paneled with carved wood. and there are beautiful Chinese carpets on the soft stone floor. The bed is just like a little house, with a wooden headboard and footboard, four posters supporting a canopy embroidered with beautiful silk patterns. Handmade lace is sewn into the canopy and hangs down to the bed like a mist of butterflies. The whole house is wonderful because we were given the best by my wife's father. It is three stories tall, very narrow, and it is part of a long row of city houses for the rich in Leipzig. We have a balcony out the bedroom door, and we love to sit out there when there is a festival and the streets are filled with the people. The house is very fine, all built of stone and trimmed with carved wood. And every evening, the servants light the fires in the bedrooms and pull the heavy drapes shut.

I turn away from the door out to the balcony and look through the lace at my wife. She lies asleep with her long honey blonde hair flowing all over the green woven coverlets, and her healthy plump arm rests over the white silk sheets. I have come home late as usual, working as usual, but she never minds. She is very happy, very content. She is secure. I never have to worry about her. She is sleeping very peacefully. We have been married for just a while, and she is only fifteen or sixteen. It makes me laugh when I think of the day we were married. I was thirty-two, and I was finally ready to enjoy myself after twenty years of hard work studying and teaching. I am well known and respected as a scientist, and I could marry a woman from a rich family. It was December of 1597, and we were ruled by the Hapsburgs. It was snowing outside, and we were in a very ornate church. She wore a white dress sewn with fresh-water pearls, and her skin was all white and creamy. Her hair was bound up under a veil.

I am really pleased; it was a great coup to get her. I was very ambitious. I never stopped working, and now I can enjoy myself. The real reason I married her, however, was not for her money. I married her because she is really free. She's marrying me willingly. I was lucky to meet her at all. She was not my student; we saw one another at a social situation, and we both were carried away by the other. I visited her home a few times, and we both decided that we would marry. Everybody is happy about the match, but I definitely feel like I'm getting away with murder, just as I always have. And it is not easy to advance yourself in this society. By marrying her, my social station goes up and hers stays the same. But the really funny experience I had with her was when I went to her house to ask her father for her hand. I will never forget that day . . .

Her father is mad. I am having trouble seeing him because he seems to be a great big rabbit, but he is stout and wearing purple velvet. He is hard to see because she and I conspired against him. She always does what she wants to do and he doesn't like it. I can hear him even now saying. "Er-r-r-ras-s-s-s-tus Hummel! How could you do it?" She's in another room, but I know she's laughing. He's basically a buffoon. He is a very wealthy merchant, and he adores his daughter.

The room is medium sized with beautiful carpets, and the ceiling is vaulted. He's walking back and forth, and I'm sitting holding my cap and trying not to laugh. He can't do anything about us, he's just venting his anger. He's not insulting me, he's just making frustrated comments about the situation in general. He's saying, "Here I am, I made all this money, built this house, I have a wife and three daughters, and you come along and want the youngest and the prettiest one."

The other daughters are only a few years older. They are handsome girls, but this one is a beauty. I know what it is . . . he figured he was really going to marry her off to a rich husband. But she's the youngest child, and she's very pampered and spoiled. But I'm going to tame her, and it's going to be fun, just like the other challenges I've faced. I'm a Leo, and she's an Aries, and it will be a great combination because we are the great love match, according to the astrologer. And he's frustrated because he knows she will do just what she wants. She's going to have to learn to quit being the favored one, but she will because she is good-natured. And, of course, she is only twelve. That is very young, but we both know it will be right for us.

Her mother is very wise and really favors me. She knows we will be very happy because she knows I really love her daughter.

And even he knows it, and he knows I'm not marrying her for her money. It's just that he figured he would really increase his wealth when he arranged a marriage for her, and we've messed up the whole plan. And then I remember so clearly the pleasures we shared. I remember the night we came together after our first daughter was born . . .

We're on a reclining couch. She's just what I figured she'd be; she loves to make love with me. We've had the child, and we're together again. We can have sex again, and it's been a long enough time. We laugh a lot, we tell jokes, and the baby is in a cradle nearby. It has a cover on it. We're eating fruit and drinking wine and laughing. Her breasts are uncovered, and I'm stroking them. She's been breast feeding the baby, so her breasts are large. Very, just very . . . just the most that a man could ask for. It's like I'm still dancing in court, you know?

I feed her some grapes, and she laughs as I put wine to her lips, and then I undress her. When she spreads her legs and I enter her soft body, she convulses with waves of pleasure, and I feel electricity in her skin. We are hot and immersed in one another. Later I sleep soundly, and she gets out of bed and gazes at the face of her daughter.

I was very happy with her and with my work. Even my death was meaningful to me. I still remember the day when I died . . .

I am sitting in an upholstered chair in my study. I can't stop looking at a brass instrument on the bookshelf that I invented, a gemma scope. I didn't really invent it, but I modified it so that sailing ships could use it in the explorations to the Western world. Everything just got more fascinating as explorers made great discoveries and many of our theories were proven correct. But what I loved most were my children. I had six of them, and I taught them myself. I just had a great time from beginning to end. I really played out my ideas and lived fully. Nothing could hold me back; it is the way life should be lived.

I'm just sitting in my study. The last thing that I notice is my instrument. I'm in a comfortable chair, and I'm sleeping. And I think that's it. I have a feeling of being bony and skinny, having lost a lot of weight. I get the sense of the study all turning to cobwebs. I know I'm going to die, and it is okay. I'm not afraid at all. My body is sitting in the chair, and I'm looking at it from above my right shoulder. I am asleep, I suppose. I've never paid much attention to religion, but I feel that other people live on, because my sense of vitality is just too strong to have it be otherwise. Death cannot be a finality. And I did what I wanted to do.

I thought about death a lot the year my wife died. That was fifteen years ago, and I'm eighty now. I just didn't expect it. She was so much younger, I thought we'd have many years together. She died seven years after the last baby was born. I had a very bad year. But once I got used to it, it was okay because we had such happiness together. But I really knew how to live. I loved to work, and having a happy family and good work is the highest form of existence that a human can aspire to. And then I was even able to teach and communicate what I loved the most. Like a star in the night sky, I began my life dancing and ended it reemerging with awareness into the cosmos.

But, imagine the confusion I experienced as Barbara, this time born into a female body once again after Erastus, then the Victorian woman. As far as I can determine, I had no incarnation after Erastus and before the Victorian woman. For reasons which I do not yet understand, I was born this time with an exceedingly strong and complete awareness of past-life experience. The reality I came into this time just did not seem to offer the hope of living life to its highest potential; the culture was just too negative, too obsessed with fear after two World Wars, to be open enough to nurture all the souls returning for the cosmic party—the Age of Aquarius. And notice, the cosmic players are all around you. So, my first reaction was a combination of feeling oppressed by the density around me, and going crazy a lot just to exit the intensive programming being applied to my growth. Predictably, the end result was a fullblown schizophrenic breakdown in late adolescence. I was supposed to organize myself into a functioning adult as I approached my twenties, but I could not understand what there was to live for because everyone around me seemed to be dead inside. As I matured, all the intense energy I felt as a child had no outlet, in fact, it was obviously unacceptable.

But, deep within myself, Erastus was screaming for some fun, Aspasia was trying to get past the Victorian woman and use her power, the Egyptian priest was literally dying in the twentieth century's ecological holocaust; and in the early years of this incarnation as Barbara, the two inner beings with the most effective inner voice power were the Syrian prostitute and the Roman landowner. The absurd juvenile sexuality of America in the 1950s offered about as much opportunity for inner growth as Lydia's small Syrian village or the more the pessimistic Roman landowner's culture. When I was 17, I tried to commit suicide a second time and almost succeeded. Everything around me began to swirl into such a bottomless black hole that I fell into like a stone dropped into a deep, dark pond. And what would it have mattered?

But, I began to live again when I gave birth to my first child, a son, when I was twenty. Then a new form of living began. a small spark began to kindle that ignited inner fires and eventually built into a rage for life, a joy just for existence.

And as I began to find joy in life, then the most powerful inner voices emerged. The shepherd is the one to speak now . . .

I have just returned from the desert after an incredible visionary experience. I am getting ready to return home. In my vision, I was instructed to live with unconditional love. I am 28, I am a teacher and a scribe; I have a wife and three children, one of them a baby. Before I open the door of my house, I am aware that I connect with the energy of the vision all the time, and it will be hard to ever feel normal again. But I walk in and sit at the round table. Everything is very crude. My wife sits at my right, wearing a coarse white tunic. She has long brown hair and olive skin on her neck and arms. She keeps her face out of the sun, and it is almost white. Her eyes are very blue. We're eating fish and carrots with some kind of sauce on the fish. We drink wine and dip bread in the sauce. It is crowded. Her uncle, an older man, is on my left, and there are other people around the table. It is a community meal because this house is connected with the Temple. My children are too young to eat at the table.

I am in a state of shock after my vision of Enoch and the goddess in the temple. I am disoriented, and I feel marked out by the experience. I feel completely different, like a completely different being, or as if another being has entered me. Now here I sit with my family. What will I do with my relationship with my wife? Does anybody notice anything funny about me? I want protection at this time so I can nurture it slowly. I am already a famous scribe and scholar, and I know that others are getting the same kind of visions I am getting. Many of us are channeling in a being named Isaiah. I am also called Isaiah. The fact that a group of us are receiving similar information validates what I see. In our culture, multiple receiving of visions is the test of their validity. I am most fascinated by the connection I see with the great Hebrew master, Enoch. In fact, that is why the man next to me came to dinner. He is my teacher. His name is Micah. I ask him what he knows about Enoch, and he answers, "The prophet Enoch is one of the ancient ones. His words are written down on a scroll in the Temple of Solomon. This scroll from the Temple of Solomon comes from the Elohim. The brothers of the Elohim are the written source."

I ask him where his own source for the writings of Enoch comes from, and he replies, "The writings that we use do not come from that scroll, but the knowledge we have is correct. The knowledge that we have comes from the brotherhood of Elohim. We hear the words within traditional teaching, in the Torah and in the Kaballah. That is the secret, to hear the truth in your heart as you read words which mask the message. Often the transcriptions are done incorrectly by the scribes, but the Hebrew language is made up of sounds protected by the Masters. The sound is heard correctly in our heads no matter what is written. If you listen right you will hear right, no matter what the theologians and scribes do to the truth."

Then I want to know whether I have been taught the correct words, but he will not tell me with people around. Later I met him in the Temple in a small room and I asked him, "I want to know if you have taught me the correct Hebrew words, so that I can receive the secret teachings."

"Yes, I have taught you correctly because you are a child of the sun. The words you know are like thought patterns imprinted in your brain, and you will always know whether what you hear is right or wrong. Listen to your heart. You will always know the truth when you hear it, which will often mean great suffering for you. But there are other issues at hand that are much more of a crisis for you. Your karma this time will be generated in your family. But remember, the way of the Elohim has been transmitted correctly by Enoch, and beware of Yahweh and the priests. Only the Masters have the truth."

I am back at my home still trying to feel normal again. Our house is opulent, I am rich, and there are reclining chairs around the room. I am trying to see my wife, but I can't because her energy is negative. But I can see my oldest son, who is five, and as I look at him, I am blinded. He is a shining being. He sends out radiating light. Children of the sun have flashing eyes which shoot out rays of golden light. I suppose he always was a shining being, but I didn't see it before. The three-year-old does not shine as I look at him with my new eyes, but he is soft and special. I see that only my oldest son is on the same frequency with me. Shining ones are the seeds of the Hebrew wisdom teachings and the ancient birthing rooms. It is not that the others are less, they are just not teachers. But my wife's face, every time I try to see her, is disfigured. Her face becomes grotesque, distorted when I try to see it. She has one eye instead of two, as if she were a Cyclopean.

I am very wealthy. I come from the Patriarchs, I am a Benjamite, my animal is the wolf. I am from Lachish, and she is the daughter from a middle-class family. I was young when I met her, and I lost control sexually. I studied all day in the Temple, and she was very sensual. I could not resist her. She is warm but untrustworthy. I am afraid of her; she is manipulative. That is hard for me, because I can't figure it out. I don't know how to manipulate, myself, and so it confuses me. I realized this gradually. We gave birth to our first child right away, then the second one, and I see that she is not good with the chidren. She is not motherly and concerned. She likes her clothing, her status, her possessions. I was 22 when I married her. She has no interest whatsoever in my feelings or my level of awareness. We have nothing in common except sex. All this was tolerable until my awareness heightened. Now I see too clearly. What can I do?

We've given birth to three special children, one of them a child of the light. But now I am afraid she will pollute him. She can't pollute me because of my awareness, but it may be different with the children. This is a complicated situation because my inner mind knows that I knew her in lifetimes before. She is a being of great power: She was a Thracian temple priestess during Aspasia's life. My inner mind knows that her purification is my issue, but my worry about my children overwhelms this awareness. And because I cannot transform her, the karma will not be resolved. It will have to be resolved eventually.

I cut myself off from her, no longer even seeing that in her inner mind I was her chance to purify herself. I remained married to her, of course, but I used my energy to shield my children from her. She became bitter and spiteful, and she resented my role as prophetic channel. I was totally alone. I became like a politician with no personal life, and I shriveled inside. I was supposed to heal her, but I did not see. I dismissed her like people we don't hear because we can't listen. I did not see her soul. My path is the radiation of unconditional love and not healing, but that still leaves behind an unhealed person. I could have at least given her help to find a space within to heal herself.

In my present lifetime, the pressure really intensified in late adolescence for me to know why I existed and what I was supposed to do with my life. But the culture was absolutely devoid of choices for children of early high aware-

ness. The only place for me with my intense connection with other levels of awareness was the insane asylum. In the mid-1950s in America, one was either "normal" twenty-four hours a day—including the acceptable attire—or one was taken away by the men in white coats for electric shock therapy or to have one's brain lobotomized. And all this was taken care of by the father gods, the doctors.

Now I suspect the Druid must have been the being in me who carried me through the miasma of breaking down and putting myself together again without being whisked away by the American father gods. As I journeyed through schizophrenia and fragmented within and began to see my own inner facets, an inner eye was being birthed in me that later became the Eye of Horus. Now I understand that escaping from the pit of schizophrenia was just like escaping the jaws of the Nile crocodile God, Sobek, for the Egyptians or avoiding the eagle to Native Americans. It is only through acute watchfulness— being fully awake—that we can become aware. And there is no way to get there without a lot of suffering.

Every dilemma in life is an opportunity resolve karma. Every difficult situation is a gift to us as a gateway to growth. And our greatest teacher in every human incarnation is our body. But this is where we are the most confused, because the body is the vehicle for the balancing of the soul. The most confusing balance to resolve is our sexuality, and make no mistake about it, your sexual issues are the key to your enlightenment. Aspasia incarnated later as male—as Ichor and then Isaiah—to balance power in the body. Isaiah missed an opportunity to find himself emotionally in what was given to him by the divine mind. The work would have to be done later. When we shield ourselves from a lesson we need, then the loss reverberates through many lifetimes until learned.

When I returned as a prostitute in Syria, and then as the Roman eunuch, I returned to dark times in history. I had to experience again the breakdown of all meaning around me, as if I was being pounded over the head by the Gods to let myself feel whole again. But, I could not grasp my suffering as an opportunity for growth. I just fell into sickening passivity.

I am 67, and I am back out in the country outside Rome again. I got back some of my family's property about fifteen years ago. The land is quite barren and hilly. I never married and had little sexual experience. This is a small farm, and I grow turnips in the dirt. I have

SENATUS POPULUSQUE ROMANUS

people working for me, and I tend the animals. We work a lot. All throughout this life I have no clear sense of anything. I feel this bland-ness and passivity, and I don't care what goes on. I actually feel cut off from parts of my body, and I felt that way even before they castrated me.

I'm standing in the room where food is prepared in front of the dry sink where the water is poured for cleaning implements. There is a jug of water and a window. I see the desiccated land out the window, and I crumple over with a violent stomach pain. My bowels are in spasm, my stomach is in spasm. I stagger and fall against a cabinet. I can't see out the window any more. I'm falling, and I bump my head. I end up on the floor in a fetal position like a raw shrimp in boiling water, the tendons and muscles pulling the shrimp into the shape of a new moon. What is the cause?

I am leaving my body, and I am incredibly relieved to get out of it. I am floating above it and leaving it, and as I am above, I feel like I com-mitted suicide. I did. I poisoned myself. I poisoned myself because the same thing is happening in Rome again! But this time I know better. I know why I can't feel the presence of my farmhands. They are gone. I cannot pay them any more, and the land will go fallow. I am behind in taxes. I cannot produce food for the people to eat. The land is barren and overused, and there is no productive way of managing it. I would have to go into Rome again and fight it out. But the taxation on the pro-ducts will not work, and the people will not have food. Once was enough for me. So, I just poisoned myself. I didn't realize the stomach cramps would be so bad.

I am floating above my body, and I am relieved to be above it. I'm glad to be out of it, finished with it. Oh—I see blue light—I am going upward and out of the farmhouse toward beautiful blue light. I now become aware that the light was always there. I always liked the blue water, I just didn't realize that blue light was up there. I am really mys-tified. I feel like I am listening to the resonance of a note just struck on a lyre. I just keep going up higher and higher, and it feels great.

I was totally caught, trapped and beaten down, and it feels good to get above it. As I rise, I make some promises to myself. I will not be passive again because now I know the truth. One way or another, passivity kills.

I just keep soaring and going faster and faster as I shed the feeling of the Roman body. I gave it up, I killed myself. Perhaps a time will come when I can fight my battles and win, but right now I am going straight up like a rocket. I go so far that I become an infinitesimal point in the sky, and then I become a circle.

I am an essence, and I am real. There are other essences around here—maybe they are stars? We are, we are like lights. We are everything and nothing, and when we get rid of everything, everything is here. That place lives in Barbara in her heart. I know the other essences by flowing into them. When I flow into them, we are one. We are absolutely diaphanous. And this is a human experience and not just cosmic. I can, in all incarnations, know essence in others and in myself. And Barbara can expand her resonance if she chooses. It is in the place we experience as nothingness, for when nothingness is there, everything flows right in. It is lightness . . . I just feel light.

We are all pulsating to the same kind of rhythm, and we all have the same light source. The source just is, that is all. And we just be with it. But the Eye of Horus is here also. It is the eye of being, and the iris of the eye is the center of nothingness. Being is the essence which I carried in the sun all the way down the Nile seven times seven times from the etheric eye in the source temple. I am in the essence when I carry the cosmic energy for the land and people. I radiate—radiation occurs between thoughts rather than in them. When I am in essence, I radiate no matter what the circumstances are outside me. First we learn to radiate in silence, then we learn to radiate when we think and speak. Then we know essence in other beings.

As I finally radiate back into my soul essence, the last thing I feel is my last memory of Ichor's germinating power. Oh God, I could not bear the desiccation of the Roman fields! In the long run, over time, germination power will always reassert itself in the fallow land. And on earth, that is the energy the Gods want from humans. When we nuture and grow, we nurture and grow God, and when we pollute and kill, we pollute and kill God.

Chapter Eleven

THE VIRTUES OF
THE SOUL

We all are journeying together, and like all true journeys, our hearts know the destinations, and our minds and physical skills merely delineate the way. The power of the awareness I have to give you now is from Aspasia, emerging out of the veil of time. And the energy I have to offer you is from Ichor, as we live and breathe together during the ultimate planetary crisis in history.

Ichor carried and manifested the germinating force for the Pharaoh, the land, and the Egyptian people. Aspasia died with the death of the Minoan goddess culture—the end of one of the great cycles—and she incarnated very quickly thereafter in Egypt as Ichor. Aspasia lived out the end of a great cycle and returned immediately as Ichor to search for balance. There is great wisdom contained in this progression: It seems that our personal incarnational cycles are synchronistic with the historical cycles of Earth. And as we seem to be living now during a time of great unbalancing, we must search for cultures that were balanced in the past. Before the corruption of Egyptian religion by Akhenaton, the Egyptians were the great balancers of human history. Many of us are strangely obsessed with Egyptian mysteries because their theology is critical to western awareness. We sense it is the "missing link." But we are painfully aware that we do not understand the Egyptian mind at all.

We do not understand the Egyptian mind because we are looking at it from our own perspective. But as the western perspective shifts now due to the discovery of the "new physics," we are entering a time when we can comprehend Egyptian theology. What seems to intrigue us the most about the Egyptians is their seeming obsession with funeral rites. In fact, we have created in our own embalming and

175

funeral customs practices which we THINK were used by the Egyptians. In the Eighteenth Century, one of the most expensive substances for healing was actually "mummy," potions made from ancient Egyptian mummies.

We are now tottering on the brink of a worldwide existentialist crisis. The existentialist dilemma is an anthropomorphic obsession over the meaning of life when faced with the inevitability of death. This straw horse dilemma is the logical end of western religion and its obsession with one lifetime instead of many. And now we have to face the possibility that a planet could self-destruct. We are paralyzed in a global existentialist dilemma. And we will self-destruct unless we look carefully at what life really is. For just as the most honorable way out for the existentialist is suicide, the same paradigm will apply to the planet unless we see that we are operating from the wrong premise.

For, to the Egyptians, life was all, and yet we think they were obsessed with death. But, in fact, if you observe their funereal books and rites backwards through a mirror, you will see that all their efforts were aimed at intensifying life forces.

If you think about it, you will notice that little information has been obtained by me on the experiences the soul undergoes between incarnations. The few glimpses into that realm, the essences, life as an angel, are mind-boggling if you can accept them as real. It is clear to me that the life of the soul between incarnations is just as real as the life on Earth, that there is nothing to fear about death, and that we can know much more about the places between if we just try. And in the passage rites to the other realm—the rituals observed by the Egyptians while the soul is in transition after death—are found our most complete record of the other places. The key to the Egyptian rites lies in the theology of the "Ba," a technology developed by the Egyptians to infuse the present incarnation with all the wisdom of past incarnations. The goal was to put the soul, the Ba, into the body, so that each lifetime experience was an ultimate learning experience.

The Christians would forbid exploration of such realities as trespassing into God's territory. But as the equinoxes precess at this time from Pisces to Aquarius, the controlling aspects of the Christian theology become deader than the desiccated flesh of a 5,000-year-old mummified crocodile. Because, unless we rise above our human perspective, we are doomed.

All ancient cultures contained esoteric teachings about the manipulation and salvation of the genetic strain. They knew about *genetic developments because once the "gods" came to earth to help the beings on this planet become godlike. Our flagrant destruction of the genetic pool with released radiation and chemical pollution is the greatest sin ever perpetrated on any planet in any galaxy. And they gave us choice, remember? We can do that if we so choose.*

The Egyptians knew that visitation to the gods, to the stars, was the only hope for elevating human awareness so that this planet will seek life over death. Today, many native people such as the Hopi and the Dogon of Africa also journey to the stars and return with the teaching for planetary survival. So. let us journey into these realms with Ichor, who worked with the Egyptian Masters . . .

I'm fairly young. I'm thin and medium tall with good muscles. I am not muscular, and for the first time I see that I am black. It is interesting to experience black skin, it is beautiful. I am Khemit. I wear royal sandals, and I wear a gold ring with a green scarab set in. It still looks strange to me because I remember that ring when it was gold with the Osirian inscription in the gold. The snake in gold holds the stone. My thick curly black hair is encased in a tight cap so that my head looks like a bald skull. I am Shem priest. I wear a white linen tunic, and oh—the sacred leopard skin—I cannot go on. This is secret. An inner voice resonates: "After thousands of years of secrets held in the universal mind, it is now time to speak of them. This seal, the Seventh Seal, is now broken."

I see very old grey stone, grey rough rock. After passing by many temples, I see a crude cave. There are columns and ledges up to the entrance, the entrance is finished. We turn to the right, and we are walking on finished stone to the edge of the cave. It's dark inside, we have to bend to go in. It's dark, moist, damp . . . not a cave, but a tunnel. I've been here many times before. As we go deeper in, we see with inner illumination. I don't like it in here. There are rats and bats living inside here. This is about the size of our bodies, and we move with hand holds while we bend. There is sand occasionally on the bottom. We are silent. I see light ahead.

There is an opening ahead, and the light starts to show on the rocks. As we come out into an opening, the opening is all angular. It has angular edges that affect my head; the receptors deep inside my brain begin to vibrate. But as we come out, there is sky, blue sky. We have gone through a tunnel and emerged out on the side of a hill.

We have just emerged out of the passageway from the priestly college where I teach next to the Mortuary Temple of Amen Ra on the West Bank. This passageway is the secret passage from the schools to the tombs. I was teaching hieroglyphics to a group of students when I was called for a ritual. We work as wisdom teachers in a large complex on the West Bank opposite Thebes. And I also oversee the burial rituals because I am Shem priest. The secret tunnel from the secret passageway in the temple to the tombs is closely guarded. I feel dizzy, I feel dazed with the awareness, because every neuron in my body is firing. For years I have supervised the message of the journey into the light for Amenhotep II on the walls of his eventual tomb. For years I have carried the energy of the inundation back to him for the germination of the land. And now he is dead. I am black, I say, not green. I am Khemit. As priest of Osiris, when my face is green, I am vegetation god. When my face is black, I am Khemit, the black fertile soil of the Nile after innundation. Life emerges from the black soil. The key is the Scarab, which lays its eggs in the dung.

The priests assisting me move behind me as we enter the tomb for the very last time. Already the tomb sealers, the dark guards of the night, prepare their materials to hide this tomb forever. We are in the Valley of the Kings, and we have a long journey into the earth to reach Amenhotep's tomb. We dug this one deep within the bowels of the earth for his protection. During the days of the Hyksos pharaohs, many tombs were disturbed.

We enter the passageway. We move deep into the earth down steps into the limestone. There are no reliefs on the walls. Small lamps light the way. We go straight, down some more stairs and come to a chamber. I see his life goods in the chamber, his favorite chariot first, and I am jolted out of my trance. Is he really gone? We turn and pass through a larger room filled with his goods. There are no reliefs. That is the way it is, for he did not pass through many transformations. We go down more stairs and carefully cross a wooden bridge designed to divert the robbers. There are the stars of Nut on the ceiling and the papyrus on the walls to fool the robbers. For them, this space will appear to be the tomb room.

And we pass into the main chamber with the reliefs we designed to show his earthly path. Amenhotep II was not enlightened, he did not transmute into the energy of Osiris, Isis. and Horus. and so the reliefs are designed to help him pass beyond just the most rudimentary stages. To pass the snake will be great for him. Beware. All who gaze upon these reliefs see his soul! His body was found intact in his sarcophagus because he has a message for your age: Transmute or die! Ahead lies his sarcophagus, and we are now in sacred space.

Nubians appear one on each side through side passageways. They wear tall striped headdresses that are cone-shaped and triangular. They wear red tunics with gold bracelets on their wrists. One of them puts a wooden staff in my right hand which has a metal flying lizard on the top. It is gold with colored wings made of lapis and coral. They put a collar around my neck which is about five inches wide, made of colored stone with the eye of a hawk in the front. It looks like a real eye, and it sits right on my breastbone. Then I begin walking forward.

I do not like to do this ritual, "The Weighing of the Heart," because my own karma is affected by the outcome. We move into the room with the gold light which comes from fires and lots of candles. The room is about twenty-five to thirty feet long, and about eighteen feet wide. There are people standing holding staffs rooted in the floor holding up candles. They are black, and to me, they are merely furniture.

I walk to the center. The three others, student initiates, stay back. I put my staff, my Uasit, in both hands, and I raise it up. I raise it just a little, very carefully, because I can feel electrical energy building. The power is working, I am connecting up with something above. Oh, I see, I am calling in all the beings who participate in the weighing of the soul.

I give them permission to be in this space.

My students are behind me observing, but I am unaware now, because my awareness is contained in sacred space. I give my staff to one of them, he stands it on the stone floor, and I turn and move forward four feet. I face a mummy in a box sitting on a platform, supported by two lions facing outward. Their bottoms are touching, and they face in opposite directions. These lions are only used when the Pharaoh has died; they are Atlantean pillars holding the axial balance. And I feel sad—very, very sad.

I'm disturbed that I feel sad. But any resistance or emotion in my body will reverberate through many of my own lives! This is really creating a problem, because I am here to do the critical ritual, to pass his heart. And I have to do it right. I move up to a kneeler in front of the two lions, and I put my hands and elbows splayed out on the kneeler. But I have to deal with my emotion, so I do something unusual. I put my hands on the sides of my head. If my emotions crack, I can't do what I need to do for him. I must make the energy circuit between the beings and the Pharaoh. If I don't do that, the Pharaoh's higher self—his Ba—is captured. But I see I have a problem with this passage.

First, I have to connect the Pharaoh's emotional body, his Ka, with his body before I can help him pass. For this Pharaoh, Amenhotep II, did not bring his Ka into his body enough during life. He did not use this body as a temple for his soul while he was living. I have never done anything quite like this, and so I say, "Horus help me." I see a vision of the yellow eye of the hawk, and once I see it, I can go ahead.

Normally, we only have to open the mouth to pass the divine breath to the other world, *em Tettetu,* for passage to the sky beings with divine Osiris. But, I have to connect in his Ka, his emotional body, to even pass him. The chances are slim.

I will call in the beings to assist the Pharaoh by visualizing them. I go down almost into the position of the child on the floor and then I kneel with my knees on the kneeler. I can't see the mummy—it is in the box—but I can see a small visualization of the Pharaoh hovering above the box. He is in miniature, and he is hovering above the chest of the Pharaoh. The more powerfully I can visualize him, the more successful I am. And what I see is a miniature Pharaoh all white and magnetized. The colors are white light and purple light. Yellow light, green light. And the light is pulsating and shooting out in all directions around this miniature visualization of the Pharaoh which I have created. I pump the energy of my being into the visualization.

Let me key in to how I do that. As soon as I have the visualization of the Pharaoh, then I connect. Even though my body is comfortable, my face is rigidly focused forward toward my visualization of the Pharaoh, and I am sending energy. I bring the energy through and around my head, the crown chakra, and bring in fire energy, red and white, red and yellow. I do it by breathing the energy from the gods into my shoulder blades, down through my spine to my feet, back up through my body and out to the visualization of Amenhotep through my hands.

It's OK, it's real strong, but it doesn't bother me because it comes in through the crown chakra, through the head, all the way round the top. It shorts out my body a little bit, but not bad. And then I send it out of my third eye and my hands. It's not light. It's magnetized thought beaming out of my third eye into the visualization which makes a

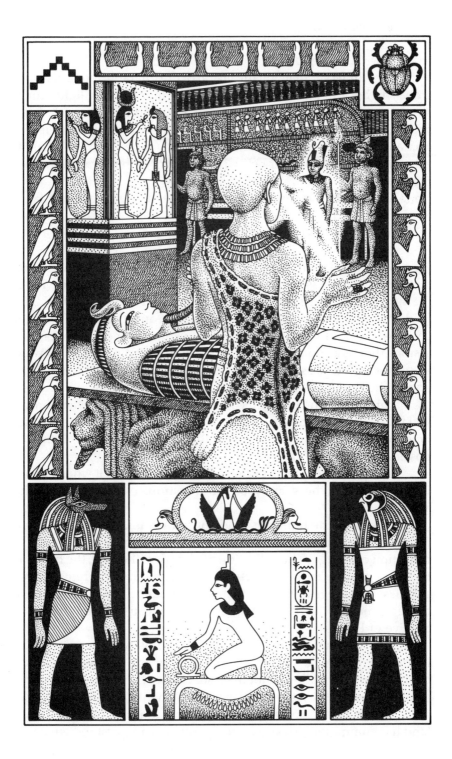

triangle with my hands.

Every time I shoot it out, the vision of the Pharaoh above his body glows; his body becomes radiated, becomes more intense light. And it shoots the color rays away from the image. And the more that I can shoot the energy from the visualization out the more I can help the Pharaoh. It's important to get the magnetic aura from the visualization and out. The further range I can throw out the aura, the greater the effect is.

OK, it really went out far. I've never seen one go out that far.

I have to ask Horus for permission here.

"May I have clearance to know the answer to a great and important secret? The reason I ask for this information is for the service of the light. During the lifetime of Ichor, when I performed this function, I did not know why. Understand? I'm asking a question now. I may not get an answer, but you understand why? I'm asking you because I assume there's a good reason to know. Master Horus, I ask you, I want to know why the passage of the soul is facilitated with the magnetization of the thought form?"

"I am Horus, and I will tell you the answer to your question only if you understand the gravity of that request, and if you agree from that time forward to be in the service of the light as much as is humanly possible."

"All right. I accept that because I already accepted it when I asked it. I understand the gravity of the question. I wish to know the answer."

"The soul of the human is made of star matter, Pleiadean matter, Sirian matter, Uranean matter. The soul of the human is merely a collection of energy. The collection of energy of the soul, the being, is the same matter as the collection of energy of all energies—stars, galaxies, and supernovas. Know this fact in such a way that you have power to merge with this the energy, and then you can know matter in the Eye of Horus.

"This information is useful to you in the following manner. Healing is not your sole work. Manipulation of the awareness of this energy through healing is not the issue. However that is how people heal. But it is not the issue. The issue is that mankind has committed a grievous error. You have been around many times before when mankind has committed grievous errors. You have understood what was happening, but you have been powerless to do anything about these errors. In this lifetime, you have power for the first time over these problems. And the grievous error that mankind has committed is the splitting of the atom and all of the things that are being done in relationship to energy manipulation. The problem is not the fact that this is happening, the problem is that the people who control these forces are destroyers. That is the problem. The only people who are going to be able to fight them are the people who can also work with this energy, but for the light.

"The point is, the manifestation powers of the Masters are greater than the power of the dark scientists. But the power can only be released by those in service of the light. The key to this technique lies in the magnetization of the thought form, which needs to be worked with—in this case, the essence of Amenhotep II. But this technique can be utilized for work on any being who needs healing, passage to another realm, or energizing. Notice that the technique is a light triangle formed from the hands with one of the seven chakras, which then creates the pyramid base with the fourth point, the thought form.

"That is your gift to the group in this lifetime. And that is where your work lies. You now have the power, now that you understand how to do this process, you now have the power to help facilitate the passage of the dead energy. There comes a time on the planet when the negative forces must cease to exist.

"Those who have the power of the light bear the ultimate responsibility, which is to help the passage of negative forces. Consequences of that work are total. A lot of energy goes into holding people back from dying when they're ready to go. And you can do that. You can hold people back. The point is, it's time to let them pass. The effect of not letting them pass is extremely destructive to the planet and to the cosmos. What happens on earth is also going to have an effect on the whole cosmos. If this planet blows up, it may destroy the whole solar system. Ultimately, the Masters will not allow global suicide, but healing power is blocked by the negativity *en masse* of the human mind."

I will return now to the weighing of the heart of the soul of Amenhotep II. I stand with the white light triangle from my hands to my third eye, and I hold the energy tight in the shining triangle. And like a pyramid formation, I am an apex of the triangle to the radiating visualization of Amenhotep. I hear his higher name in my inner ear—

Aak-he-per-u-ra—and my hands and third eye are hot like liquid platinum.

Now the energy changes. My heart, meaning heart chakra, begins to pulsate. Begins to glow like a coal. It's yellow, red, just like a coal in a fire. And it begins to get hotter, and it begins to become white. There's a triangle from my hands, there's a white light in my chest. And the triangle of light is forming more perfectly. I'm using some kind of power, mostly a letting-go power, to get it to be a perfectly formed triangle with no holes in the light. You know how when you have a light beam and it won't form completely? So what I'm doing now is forming it. OK, I got it. Now the visualization of the Pharaoh stops being all full of power, and it disappears.

And now a black shape appears that is very much like a bird. I don't really see it clearly. I see a wing, I see the whole bird, and a miniature face of the Pharaoh is the head. It's part of the Pharaoh's body, and it just sort of separates itself. It's half out of his body and half in. But still connected to him. And now it's important for the beings to connect with this. This is the passing of his soul. And I'm really curious right now. I'm holding my triangle tight, good, everything's fine, it's under control. But what I'm wondering is who is there. Which beings are here?

"I am Seth of the Seventh Seal. I will speak when I hear the words of the other four archangels. This judgment is not merely an individual passage, it is the survival of the pharaonic line."

"I am Raphael. My tongue is tied now by another being. I cannot yet speak."

I announce as Shem Priest to Raphael (Qebhsennuf), "In the name of Horus, Qebhsennuf, you must speak, for you are the guardian of the heart of the pharaonic line."

"Yes, Master," the guardian of the heart, Raphael speaks. "I must maintain my silence now, for the only voice I hear at this time is the voice of another being, very dangerous to Amenhotep."

"Master Horus, what am I to do now?" I say in my heart silently. All during the life of Amenhotep, I knew he was captured by the will of others. That is why he has so few reliefs, for the one thing that must never happen is to have the priesthood lie. We fabricate for the people; they will think Amenhotep is like any other Pharaoh, human as well as divine. But here deep in the temples and tombs, the truth is on the walls so that the priesthood will never lose the teachings of the path of consciousness transmutation. If we ever do, the human race is no different than the animals. All the teachings about the soul of each Pharaoh still exist on the walls of Egypt, awaiting the Aquarian Age when the priesthood will incarnate again to protect the wisdom.

So. I stand facing the Pharaoh, holding my energy triangle in place as I feel heat from the other two archangels on my right side, Hapi/Michael and Tuatmautef/Gabriel.

From Michael: "He was a good Pharaoh. Already when he was born, the corruption of the pharaonic line was in place. A Master has not been Pharaoh for many years, and the last Master who will come, Seti I, will bless Amenhotep II. I say, give him passage to bless the kingdom."

From Gabriel: I shout to the tops of the mountains and over the desert and down the Nile, give him passage, great gods, he is Pharaoh, Lord of the Orbit. He had a great and wonderful heart, but could not cope with the disorder of the times. Who can cope when the last planet is farthest from the sun every 3500 years? With his heart, he fed the hordes who had fled to Egypt when the Aegean was inundated by the great volcano. He understood that Egypt escaped some of the effects of the cataclysm when Thera erupted, and that Egypt was meant to be a refuge. He did not deny the people the sustenance of the Nile.

"He was just so busy that he did not change his awareness. And, how could he anyway? His grandmother instructed his nurses and teachers to restrict him. He was never allowed to feel anything, to touch anything, so how could he grow? His body was too restricted, and his time too occupied. He deserves enlightenment for each mouth he fed. Amenhotep II felt the pain of the people and Geb, the earth god."

And now Amset/Seth speaks: "He gave into his passions. He never cared for anyone but himself. He played the Pharaoh's office because he liked power. He never cared about anyone but himself. There is just no way I can sanction the divine right of the Pharaoh in this case because it corrupts the issue for the future."

Now it is time. I am the fifth force as Shem Priest. That is the role that I play in this ritual. Please understand that if I can infuse his Ba with all the knowledge of this incarnation, no matter what history records, this being will return again with his life records and the power to infuse the body into the soul. The salvation of each soul even predominates over the pharaonic line. "Master Horus, what do I do now?"

I suddenly go rigid as I feel a jolt of electricity shoot down my legs and connect to the limestone beneath my feet. I raise the palms of my hands up so that they are facing the Pharaoh, and I lean slightly forward and feel stabs of power in my shoulders. Rods of power are shooting out of my palms and electrifying the hawk above the Pharaoh's body. And the tomb is shaking as if there was an earthquake. It was as if I myself was a lightning bolt. I hold it for a moment, feeling it is my death, and then I feel a power welling out of my throat in a thunderous voice: "Know ye now that one lifetime is never the answer. Know ye now that this Pharaoh is not passed, that he will be passed during the reign of Seti I, my son who will come to Earth. Know ye now this lesson: All that I care about is the work of the Ba, the life of the higher self throughout time. I do not care about the outcome of this one life."

And out of Raphael comes another voice, the voice of Hatshepsut, now dead many years. "I will not let go, never!"

And the electricity intensifies in my body as the voice thunders out of me again. "No, Hatshepsut, you will never let go, and you are one of the condemned ones. You will have your last chance when you return in the male body you desire throughout eternity. You will return as Amenhotep IV and change your name to Akhenaton. May the gods have pity on your soul. There was never any hope for you."

And lastly, Horus speaks through me as Shem Priest so that it can be heard in the annals of the karmic record book. "I say he is not to have passage. But his mummified body will remain protected by me for 3350 years. He is to return again. He is to return again of lowly station with little power, and he will have a good heart. And with this heart, he will connect with his higher self, and he will be humble. He will not be someone that anyone else would know was a being of great power. But he will be born as a person who is of great heart and great consciousness."

Everything behind me dissipates, and I stand with my energy broken. The Pharaoh cannot undertake the journey to the star waiting for him so that he can beam wisdom back to the Kingdom. Later we will have the usual public rituals, the inscriptions in his mortuary temple depicting the journey of the twelve hours will be the most complete ones in the Kingdom, and the people will believe the divine connection has been made. But I know it is the beginning of the end.

Why has this happened? During my time there has been much priestly intrigue, war, even famine. But I know what the viper in the tent is, and I am very sad. The invaders over the last few hundred years have infected our ritual. We are losing our power to make our connection to the gods. The Age of Taurus is over. We will not have the power of the fixed age again until Aquarius. And in the Age of Aquarius, the powers of the Egyptian priesthood will be birthed in many men and women on this planet.

Someday maybe people will find their way back, but this time the journey cannot even be undertaken.

As always, I will serve the brotherhood. I am the carrier of the vulture, of Anubis, of justice, and that is why I pass the souls. It is my neter, my energy form. Balance is all that matters. But I was deeply shaken by this experience. I will go to my master's compound and talk to him.

He lives in a small house in a compound with other teachers. His house is old, with columns in front. He has a metal bar on the door that I hit hard, because he cannot hear very well now. I hear him, shuffle, shuffle, he opens the latch, and we walk through the front reception room with benches all around the edges. We go down a hallway into his main room, which has a wooden table and chairs, reclining couches, and a little fireplace. There is mead in a beaker on the table, and he pours it for us in pewter goblets. I'm tired, and the mead is very sweet, very thick.

Oh my . . . he is completely clairvoyant, I discover, for I have not told him about Amenhotep's soul, but he knows all about it. He says, "I knew about Amenhotep's problem all these years. I tried to change him. But what you need to know now, Ichor/Horus, is why you were selected to pass him."

Mena then goes into a trance and begins speaking as if he were drugged. "Time is spherical, Ichor. You are sad because later you will encounter this being again. And in your next encounter, you will not fail. From all experiences the soul learns, and what you have learned now will enable you to succeed later. You know that karmic connections are present only to teach us lessons. We all manifest the lessons we require. There is no confusion about who one learns the lesson from. What one lives with in order to manifest the lessons is absolutely irrelevant. When you have attained this awareness, you will experience life's journey with detachment. You will be fully in the world as you are in spirit. You were chosen to weigh Amenhotep II because the

Lords of Karma chose you. All is resolved in the end. You have made
the journey to the star beings many times before, and you will again.
The connection is never really lost, it is just that attraction, allurement,
cannot exist without separation and tension. This Pharaoh, Amenhotep
II, was experimenting with a form of higher awareness that will be
understood at the beginning of the Aquarian Age. At this time in
Egypt, we had mastered the techniques for journeying to the stars. At
a later time, the stars will journey to the humans."

But what could this possibly mean to any being contemplating the
beginning of the Age of Aquarius? Actually, the answer to that question is astonishingly simple. The fixed ages, Taurus, Leo, Scorpio, and
Aquarius are the ages of manifestation. The cardinal ages, such as
Aries, approximately 2000 B.C. to 1 A.D., are the ages when new
powers are developed, and the issue of the Age of Aries was the meaning of free will for the human race. The mutable ages, such as Pisces, 1
A.D. to about 2000 A.D., are the exploration of these new powers in
relationship, and the Age of Pisces is all about the power of love and
the ways in which our free will is limited by other beings. And now we
enter into the age when the power of love, the power of free will to
choose God, will be manifested. And so, now we will have the revelation of spherical time, the knowledge to alter the hologram, the technology
to bathe our body cells deliberately with the power of love.

And the issue is technological. Humans are curious beings. Their
only limits seem to be self-imposed. The glue that holds the whole cosmos together is love, cosmic allurement. And now the last barrier to be
broken through is the barrier of fear. And that is, simply put, the key
issue of the Centaur's Eye. The only barrier keeping you from the total
awareness existing in you is where the optical fibers connect with the
brain. Fear lurks there and blocks your sight. And that is why the
ancients all say the final barrier is always being blinded by the light
when you ask for initiation. Aspasia is the key, for the inner illumination
brought her through the labyrinth . . .

I am barefoot, and I wear a sienna brown cape. I am naked under
my cape. I am so filled with energy that I can barely see. My upper
body is energized, my hands, the top of my head. I feel a roaring
within myself. It is very hard to go back into that now. I will go back in
time, back to the entrance steps to the causeway of the Delphic Oracle.
It is too much to begin this close to the source.

I am a visitor here, I've never been here before. I stand on the staircase facing the people who are in front of me and all the way down the hill. To the left, I see rocky hills and a blue sky with a few clouds in the distance. I can see water far off to the right in the distance. The people come from down below up a winding road on the right side.

To my left stands Dionysius. He has wild dark hair and he wears a skin, a panther skin. The others wear berry-colored robes. There is a young woman next to him with long brown hair. On my right are two more, two men. One of them is fat, and the other one is a small wiry black man. Lucia is here, also on my left.

I am now thirty-seven years old. I wear only a white cotton tunic. There are not many people here, maybe fifty. The four with me indicate that it is time to move to the oracle. I turn and begin walking towards it, with them right behind. It's cold and breezy. I'm here because this is where the earth speaks in a voice. I came here to Dionysius because of my vision in the sheep intestines. Neither one of us has official access to this oracle, and we aren't sure what the Delphic priests will do as we approach.

We waited a few days for the sign, and it came three hours ago. There was a groaning in the crevices, and sulphur has risen from deep within the earth. The earth will speak now. I am drawn here by instinct like an animal. As we approach the oracle, there are other people milling around. The temple people are up there guarding the oracle at this time.

The three of us—Dionysius, Lucia and myself—come close to the oracle. The fascia is in front of it, and I feel frustrated. The oracle itself is behind the fascia in a hollowed-out area like a small cave into the mountainside. The fascia is about four by six feet. Tall thick columns line the two edges of a stone platform in front of it.

I am walking onto the stone platform with the columns on each side, and I begin to feel very strange. Everything becomes deathly silent, and I'm not aware of people any more. I feel the power of the oracle in my head, a power I have never felt before. It is deep in the center of my brain, it vibrates at a high frequency, and it is affecting my eyesight and hearing. I am not hearing and seeing in the same way, but I can't explain this. I feel energy through my whole body, but it's not a light energy. I also feel very disoriented, because I feel this swirling power all up around in the sky. It's like a whirlpool of energy, not that strong, I just haven't felt like this before. I am so confused, I cannot explain it to you. Let me go out of body and look from behind so I can see better.

Aspasia has moved up onto the platform which is normally forbidden. Everyone drops back, including Lucia and Dionysius, and they watch the four temple guards closely. The oracle has not been heard by a priestess for a long time, and Aspasia is not a Greek. The temple guards face each other and raise their hands so that their palms are facing, and they watch Aspasia as Dionysius moves to come forward. There is a gnashing in the rocks from a deep subterranean place, and the sky has become a whirlpool of swirling steel grey clouds that appear to be sucking into a vortex and disappearing.

The temple guards gesture to the people to move back, their eyes are wild as they fall back stumbling over one another. Now two of the temple people move up with Lucia and Dionysius behind Aspasia and in front of the columns. The other two temple people go into a small building on the right behind the columns, and they bring the robe.

I take off my dress as suddenly electricity jumps in the cotton. It is painful. I drop it off and step out of it, and they put the earth robe with blue Atlantean stars on my shoulders.

Now I feel different. They put the robe on quickly, and they take their hands away. They get out of there and leave me alone. But now I go—I walk forward fairly quickly again. I don't go slowly. I go up there and kneel again.

I'm starting to feel the energy come now. What I feel like doing is getting as close to the oracle as I can, but the same thing happens. I have to stay behind the fascia. And so I go up and get as close as I can by sort of kneeling sideways—what I try to do is get my right ear, right side of my head, as close as I can. It's cold, too, so I take the robe and sort of wrap it around the backside of my body. Now it—it's so strange. I feel so much like some sort of naked animal. But I feel so drawn to it. It's very confusing to me, because it's not an energy I know. I feel very much in limbo. I want to claw the ground.

The oracle is a little hole in the ground, not in the side of the hill. I'm afraid of being possessed, I'm afraid of letting go into it. The problem is that this is the place of the age before. This is the place of the age 2,000 years before this one. And I'm not the only one who's afraid of this place. Many people are afraid of this place. They're afraid to destroy it, to bury it, or to ignore it because of what would happen to them if they did. But nobody knows what to do with this place. It is very ancient, and the problem is that the fascia does not belong here. They put it there to seal it off. The hole has always been there. The hole has been there for at least 2,000 years. This fascia is really new, less than 100 years old. And it's wrong. It's a mistake.

I can't lower my ear to the opening because of the fascia. Let me see now. I understand. I'm there, and I know that this barrier is wrong. The barrier is false. But if I were to climb over it or walk around it or try to crawl through it, they would kill me or something. And the sense is of the males. The males did this. The oracle had been accessible only to females. Now, this thing makes it accessible to males too.

It's frustrating going to a sacred place when I know the energy is there and having bars in front of me. I'm beginning to feel the power, but I feel like a lion, a caged lion. I feel like they will kill me, the temple guards, if I do what I have to do. When they put the robe on me, they couldn't even feel the power themselves. They've lost all contact with that robe. I want to tear that fascia down.

Something strange is going on behind me. Dionysius can read my mind, and he hears my frustration with this barrier. He knows he has to do something or we are going to have an absolute impasse at a crisis point. We are at the end of a long cycle, and things have to be finished at this time. Behind me, he begins routing everybody away. He's clearing them out of the sacred space because something is about to happen here, and they are not going to be allowed to stop me. He clears them out.

Dionysius comes up behind me as I feel overwhelming power in my hands. He puts his hands on my shoulders over the robe, and he energizes the robe. The energy hasn't been in the robe for a long, long time. My hands are through the opening now, and the energy is so strong that it is like grasping lightning. I put my hands over the hole.

I've broken the taboo, and I feel the overwhelming wolf energy, with Dionysius behind me over my shoulders making some kind of circuit. He is protecting me from the negative energy on the outside that seems to want to suck down into the hole through my hands. It sucks out of my hands, up my arms, into my heart, and out the top of my head. Behind us, the vortex in the clouds is so intense that the people stand rooted and magnetized to the soil for fear of being sucked away. The connection has been made for survival, survival of the people from the other planes. Even though most of them will die soon, they will pass to the fields of the gods. They are also a part of the circuit I am making with Dionysius. No energy is possible unless it is in a circle.

But I begin to feel like I'm fried. Somewhere the circuit is broken, and I feel the force of the negativity. The back of Dionysius is against mine, and he is looking out through the columns. He is angry, very angry. But I feel something in him break as I draw energy from the oracle. It moves to him, and he circles it out to the people on a psychic level. It just feels incredible in my hands. So we're holding this incredible power, and there are even electrical storms out there beyond the people.

Dionysius raises his hands, he stands tall, and suddenly the temple guards become empowered. They are jolted because they've never felt power before. They go back to that little crypt or vault, and one of them gets a robe and the other a crown of thorns. No . . . it's not a crown of thorns; it's a crown of vines and grapes. And they bring it. They are in a trance, a total hypnotic trance. They are transfixed. They also carry a piece of cloth that is old, 2,000 years old, and they carry the crown on the cloth. And then one of them brings a red robe, a robe dyed with berries.

I am in front of the oracle, Dionysius is behind me with his arms outstretched with an ecstatic expression on his face. It has been 2000 years since he felt this energy. Electricity crackles now from the mountain peaks, and the temple guards are moving in front of the column with the sacred power objects from the crypt that have not been brought out for a long time. They are under our power. Under the power we are bringing from the oracle.

The three come. The fourth one walks behind the three, and he shuts the door. He's the black one. He comes behind the three. The first two carry the crown, the third one carries a shield with an eight-pointed wheel on it, and the black one carries the cape. They stop—the one with the crown stops behind Dionysius. And the black one is in ecstasy; he shines like the full moon. Finally, the right thing is happening. He comes and he puts the crown on the head of Dionysius, and then the other two—they do this very quickly because it has to almost be done together—they get the robe and give it to the black one, who puts it on Dionysius' shoulders. The little black one—this is very strange—he goes around in front of Dionysius, and every time somebody does something like this, I'm getting these jolts in my hands that are really almost too much to take.

He goes in front of Dionysius and he—first he kneels—he's having a hard time, he's reeling as if he's in shock. He kneels and then bends down in front of the shield, and then he gets into the pose of the Sphinx. That's the yoga position where he puts his head on the stone in front of Dionysius, and he puts his arms down, out in front of his head, to the stone. He's on his knees, he lowers down to the stone, and it's a prostration of complete acceptance. Once he does that, I feel better. The problem with this energy coming into me is it's like electrical short circuiting. So then it calms down a little bit. Now I feel the flow, and not like I'm being short-circuited. Now I feel a flow. He is one of Dionysius' people from another time. He is a guardian.

Dionysius lowers his hands. He puts his thumbs together in prayer position and bows. The black man is empowered then. We're really pulling something off here. The black man comes back around, and he gets rid of those other three. I don't even know how he does it, and I don't care. He can take care of them, and that's his job now. He takes care of them.

What we're about is calling forth all of the earth energies for the people. The connection we're trying to make is making this with two together and not with one. When two people work together to the deepest degree, there is a connection at all levels. But, part of my confusion is that Aspasia has not connected with the earth energy before. She could not do it without Dionysius.

So, Dionysius bows to the black temple guard. Dionysius stands up straight, and the energy in my hands is turning them to stone. Dionysius walks up behind me, around the side of the fascia to my right side, and my hands feel electrical jolting in the stone sensation. Dionysius gets down on his knees, and he puts his hands over my hands. The energy shoots through my arms and heart, and now the oracle is ready to speak.

The oracle says, "You may ask me questions."

I reply, "I want to know how we can make the oracle speak to the people again."

The oracle answers, "First, you have to ask me three questions."

My first question is, "When will we come here again to make the oracle speak to the people—not just to us, but to the people?"

"I will speak to the people when Aspasia sees that the conjunction will occur. Aspasia will be able—she has the tools to know the time of the conjunction. She will then give the order through Dionysius that it is time for the oracle to speak. That is when."

Dionysius says, "The earth powers are the strongest powers to the human. There are four different powers. But the earth power is the strongest in me, as the god of the earth. I, Dionysius, can call forth the powers of the earth speaking if Aspasia calls for the energies of the planets. Only when the vibration of the polarities is struck and vibrates can I speak to the earth energies. We are here together, and I ask the earth energies to speak to Aspasia and to tell her something that she must know."

The oracle says, "Aspasia now has to be connected to the earth energies. Aspasia must now channel the energy in all four directions instead of in three. She always channeled in three.

"She has made this connection with Dionysius in this life-time because this is the passage of the male energy to the female energy. In the time before, he was her teacher. She was guided by him. Now in this lifetime, this is the time of the connection. The connection has nothing to do with the human plane. This is the connection on the universal plane, the plane of the one.

"Listen now and understand what I say. Soon a cataclysm will overwhelm you. The goddess religion is in power now. The goddess power will be blamed for this cataclysm, but no one on earth is responsible. It is simply an extraterrestrial cycle which manifests every 3500 years. The patriarchy will assume power because the next culture will assume that safety exists in patriarchal order and control. And then the patriarchy will be blamed in a similar way when the cataclysm cycle repeats around 2,000 A.D. Humans will only be free when they recognize natural cycles and let go of fear when they understand they will reincarnate anyway.

"But the energy connection in the polarity is something that has to be made at certain times. There are certain times when the gods demand this of the earth. The earth lies fallow sometimes for a long, long time, and then the connection is made again. It will always be like that. That is what keeps the earth alive instead of becoming an old hag like the waning moon."

So that is the second message.

Dionysius asks the great and divine and true oracle for the last message. The oracle says, "It is this connection, the connection of all four kinds of energy, that causes the beginning of the fifth energy, which is the center. The center is only given to people together, or in groups of people, certain groups of people. Because otherwise, the center can destroy. The center is given to these two people now because they must be able to take the energy and do with it as God wishes. This energy will never destroy them. It will never destroy them personally.

"There will be times, many times in many lifetimes, when this energy will not come to them, but when this energy comes to them, it's not something to be afraid of. When this power comes, it seems like there is no free will, but it's the greatest free will. It is the gift of being one with the universal one without the interference of free will. It is the universal center that all humans may know if they let go of fear."

In only a few months it happened. Dionysius and Aspasia returned to Delphi once more as the great cosmic event foreseen by many Aegean seers approached. And then, finally, she returned home to her family to watch the sky with her daughter. Aspasia leaves the following account for the record.

My house is filled with people, the yard is filled with people, the rocks are filled with people. They have come for the only safety they've ever known, the Thasos Oracle. It's dark and many have come here because this is high ground.

Just as it's happening, I'm standing out in the back yard on the steps again, and I'm watching the sky. We realize that it is happening; we've seen the comet in the sky for about two or three weeks. It's been coming closer and closer—well, it seems to be closer to us, but it's not really coming closer to us. It looks to us like it is, every night we look in the night sky. But all day the air was thick. What I'm concerned about is that I made a mistake. I should never have told—none of us should be where we are. We think this is high ground, but it isn't high enough. We're only two or three hundred feet above the Aegean.

It's nighttime now. I can't see the ocean, but any time I want to look at it during the day I can see it. We're looking at the sky, because the first feeling is that it's coming closer. The first sensation I get is the sky seems to be getting really red, a strange red, almost blood-like quality to the sky. And then our hearing is almost destroyed by an incredible imploding blast! A few people fall, clutching their heads from the pain. What could it be?

Oh—the earth is beginning to shake. There is a rumbling sound, a sound of rocks crunching underneath where we stand. Some fissures develop in the temple building. We feel very strange. The air thickens more. As a group, our consciousness centers. It is a mistake to be here; we know it, but there is nothing we can do about it now. We are just becoming fascinated and centered in the power of the Mother, as she seems to be writhing like a woman near orgasm. We hold our energies and watch, all aware that we are chosen to observe cosmic chaos. We are hypnotized.

I can see the comet in the night sky. It is deep red, fiery, and it has a long yellowish-blue tail. It looks beautiful. It looks like a snake, a dragon, like a thrashing angry god of fire. It is blood-red black in color. It is going close to Mars, it is very, very close. I am afraid the comet will collide with Mars. We're all afraid it will hit one of the bodies. I stare at it and wonder what it is. It is close to Mars; this must be retribution for war. Whatever happens, I feel like we deserve it, feel fatalistic. As it moves closer to Mars, we can't see it any more because the ground shaking intensifies so much. And we are losing our nerve.

My main consciousness is trying to be strong and keep people from panicking. But we're really shaking—the grass is opening up. and the rocks are emerging from underneath. And people are getting thrown against the sides of things and getting badly hurt. It's an earthquake. I take one last look up to see if it hits Mars, and it doesn't hit but passes really close. And as it passes closest to Mars, the shaking reaches this intense level. That's the last time I look up. Now we think it's going to hit us. And now we panic. And we're panicky anyway because the lawn is being ripped to shreds because the rocks are rising from underneath. And the people around me, their heads are smashing, being broken against the rocks.

The temple is coming down. I can hear people screaming inside the temple. I am out in the back. People are clutching at my shoulders and screaming. Trying to keep their balance. People are really trying to be brave, but you can't just stand there and keep your energies focused when you're getting shaken all over the place.

It's like standing up in a boat in rough waters. The stone is shaking around, and I'm trying to stand on it. The rocks under the ground are viscous. I feel muscle power in my knees, and I'm staying afoot. I'm very much aware that I'm going to die. Definitely. There's no way anybody's going to get out of this. So everybody else seems to go down before I do, and then I go down.

The rock pitches me forward, and I fall out in front of myself, and then I'm on top of some people. And people are clutching. And then the rocks come down. The house behind is crumbling, and the rocks come down on top. I'm obviously going to get smashed, and I'm afraid. But I'm also curious about what's going on around me.

I think what happens is I don't feel any pain because I've been hit right on the back of my head. It's like instant death. And I immediately get out of my body, instantly, because I want to see what the water is doing. And I'm curious about what the ocean is doing, what the rivers are doing, because it seems to me that if I'm going to understand at all what happened here, the tides and the ocean will tell me what happens—whether this thing is going to land in the Aegean Sea or what is going on.

All of my energy goes into getting above my body immediately and getting a little bit above the situation so I can see what's going on. There's a lot of screaming and yelling. and I'm still aware of the terror and agony around. But I want to see, I'm above the city. Most of the buildings are totally destroyed, and a large fissure opens up right through where the center of the city was. And the Aegean Sea seems to be—it's sloshing all over the place with great waves, and the fissure fills with water. I can rise above it, and it's like an act of seeing. And that's what I want to do. It's like over there on the left-hand side is the Euxine Sea and the Straits of the Symplegades. Far in the distance, I see a volcano shooting lava and smoke into the sky where the island Calliste was.

I have a map, a visual consciousness of the place where I live—Greece, with Mount Olympus and Mount Athos up to the one side, and I can visualize the Euxine Sea in a map-like sense. It empties into the Aegean Sea through the Symplegades. It's like it just sucks right out. So I think that the level of the Aegean Sea goes down. First it goes up, and the fissure fills up with water. Then it goes down. The fissure is huge, like it was two hundred feet up, and that was the high point. It goes down three or four hundred feet.

So what happened is the water level didn't go up. The fissure was just so deep that the water went down into it. Right through the middle of the city where a section of earth collapses into the ground. It just splits open, just like a fissure. And the water rushes into it. And the Euxine Sea just empties out, it's like a bowl, it just empties out of water. So the Aegean Sea heaved high. There's a feeling of water rushing out there and down into the area where our city was. And then that's that. And then I lose interest. I hear a siren calling in the distance. I am aware of leaving the quaking land and the sloshing sea, and I shoot straight up into the blue light that always waits for my return. And next I hear a clear and prophetic voice that seems to be speaking to the millions:

"The mass consciousness works through such means as weather and geophysical disasters, not for the purpose of righting imbalances, but allowing people to demonstrate to themselves choices which either show them their life has reached a dead end (in which case, they now have an opportunity to leave it cleanly), or to cause them to bring to themselves that strength and force of character which would allow them to complete the lessons the inner self requires of them. This would be true regardless of the choice the mass consciousness makes of what probability to realize or what combination of probabilities to realize.

"This planet which you experience, and many high-level spiritual individuals experience, is the central Earth among a large number of probable earths, each one of which explores one or a combination of several of the experiences we mentioned.

"This planet is emotionally unstable precisely because it literally has superimposed on it ghost figures of several realities happening powerfully on other earths in these various different systems. Individuals who are at that stage of awareness where they can participate in this reality and others frequently get visions of disasters such as the ones you perceive because they are tuning in to what is happening now on one of these probable earths. For a period, then, you have shifted your focus so that you are actually present on that planet in its current line of development. But you will always come back to this one, because the most powerful lessons for the particular kind of consciousness you've developed are to be learned by your being able to maintain as many possible versions as you are capable of accessing without burnout.

"The key awareness that is yours now is that you must hold all these levels of reality in your heart. For no one knows what will happen next. Even the Masters say they know nothing of the future after 1996 A.D. At that point, a crisis will occur in the accumulation of all human actions which will create a new reality which will be free of imbalance. Christ planted the seed on your planet, but the theologians and priests obscured his revelation. But all will be seen in time."

Chapter Twelve

THE VISION OF
THE CHRIST

The goal of Egyptian theology is to control the Ka, the double or emotional body, to keep it in the body during an incarnation, and to imprint the earth records of the whole string of incarnations thoroughly into the Ba. The ideal result is that the individual human being can live a lifetime aided by the wisdom of previous lifetimes, and the soul of the individual will have free will as a result of the understanding derived from non-dimensional insight. Since time is spherical, then all awareness of past-life wisdom can be imprinted upon present consciousness by means of initiation, and the soul itself can see the purpose of the incarnation and enter service to the eternal source, the God force.

Higher initiation is the infusion of past-life powers into an individual who is carefully trained for such total awareness. The present time is all that matters: it is only now that the cosmic wind can rustle the eagle feather. All awareness is in the body, and all you have to do to open yourself to other levels of awareness is listen to your body. For example, next time you've climbed to the top of a mountain and are transfigured, attune yourself to higher centers in your inner brain and notice which neurons are vibrating. Feel the place and level of vibration in your head when you are having an experience of higher consciousness. Learn to use those old perceptive organs that have been lying fallow for so long.

Or, try out your heart if you want truth. Next time you feel pain in your chest or lungs or heart, go into the place of pain to find your inner knots. You can move through them if you wish. Egyptologists puzzle over the canopic jars where the priests tried to preserve the internal organs of mummies. But there was a good reason for all this effort. The Egyptians knew that the seat of the emotions is the bodily organs. They

knew the way to clear emotional blockages and unresolved karma was
to clear the body organs. The Egyptologists puzzle over the way the
priests sucked the brain out of the cadaver, and the Egyptologists say
they threw the brain out. I doubt it. They must have returned the brain
more totally back into the environment than any other part of the body.
Possibly the sacred hawk Horus ate the brains. The knots and pain in
our bodies are where the deepest secrets lie. And that is where the sec-
ret of the Hebrew prophet emerges—from a place of pain in the body of
the druid master.

I am thirty-two years old. It is daylight with grey haze in the air,
and the field I stand in is of lichen with green moss and grey rocks. I
have on a gray cloak. Now I see it is misty, rainy, wet. It is a very windy,
stormy night. I am alone.

I walk by grey stones coated with lichen as I wrap my cloak
around my shoulders. I walk a little further to a cave, and I look over
my shoulder. As I look to see if any body's around there, I have a
vision of a red eye. It's not really there. I hurry faster. I go to the
entrance of the cave and enter. It's wet, watery inside, and I go a little
further into the cave, and I can hear water. I can hear the water and I
should go a little further in. It gets a little bit cramped. There's a spring
inside. The spring is running heavy because it's rainy this time of year.
I've been here before; I sit down with my hands on my knees, and I listen to the sounds of the water. This is the spring that speaks, this is an
oracular spring. I feel little spinning balls in the middle of my skull
behind the sockets of my eyes. And this is a spring that has not been
disturbed. I have reached another level after attending the moon service at Avebury. Now I can hear voices by listening to the water.

Let's see, what did I come here for? The reason I was worried outside is I don't want anybody to know about this place.

The sacred springs are closely guarded by the Masters, who use
silver wolves to watch them. I am the conduit for much necessary
information. That's one of the things I do. I listen, and I find out what
needs to be known. And then I take appropriate actions based upon
what I find out at the spring. The water trickles and I get information.
This is the rite of Lykorea.

I am here to find answers to questions about the English court. I
am from the Rhineland, but I work with a secret brotherhood in
England and I'm involved in the high court. I am a Druid. The court is
not Christian. My group is the Liber Frater. Part of my work is dif-

ferentiating people. If their energies are good, if they are trustworthy, then I can give them messages. I evaluate people in relation to the greater purpose. The brothers are with me, and we have a plan. We also work with Masters from other planes, and I recognize other humans working with the Masters by their eyes. Also, when I meet someone working on the plan, the place between my eyes on my forehead always gets hot, or my crystal heats up.

I don't think anybody else at this time gets information the way I do, and sometimes I feel very alone. That is the real cross of my work. But I also have this method of getting information from the water in the cave, and I don't think other people get it that way. I will never know, because things like that are not talked about. I wish to explain at this time how initiatory secrecy functions. Past secret knowledge can be communicated, but contemporary masters and techniques must remain secret. We pass secret knowledge to you from the past to stimulate contemporary people who may possess unrecognized intuitive skills. That is how we activate the super conscious. But contemporary initiatory wisdom is always absolutely guarded because the power is lost if any knowledge is shared. So, initiates lead a lonely existence on the human plane, but they are in communion with the divine forces.

I'm here tonight because I need to know whether the king's brother is trustworthy or not. As Masters, we always observe, influence, and instruct those working with the kingly role in order to help the people. The kingly role is a potential conduit of divinity or an immediate hallway into oppression. Thus, kings carry heavy karmic burdens. The king's brother is in love with the king's wife, and we are afraid the king's brother is going to cause the death of the king. I am here to learn whether he will kill the king. And I come to learn whether the king's wife is unfaithful with the king's brother. The king is Sigebert, and his wife is Brunhilde. The name of the king's brother is Childe.

So, I put my hands on my knees, and I am in a squatting position on a ledge in front of the trickling spring. I listen. I listen to the sounds of the water trickling out of the rocks, and it makes a mesmerizing, burbling sound. The rocks glisten. The energy comes into my shoulders, into the back of my shoulders. And I feel like turning. As I listen, my head jerks to the left, and I feel energy coming into the right side of my neck. And the knowledge comes to me: Childe is thinking of murdering his brother—Brunhilde does not love Sigebert, she never did, and she is a manipulator. No one knows what is going on. It only occurred to me to wonder when I saw Brunhilde looking at Childe strangely in court one day. And there are lots of rumors in court, but there always are.

So, I listen more. She never loved him—which I did not realize. She is plotting while she has an affair with Childe. That is outrageous, because she will have a child by Childe instead of her own husband. And Childe is ambivalent, torn up, and he doesn't want to kill his brother. But she, she has no emotions about it at all. At this time, she is trying to manipulate Childe into killing Sigebert. I am concerned about the effect of this situation outside Britain now that I understand what is going on.

If the monarchy weakens in Britain, then the invaders from the north and east will move right in. They are always poised to move in. The monarchy is mixed at this time. Some are Christians, some are influenced by the Druids. The Roman Mithra cult is stronger in the Rhineland than here, where the Druids still have some power. So, when I am in the Rhineland, I am a secret Druid Master of the Liber Frater and a Roman priest in public. Here in Britain, I am a Druid, and I am known because I participate in rituals such as at Avebury. But, my work as an adept, that is always secret. I have a lot of power in the court, the high priesthood of the Druids wields considerable influence in court at this time. As for the king, he doesn't seem to believe in anything.

This is basically an agnostic age. Those who are mystical participate in Druid rituals. People might attend a Druid festival, but they mainly come to eat, and they like the energy. They also come to court festivals occasionally to eat. My reason for being involved in the court is not because I am a Druid. I influence the court because I am a brother, a Master. We always have to influence politics. I just need to know what is going on all the time in case I get an opportunity to improve the energy. So, I am working to keep energies in good shape, and if Childe is going to murder his brother, then I will do what I can to minimize the resulting difficulties.

I'm concerned about what effect this will have in the Rhineland and in Gaul. This is interesting. At this point, I focus on a rock formation opposite where I'm sitting. There is a shelf, and there's a hollow area in back. It's hollowed out in the rock, and there is a little carving on the rock of a cat-like face. And at the bottom of this face, there are small stones and some quartz crystals mixed in. I focus on the rock backing, which is about five or six feet across. The spring is on my righthand side, that's why I can hear it over here. And as I watch, I unfocus myself by staring at the water running over the shining rocks so that I can see impressions on the back of the rock.

What I'm doing is calling in people from over in the Rhineland to check out what the situation is here. I want to know what the effects of Sigebert's murder would be. So the first thing I can hear are the names of the ones I'm calling. I'm calling—this was the name I thought the priest was going to be named that we got into the first time. I'm calling Rurick, and I'm connecting with Lucca, the one before. Now I put my hands on my head, press my head slightly, and look—kind of peer through to the back of the rock. And I have them visualized. I can see Rurick's eye very clearly. So as I visualize them, I send them the whole thought form of the political situation with Sigebert, Childe, and Brunhilde. They get it instantly.

The spring becomes more active at this point. It's more water, and the spring becomes extremely active. The stones are moving. And it's very clear to me that this situation is very ominous for the Rhineland. The tribes from the north and east will move in more quickly.

Now my right arm is in terrible pain. It really hurts. Right at the elbow. Well, I'm tuning in now to what they're doing. And Lucca—I can't explain this, but whatever he was doing he stopped. And he has a ring. It has a red carnelian stone in it or something, and he rubs his ring slightly, and he knows. And my right arm is being possessed.

A voice manifests in the deep passages of the etheric plane with a clear message. "Go into your arm, go deeply into your arm to withdraw the knife of awareness. For at this time, we tell you, you have to cut through the final layers for the heart."

This arm in the cave is possessed above my elbow up to my shoulder. It is stabbing me, stabbing me, some form of myself stabs me. It stabs me because I am trying to affect things more than I am supposed to now. The stabbing comes from another lifetime . . . a lifetime before this time. And I see the face of the glistening rock, in the face of the pool, I see myself with coarse bushy hair, with light radiating all over the top of my head, and I am bald on the top of my head. I am large, with flowing robes, and I have light blue eyes with a strong face. I have prominent cheekbones, a large chin, strong teeth. I am standing holding a wooden crosier in the wind, and my robes are flapping. I move into that body.

I see myself now as younger, standing in the wind with my

shepherd's crosier. I have very dark hair, and I am a powerful being like an intense storm. My name is Isaiah. I hold that staff, that crosier, very hard. I hold it hard into the earth to get my power. And the place of holding the magnetic energy to the earth into my being is in the muscles above my elbow.

I go back and enter the Druid in the cave, who comes after my time, and I have a question for him because the history of my time was so utterly tragic. I ask the dripping water being heard in the mind of the Druid Master whether or not it is futile to tamper or meddle with things that other people are going to do. Specifically, is there any such thing as trying to meddle too much?

"There is no limit to your influence if your intention is good.

"But back to the pain in the arm. The pain in your arm is coming from trying too hard to influence events, from caring too much about this political dilemma now so far back in time. The Druid Master loaded Lucca with information, and maybe he should have waited a while. But, everything is so critical, something must be done immediately! But wait, there is another form of fear, a more subtle one, but it is still fear, fear coming from negative past-life experience."

The pain in the arm went away when the source was identified.

And so we have arrived on the threshold of the crux of the matter—power. We are at the end of the Piscean Age for which the Crucifixion is still the most potent symbol. Christ started it as the Master who attained his full potential reach into matter and was put on a cross for it. He was followed by two thousand years of searchers who are now in incarnations again after two thousand years of experience being garrotted, burned at the stake, hands and genitals cut off, and lately radiated with atomic weaponry. Does anybody think we've had enough? Isn't it about time to enter into the places of pain to find our power? There is no question about it any more. It is a matter of survival.

But now we're going to grasp hold of the most difficult problem. Before the final goal can be attained—the taking on of one's full power—we must take one more journey into the personal labyrinth. And the personal labyrinth, the emotional body, must be fully explored in each incarnation if we seek inner illumination. And it is in this area that the Egyptian theology of the Ka, the double or emotional body, is so subtle. The ancient Egyptians actually understood the block to higher awareness that almost all of us are fooled by. The Egyptians spent a lot of time trying to ensnare, to hold, to keep the Ka embodied.

For they had learned from the Masters of ancient days that the way we avoid going into pain to obtain full illumination is that we let the Ka, the emotional body, jump out of our body.

The Egyptians were forever making bargains with their Kas, making offerings to it, to stay around. And if you wish to progress, try keeping your emotional body totally present in your essence. Your emotional body is your teacher if you can just allow it to stay with you.

And some reflections on Christian history are appropriate at this time. Now can you see why the Christian church has gone to such lengths to eliminate the theology of reincarnation during the Age of Pisces? If you carry your earth records in your Ka with you from lifetime to lifetime, then you do not need a church to tell you how to achieve God. You already know more about our successes and failures than any priest could possibly comprehend. You, each one of you, is a shining storehouse of wisdom.

And just as you must ascertain which parts of your brain are responding when you have higher consciousness experiences in order to train your awareness, so must you learn what your astral body feels like in order to learn to control it. But there are also advantages to controlling the emotional body, because the astral body is also a great traveler if you learn to stay with it. It will take you wherever you need to travel for whatever experiences you need. Your emotional body is the part of you that can connect you with other levels of existence if you can clear it of past-life and present-life trauma so that it is entirely free to interact in your consciousness and connect with other realities. It is just filled with long strings, going far out to intriguing places that you never dreamed existed. The Priest of Enoch is shouting now to tell you his secrets, because he was around at one of the precessional changes, the Age of Cancer to Gemini in 6700 B.C., and he has a message about the precession from the Age of Pisces to Aquarius. And since we are on the verge of the precession into Aquarius, Enoch is allowed a revelation.

I wear gold and blue sandals, and my legs are bare and hairy. A kilt comes to my knees. I am large, slightly overweight, and I am a male. I have no hair on my head. The skin on my face is loose and fleshy, and it feels cold. My nose is long and straight, and my lips are thin and tight. I wear a collar that is turned up at the shoulders. It is metallic, with jewels set in it. The jewels are sapphire, emerald, ruby, dark rudalite crystal, topaz, amethyst, and clear crystal. And the garment on the upper part of my body is like armor. The collar stands up and is an energy shield under my ears. The armor is around my shoulders, across my chest, and it is smooth. I wear a shirt under the armor that is woven with silver threads. Everything is metallic, blue and silver. I wear a belt around my waist that is about four inches wide, which has seven or nine energy conductors in it. They all work the same, and they are activated at this time. Then the metallic armor is below the belt with the skirt under it. It is a shield around my hips as the upper part is a shield for my shoulders. The skin on my hands is white with dark hair. My hands are thick. I have no rings, but I have energy transmitters on my wrists. They are three inches wide, with an inverted jewel in each one. It is metallic, maybe aluminum, and it is concave with light inside. It is white light, and I don't usually wear this attire.

I stand on white stone which is a half-moon-shaped circle, and the 180-degree side of the circle is in front of me with the straight line behind. It is polished, and I am two-and-a-half feet in front of the straight line. This half-moon is within a bowl—on the inside bottom of the bowl with the rim opening out to the sky. It is like I stand in a rounded cone with my head and neck above the rim of the cone. And the cone is elevated. All I can see now is the sky. There are a few clouds and no vehicles flying about at this time. But, we must go back to the wrist devices.

This is Atlantis, but the wrist devices are constructed of lapis lazuli and coral. The concave jewel is Atlantean, and I am in Atlantis. But I use these wrist devices to reach the Egyptians. The Egyptians are later in time because this is 6700 B.C. over the Gobi Desert. But I can go backward and forward in time.

I am protected from the sound power outside at this time with my shields. My shields are made with my own visualization. In this case, I see myself encased within the inside of an amethyst geode. They transmit sound energies into this cone. and I would be destroyed without shields. The shields are time protectors also. So, I maintain my physical integrity while I experience this energy. Since this is an issue of time protection, I would disintegrate holographically without my shield. I would dissipate like an image no longer in the refractory field of a mirror. Of course, what would it matter if I did? But I have come to deliver a key message to your age through the veils of time so that you may know that the time has arrived for you to comprehend the visit of the Master, Christ.

So, I am inside the cone, and I am also aware of what goes on outside. This cone is resting on the top of the step pyramid, the oldest one on the planet at this time because so much was lost in the flood. This one still works. We only come to this pyramid at the right time, the precession of the equinox, in this case from the Age of Cancer to Gemini, 6700 B.C. It is a time of great quickening in the awareness of earth. But, please note, as you listen to my activities, that these times at the precession are critical dichotomy points when many forces blocked from earth can affect the planet. But, let us not be so complex so soon.

Now, most of what is happening down there around the pyramid is astral, and I can relate to it. I don't know what is inside the pyramid at this time, but there is a piazza all around it made of polished white stone. The step pyramid is four-sided. I am with my people at the top, and we are astral, so that the priests below can make contact with us. If we manifested on the physical plane. We would destroy all beings below, so they know us in their hearts and through their third eyes. And they have been thoroughly trained in occult verification. We taught them in their dreams to trust their hearts and uraeus as much as their eyes and ears. We would destroy them on the physical plane if we manifested, because we would be tampering with the earth laws of time.

The laws of time are the cosmic law, that allow the ultimate manifestation of the divine plan through evolution. But each new form is meant to birth in its proper time. If the laws are tampered with, great destruction occurs, destruction on all planes even. And the destruction of one molecule, one being, one form by the Masters is not to be allowed. But, we are always anxious to make a breakthrough to humans because it seems to us they progress so slowly. But we only manifest obeying the laws of time. We wish to interfere often, to make consciousness evolve, to encourage love, positive force, or action. We always strive for the ultimate development. That is why we exist.

The laws of time supercede the laws of karma. Few understand this at all, because many experience the laws of karma but few comprehend the laws of time. You can't live time, for example, as you can live karma. Time is the dimension that makes everything exist on all the planes. One knows cause and effect, so to speak, but rarely can see the progression because it is not linear. The divine mind which loves all beings is not linear as the human mind is. That is what is meant when you can understand our teaching that the Master, Christ, has always existed and always will. The only question is how much an individual knows Him.

You don't experience time, you only experience the passage of it. But you do experience cause and effect even though you create great religions and theologies in order to avoid that truth. Christianity is designed to ignore cause and effect: the Law of Karma. You could alter all existence in what you perceive to be a moment if you just could hear what I say. You experience the accumulation of emotional memory in your body, and that is where I exist to teach you. The point is, the reality of time is subtle. Let it go, and suddenly you will be God.

If you could see what I mean, then you could grasp something you already know; that the connection of time to the physical plane is where the plane of one exists. You all talk about it constantly, that all exists in a given moment, that there is no time, et cetera. But, few of you use the power inherent in that law. Think about it: You carry within yourself, in your body, the timeless awareness. Therefore, since time is form, you know how to manifest; that is, to make something happen at the right time. The right time is when a certain matrix of energies is present which has potency to become form. The matrixes are constant within the center of a being. That is what life is, and everything radiates out from that. And therefore, energy can be experienced, enhanced, and directed.

So, observe. I am located in this one cone at the top of this step pyramid at this specific time for a particular reason. At this juncture, I am able to use physical forces even though I am not actually physical as you understand it. And please do not fear us. Use your protective energies against your black scientists instead.

So, let us proceed with the action. I am conscious of what everybody is doing. Just like when I read the oracle at Delphi later, I need to know at all times what is going on. The purpose of the cone is to take the focal energies—the energies of the polished half-circle at my feet—and make them spherical. We flew the cone and put it on top of the step pyramid. We have to be incredibly conscious of not crossing the karmic path of any individual being below, and yet we must maximize this moment of the precession from Cancer to Gemini. The priests down below cannot see us, so I must tune into them. They are aware of me, but they cannot see me. They are more physical than I, but they share in my consciousness in their priestly office. They manifest perfectly in their office.

They try very hard and often they fail. We try hard to tune into them and organize them and restructure them in whatever way we can. And will is an issue. They have to give us permission to influence them. Sometimes we wait a long time for them to give us permission, and it is exhausting to watch them all the time. We mostly reach them through the mind, not the heart. I do it with the wrist devices. The disk that is in each wrist device is the same device that Ichor saw in the top of the small pyramid at Philae before he began his journey down the Nile. The substance in it is liquid, not solid, but it becomes solid in the wrist device and forms the Eye of Horus, the manifestation of the divine in time through light.

As I look into them, I can see the refractory angles, and they look like the tops of cones. It is like looking into a silver beehive, and I can see very clearly. They are also my eyes. If I were to look out in front of me into my eyes, that is the iris of my eyes. So the sound action of the cone causes the mercury to solidify in the convex lens. The physical senses are transmitters on the physical plane, but it does not occur to us that our senses can actually affect matter. We are lazy about our thoughts, because we underestimate what is going on. The Egyptians address this issue when they say that Amen, the invisible one, is the Ba—the soul in all things. Notice what you say at the end of your Christian prayers.

So, you can see all levels of reality if you master the awareness that you can SEE time. It is the simplest and the most occult fact about Earth reality, and only astrologers are trained in this principle. It is easy for them, and that is why they are masters at maximizing the moment. Or time can be SEEN with the I Ching. And it will also be useful for you to know that learning a divination skill is absolutely essential for the attainment of mastery. So, the eye is the key to energy transmutation or the way in which thought forms are manifested. The actualization of time is like the manifestation in time of a thought form, and the structure of the eye is the key to the way this works.

Look at it in terms of place for more understanding. First, if you study a duality, seemingly you can see more on the physical plane than if you view the oneness of it. If you make it into a four-sided issue you can see more. If you look at it in twelve ways, you see more. And if you look into a 360-degree circle you can see even more. And if you ponder that the eyeball itself is a ball like a crystal ball, that the surface of the eye is convex and brings in the light; and the thought form is accessed on the convex surface within and travels into the brain stem, you can see how a thought form is manifested. So the key to actualizing what you want is to meditate on the action of the eye. And the key is also intuition. Just as the eye sees and transmits, so it is that we know what matters intuitively. And that is also why the Egyptians revere the uraeus, the third eye, and the Eyes of Horus.

So, back to the cone and the connection to the priests and priestesses on the ground. Now angels appear in the sky above the cone. They are diaphanous, white and blue, and they vibrate. They are mental, I am astral, and the priests below are physical. We are all working on a harmonious level, but my function here is to link the mental and physical. It is actually a hard job when I think about it, because it means infusing the physical level with an idea so that a change is possible with the physical plane. And it only works by manipulating the astral connection. It is mainly the way the Masters work. And humans can link the mental with the physical by immersing themselves into their emotions. But enough talk, let me show you how it works.

The angels need to connect with the priests and priestesses down below, but the angels are all playing in the sky. They are swimming in the sunlight, and I have to get them to be serious. Nimbah, a priestess of fire, is down below, and she is the key. So I enter her awareness, she stops dead in her tracks, and she lights the fire . . . whoosh, in a disk. People who are attuned to the Masters stop dead in their tracks.

Suddenly, all the priests and priestesses stop what they are doing as if they hear the wind, and sacred time begins. For them, hearing the wind is like hearing the music of the spheres. This is why eagle feathers capturing the wind are sacred. The wind activates the divine plane when it moves the soft down of the eagle feather. And an angel moves over each one of the priests and priestesses. They move to each one of the corners of the pyramid and one in each place of the middle between the corners. They stand and move their hands up to raise energy, and they begin to walk forward.

Now I see why this is so miraculous. We have been having so much trouble with them. They are idiots; they have been using the top of the pyramid for sacrifices. But they just move right into place for the first time in their lives as if they knew it all along. The pyramid feels their power and comes alive with energy. It is the exact moment when the equinox precesses out of Cancer into Gemini, the eight priests and priestesses are connected with the angelic plane. The pyramid is becoming less dense and pulsating with white light, and I am ready.

I transmute my whole essence through the irises of my eyes suddenly to the place of Gemini in the higher mind, the domain of The

Twins and the manifestation of the duality. Every fiber in my essence begins clicking over into a new place as my wrist cones and waist energy activators send out a massive cosmic signal to all Earth beings. Suddenly, mysteriously, the symbols will change from The Crab and the moon of Cancer to the activation of the human mental plane of Gemini needed at this time. As the signal radiates out above me and down to every place on earth, as the priests and priestesses move to the pyramid, an incredible wave of sound moves through space, through all the spheres and galaxies, to all supernovas, and the cosmos is forever changed. Remember, Earth is the place where symbols exist in the cosmos. A New Age has dawned, and the last connection is a new thought in the Divine Mind. Gemini is here. And the next mutable age when energy moves quickly through the human plane from the Divine Mind will be the Age of Pisces, 100 B.C. to about 2100 A.D.

We move from the change into a New Age thousands of years ago to the final vision of the Eye of Horus in the body of the composite being, half animal/half human, the Centaur whose name is Cheiron. And the final vision is a vision that we all know well in one part of ourselves and reject in another part of ourselves. Yet the vision of The Christ is a centering experience for us as humans, and it is a vehicle that can carry us to the stars. But how can we see with our eye?

You are a being composed of vortexes of energy with so much space between each part that you are actually nothing. You only know yourself by what you have experienced and felt. And your organizing principle is polarity. Some call it ying and yang, positive and negative, male and female. Because your primary way of experiencing is emotional or astral, it is only by experiencing the full range of masculine and feminine that you come to feel your vibrating mass of energy particles. Remember, from one molecule to another in your body, the distance is greater than you can envision. Stop for a moment, close your eyes, listen to the cosmic silence of nothingness within your being. And then start again and move on the polarity into experience.

You are dulled, you know. You have allowed yourself to exist only in known patterns and familiar circumstances to avoid your emptiness. But, Christ is between your molecules! Let the patterns go, let the first awareness you find from emptiness happen to you, and then simply say that it is. And, that is occult verification. Every time something

happens to you that comes from the unknown place, from the nothing-
ness within, then learn to say it is. And then, when you see The Christ as
I did last year, you will know that you saw Him. Last year in 1983, I
finally found out what it was that I had been dreaming about for
forty years . . .

I am tall with a strong body. My hair is black with grey mixed in, it
is coarse and curly and wild. My face feels rough. My eyes are intense,
they are bright and piercing, my brow is heavy, and fire comes out of
my eyes. When I first came into this body, all I could feel was all the
energy. It is the energy of light and fire mixed together, not electrical,
more like magnetic light energy. I feel less dense than in the incarnation as Barbara. My body feels very balanced, as if it is in perfect health,
but shooting with magnetic force. The energy is distributed everywhere in the body, and my eyes are full of energy. They are disturbing,
powerful, and people don't like to look in them. The shining ones
have always been identified by their eyes. I feel very self-contained. I
must have amazing shields because I radiate all this energy out, yet I
feel like no one can penetrate it. This energy feels very extraterrestrial,
very much as if it is from another place, but it is fully contained in my
body. This body is fully formed and developed for a purpose, and this
purpose is sharply defined. I am not in the body. I am right in the
energy field on the edge of it. This energy field is of intense white light
with no penetration through it. It is a solidly knit, dense etheric web of
intense white light.

I am up on some rocks, and I am herding sheep. Sheep herding is
a religious function, it is a practice of genetic protection. This is my
highest work on this planet from my other place. I am a shepherd. A
shepherd is the highest manifestation of energy on the planet. Taking
care of the sheep on the physical plane is my way of balancing these
awarenesses. It is a grounding on this planet. It is soothing, and also,
sheep herding is a way of communicating with my people—my people where I came from. And, watch out whenever it seems that extra-
terrestrials are stealing or mutilating the sheep and cows. It is a
sign of doom.

At this moment, the Master Melchizadek wishes to inter-
vene, and we would ask you to relate to us for the good of
the planet earth at this time, a time when you had overt conscious contact with the people from the place you came

from . . .

Yes, Master. I am standing by a rock, a large rock, twenty feet tall, ten feet wide, whatever. The rock is on the edge of a cliff, down from the top of the plateau slightly, the top is above. The wind is hitting the rock on my side of the rock. In other words, it's blowing onto me. I have come here because I was called here for a meeting. This is a level of intuitional awareness that functions in the brain, in the place where messages are sent. So I came here because I was called, and as I wait, my time comes—way up above on the righthand side, up in the sky, there is a light explosion.

This is in the night, in the middle of the night, about two in the morning. The stars are very intense. There is no moon. It's cold. This light intensity that I see up on my righthand side seems to have lines projected down toward me. Some of them touch me, some of them go to my side. It's making me shake. It's very powerful. I have never seen anything like this—could it be angels? It's something else, but the only way I can see it with my physical eyes is as angels. It's an energy force that I can't really see.

My conscious apprehension is that it is the angels coming down. But I can also access levels of comprehension that are beyond conscious levels of awareness. It is the Annanage coming, and that is how light and sound fuse in my consciousness. It is in some way going backwards through time. I have called it to myself somehow with these connections I made.

It is coming closer. I can see it now. It is shaped like a saucer. The main body of it is an intense purple color and it has metal sheets over it with white lines in it. It is moving toward the top of the plateau up above me, and as it comes closer, it is shooting out very incredibly powerful light, power sound beams: "tchoo, tchoo, tchooo." In that frequency, but they're mostly light. That is the way it deals with the changes in frequency of coming into this density. That's what the vehicle is for. The beams align it. The vehicle creates an energy field around it so it can move in. If someone was watching, they could see this, too. It's late at night and very far away from anything, so chances are no one sees it. I've never seen it before. I was aware through mental communications of my connections, but I've never seen the vehicle before. It's beautiful.

We are not technological, but they are very technological. I would have no way to describe this in my own reality, but these things exist

in Barbara's reality, so I can describe it. That is why the descriptions of vehicles in the Bible were not taken literally until such vehicles were discovered again. OK, so it moves. Now it hovers above the plateau. It stops shooting off those magnetic sound light waves, and it hovers. and then there's a center hole in it. I am about twelve to twenty feet down from the top of the plateau.

I want to go closer, so I turn and put my hand on the rock. And I take my hand off fast. The rock is magnetized. And I feel burning and electrical crackling in my feet. I took my sandals off a minute ago. I'm standing barefooted.

There's a hole in the bottom of the vehicle, and as I stand and look at it from where I am, a circular shot of light force comes out of the hole down to the ground. It's like a shield of light. It's like a magnetic shield light force. And it forms a circle on the ground on the plateau above me. And I want to go up there, but I'm afraid to touch the rocks again because it's all electrified. So I wait. And into the electrical force field from the body of the ship—this is amazing!—a shining one steps down. He is white like an angel, he is a shining one in white robes. I wonder if he is the great Anu.

I can see through his body, but his body has a solidity of light. His hair is medium brown, very full brown—the most physical thing is his hair. But his hair also is shining. And his face is all light. I can see blue where the eyes are, but that's all I can see. He is standing in the light circle. The ship goes back up, and it's strange, it's like "wsssht" as it goes back up out of sight. It goes up and then over sideways, backwards or something like that. On the ground now the shining one is standing. I touch the rocks again, and they're no longer full of electricity. He just stands there, and I know I'm supposed to go there, so I climb up a little path, a few rocks, and I'm right up there. As I approach him, I feel that my energy field right outside of my body is similar to his. The energy field—the light body right outside my body—is pulsating in a harmonic in response to him. And now I know that harmonic response is His wave-length.

He seems to be having difficulty seeing. There's such intense light around him. He raises his hands in the power position, with his palms facing me. And at that point, I'm still looking at him. I can see his face. His face is—I think what I'm seeing is my physical apprehension of his face. It's like it seems to take a form that is a conglomeration of what faces are to me. His face looks Semitic. I'm conscious of organizing his face in a way that is seeable to me, and it's necessary for me to see his face.

He is all light, very intense light. So as I see the physical face—which is very Semitic with a brown beard and brown hair—his eyes radiate a lot of light out and I connect: I see his eyes because I need to see his eyes. It's not like I'm really seeing his eyes. I look into his eyes. When I look into his eyes, it's just this incredible vortex of energy shooting out. I go to the center of them. His hands are still in the Power position as if he's trying to orient himself. It's as if he's trying to orient himself from here. Then, as soon as I look into his eyes, I prostrate myself on the ground. I'm on my knees. I put my hands out, prostrate myself on the ground.

At that point, he moves his hands into a position so the energy comes directly out of his hands. At that point, time stops. My existence in that dimension of time and space disappears. I feel very peaceful. He then indicates to me with his vibrations that we are going to communicate with each other mentally. Not with him thundering at me or something like that. He does not assume a human form very much. It's a little hard to imagine communicating.

He says, "Isaiah, I have come to call you. I have come to manifest your other body into your present body. You will live this lifetime with the light body infused in your being." Now, this is very unexpected information. I obviously don't understand, but I don't say anything. He says, "You have returned—this is your second incarnation. This is your second incarnation on this planet from the Pleiades. The first incarnation was as the priest of Enoch. And this is your second incarnation to do the work of Enoch on this planet.

"You will have a third incarnation on this planet as Barbara." (I am fascinated as I stare at the pulsating white light with my intense blue eyes, because a question that has always burned inside is finally answered . . . I have felt so totally embodied on earth and simultaneously so far away, as if I also lived on a star.) "You will carry the light body of your place—the Pleiades—on the physical plane on earth. I have now come to give you your instructions.

"I am The Christ, and it is through me that you may know that I am always present, just as all your lives in the past and future are present in your essence at any time. I am the Son of God, just as you are the Child of God, and I am of the Holy Trinity with the Holy Spirit. All the power is in the triangles as it is in the essence of the three of us. We radiate our energy to you so that you may move closer to our essence, the light. In your physical being, you are now to infuse the light planes into human reality unconditionally. It is your work. If you would like to ask me questions, simply form them in your mind, and I will know what you ask. And the answer will be yours. So it is throughout time for those who ask and listen."

My mind forms the question, "Master, how am I to do this work?"

"You are to pulsate magnetic energy and ground magnetic energy into the physical plane from the light planes in order to increase our Trinitarian maximization of energy on the physical plane. You are to accomplish this end by staying as close as possible during your incarnations to the human religious power source."

In my mind the question forms. "Master, how do I identify whether the power source is your power source or not?"

"You do not have to worry about this question. You are able to know in all situations whether the energy is from me or not. Trust your awareness. All energy that is not from me is energy that we fight to dissipate. The energy that we fight to dissipate is very large and very all-encompassing on your planet, and in our realms it is like a pea. But, if you do not ground and diffuse, magnetize our energy on the earth plane, the earth plane will be destroyed in some form. You will be overcome by that other energy which causes human beings to do things which destroy them."

The next question in my mind is, "Master, if I hear you correctly, you mean to say the power sources are corrupted in various ways, and the only connection for you on this plane is through those power sources. (He communicates to me that I understood him.) Then my question is, "How do I use the power sources that are available to make the connections?"

"You must proceed with your judgmental abilities based upon intuitive perceptions toward the correct source. You must connect, you must do many things with this source. You must protect this source as far as information is concerned. There are many levels here for doing this. You must work to get the correct words through to the humans by means of writing and by means of speaking. You must exist as a purification force. In all rituals that you participate in, you have the power to purify participants in the ritual, and you have the power to affect to some degree the priests and priestesses, the transmitters of the power. You have the power to go to the temple to purify.

"And you also exist to radiate unconditional love to all beings

and all people that you encounter. The magnetic force of the purification of unconditional love is my way of reaching to the human plane.
This lifetime as Isaiah will be a lifetime of unmitigated tragedy. As you
follow my instructions in this lifetime, you will not succeed on the
physical plane. The negative energy forces will overcome the earth
plane—not you, the earth plane—in almost all situations. Even my
energy sources will be hidden and taken from the people.

"You will be able to get your words through. Your words will be
protected by my light. Your words will never be lost to the people. In
this lifetime, the negative forces are stronger. But later, the time will
come when the negative forces will be defeated. The whole meaning
of this lifetime of Isaiah is to identify the negative energy forces so that
the battle is won in the third incarnation. The third incarnation occurs
after my incarnation as a human, as Jesus of Nazareth. It is a change of
age to Aquarius after my Piscean incarnation, and many humans will
incarnate the light body into their physical existence, and they will
learn to dissipate the negative forces. Listen carefully now, in your
third incarnation as an Enochian, find hope and connection in the
many, many humans who have found my light. When that time comes
for you, the water-bearer, Aquarius, will energize the planet. The
Egyptians knew the secret because, notice their god of the Nile, Hapi,
was represented by the hieroglyph of Aquarius. But, Aquarius is fixed
air, permeating and grounding all. Wait for the water-bearer."

Then he dissipates. I feel great loss. For a moment, I was connected with a part of myself that always existed in my deepest self. I found
a way to a place inside that is my essential being, a place I return to
continually throughout all time and space. And now, like the cruelest
vacuum on the planet Earth, I am left alone. My deepest self is gone as
if I never knew it. Yet, I know I found a place that will direct me
throughout time.

Now, like a sheep gone away beyond the mind of the shepherd, I
am totally alone. Only thousands of years later as a little girl climbing a
brick tower in Michigan, only then will I find the light again.

SUGGESTED
FURTHER READING

After experiencing each regression, I investigated various original sources from the time of the regression and considered the opinions of archeologists, historians, and scientists who had done work on the periods I had lived in.

The following is a list of sources which relate to my experience and some information on why they are relevant.

CHAPTER ONE
The focus of the first chapter is psychological and helps the reader enter into what the process feels like. Experiencing regression is like peeling an onion, and the outer layers were what made me cry. The first chapter breaks into pain to clear the constriction in my body so that inner growth was possible. Therefore, the books which are relevant are mostly psychoanalytic.

Arroyo, Stephen, *Relationships and Life Cycles,* Davis, CA CRSC Publications, 1979.

————————————, *Astrology, Karma, and Transformation,* Davis, CA, CRSC Publications, 1979.

Brown, Norman O., *Life Against Death,* Middletown, CT, Vintage, 1972.

Fox, Matthew, *Original Blessing,* Santa Fe, NM, Bear & Company, 1983.

von Franz, Marie Louise, *Puer Aeternus,* Santa Monica, CA, Sigo Press, 1970.

Groddeck, George, *The Book of the It,* New York, New Americn Library, 1961. This book threw me hard into the awareness of mind in the body.

Hall, Nor, *The Moon and the Virgin,* New York, Harper and Row, 1980. This book forced me to enter into the interior, the feminine, in my mid-30s. When I entered into regressions, it served as an unconscious feminine guide as I travelled a road with many potential pitfalls.

Horney, Karen, *Self-Analysis,* New York, Norton, 1942. This book helped me to accomplish self-analytic work on my own between regressions.

————————————, *Our Inner conflicts: A Constructive Theory of*

Neurosis, New York, Norton, 1945.

Moss, Richard, *The I That Is We,* Millbrae, CA, Celestial Arts, 1981. This book caused me to know that I could no longer tolerate remaining separate.

Reich, Wilhelm,*Character Analysis,* New York, 1933. This is a seminal work for New Age healers. Reich demonstrates that we can observe the inner conflicts of people by observing body characteristics. Therefore, he establishes that psychic conflicts exist in the body since the effect can be observed. Therefore, New Age healers can enter into the place in the body where the conflict resides and clear it.

_____, *The Function of the Orgasm,* 1927, New York, Simon and Schuster, 1974.

_____,*The Sexual Revolution,* New York, Farrar, Straus, and Giroux, 1974.

Reik, Theodor, *Curiosities of the Self,* New York, Noonday, 1965.

Wilhelm, Richard, *The Secret of the Golden Flower,* New York, Harcourt, Brace, Janovich, 1962.

CHAPTER TWO
The focus of this chapter is transformative. Often the neurotic depressive elements of the psyche have a strangle hold on the transformative elements. Often when the negativity is cleared, wonderful mythic contents of the psyche arise and mesmerize the discoverer. This can be a dangerous phase of any form of analytic healing because the client can get "caught" in the story. Some therapists call this process ego inflation. This is the reason the onion image is a good one for past life regression: I was aware I had to keep moving into the center through all the layers. The contents of Chapter Two are fascinating in light of archeology, ancient history, and esoteric tradition. So, the sources I investigated are mostly from archeo-historic sources with heavy emphasis on esoteric literature. I list the Druid and Egyptian separately because each list of sources is so lengthly and readers may have an interest in one or the other.

The Druid Priest in about 500 A.D. in Britain and the Rhineland:

Adkins, Lesley and Roy A., *A Thesaurus of British Archelology,* London, David and Charles, 1982.

Barrow, R.H.,*The Romans,* Baltimore, Penguin, 1949.

Bord, Janet and Colin, *The Secret Country,* London, Granada, 1976.

_____, *Earth Rites*, London, Granada, 1982.

_____, *A Guide to Ancient Sites in Britain*, London, Granada, 1984.

_____, *Mysterious Britain*, London, Granada, 1984.

Branston, Brian, *The Lost Gods of England*, London, Thames and Hudson, 1984.

_____, *Gods of the North*, London, Thames and Hudson, 1980.

Brennan, Martin, *The Stars and the Stones*, London, Thames and Hudson, 1983. This is a little known but definitive book on archeo-astronomy.

Burl, Aubrey, *Prehistoric Avebury*, New Haven, Yale University Press, 1979.

Cathe, Bruce, *Harmonic 33*, Australia, A.H. and A.W. Reed, 1968.

Caesar, Julius, *The Battle for Gaul*, Boston, David R. Godine, 1980. Translation by Anne and Peter Wiseman.

Chadwick, Nor, *The Celts*, England, Penguin, 1984.

Cumont, Franz, *The Mysteries of Mithra*, New York, Dover, 1956.

Cyr, Donald, L., *Stonehenge Viewpoint*, Santa Barbara, CA 1985. See article, "Skies of Early Man," p. 67.

Dyer, J., *Prehistoric England and Wales*, England, Penguin, 1981.

Hitching, Francis, *Earth Magic*, New York, William Morrow, 1977.

Josephus, *Antiquities of the Jews and a History of the Jewish Wars*, Philadelphia, David McKay, translated by Wm. Whiston, no publication date.

Lewis, Archibald R., *Emerging Europe A.D. 400-1000*, New York, Alfred A. Knopf, 1969.

McMann, Jean, *Riddles of the Stone Age: Rock Carvings of Ancient Europe*, London, Thames and Hudson, 1980.

Mitchell, John, *Secrets of the Stones*, London, Penguin, 1977.

_____, *The New View Over Atlantis*, New York, Harper and Row, 1983.

_____, *the earth spirit*, New York, Crossroad, 1975.

Newham, CA, *The Astronomical Significance of Stonehenge*, Wales, Moon Publications, 1972.

O'Brien, Christian, *The Megalithic Odyssey*, England, Turnstone Press, 1983.

Piggott, Stuart, *The Druids*, London, Thames and Hudson, 1975.

Pogacnik, Marko with William Bloom, *Leyline and Ecology*, Glastonbury, Gothic, 1985.

Rutherford, Ward, *The Druids: Magicians of the West,* Wellingborough, The Aquarian Press, 1978.

Sharkey, John, *Celtic Mysteries: The ancient religion,* New York, Crossroad, 1981.

Spence, Lewis, *The History and Origins of Druidism,* New York, Rider, no publication date.

Wallace-Hadrill, J.M., *The Barbarian West: The Early Middle Ages-A.D. 400 1000,* New York, Harper Torchbooks, 1962.

The Egyptian Priest in 1400 B. C.—Eighteenth Dynasty under Amenhotep II:

Aldred, Cyril, *Egypt to the End of the Old Kingdom,* London, Thames and Hudson, 1965.

Budge, E. A. Wallis, *Osiris and the Egyptian Resurrection,* Vols. I & II, New York, Dover, 1973.

_____, *Dwellers on the Nile,* New York, Dover, 1977.

Erman, Adolf, *Life in Ancient Egypt,* New York, Dover, 1977.

Fagan, Brian M., *The Rape of the Nile,* New York, Scribners, 1975.

Haich, Elisabeth, *Initiation,* Palo Alto, CA, 1974. This book is the most similar book that I know to EYE OF THE CENTAUR.

de Lubicz, R.A. Schwaller, *Symbol and the Symbolic,* New York, Inner Traditions, 1979.

_____, *Sacred Science,* New York, Inner Traditions, 1982. This work is a great source on ancient Pharonic wisdom.

de Lubicz, Isha Schwaller, *Her-Bak: Egyptian Initiate,* New York, Inner Traditions, 1956. This book is closer to the mentality of Ichor than anything I've yet found. I've read it five times and still barely grasp its profundity.

_____, *Her-Bak: The Living Face of Ancient Egypt,* New York, Inner Traditions, 1954. This is a fine work, but not as remarkable as the first Her-Bak.

Petrie, W. M. Flinders, *Religious Life in Ancient Egypt,* Boston, Houghton Mifflin, 1924.

Sety, Omm, *Abydos: Holy City of Ancient Egypt,* Los Angeles, CA, LL Company, 1981. Omm Sety lived near the Temple of Abydos from 1933-1981. From her earliest recollection, she felt a close affinty to the ancient Egyptians, especially Sety I. She married an Egyptian and had a son near the Temple at Abydos whom she felt was a reincarnation of Sety I. Since Abydos has a megalithic Osiris temple called the Osieron which is much older than the Abydos Temple, and it was exceedingly ancient in the time of Ichor in 1400 B.C.; I surmise that the Abydos Temple is the original site or a continuance of a special place for helping people to get in touch with their ancient ancestors such as Osiris. I was extremely moved by this temple and understood it very easily even though I have not recalled a lifetime during the time of the construction or use of the main temple. Ichor used the Osieron for a special ritual when the Inundation was especially high. Possibly there was an older temple where the present temple is, and Sety I copied it. I knew it very well.

Tompkins, Peter, *Secrets of the Great Pyramids,* New York, Harper and Row, 1971.

Spence, Lewis, *Myths and Legends of Ancient Egypt,* New York, Farrar & Rhinehart, 1911.

Steiner, Rudolf, *Egyptian Myths and Mysteries,* Spring Valley, NY, Anthroposophic Press, 1971.

West, John Anthony, *Ancient Egypt,* New York, Knopf, 1985. This is the best guide to Egypt for those interested in the sacred mysteries.

CHAPTER THREE:
The focus of this chapter is the breakthrough and empowerment of Aspasia. Since Aspasia appears in other chapters, books chosen here which I pursued for background on Aspasia will be limited to the experiences she had in this chapter. Later, there will be more information relating to the Late Minoan regarding Aspasia. Since her culture was destroyed by the eruption of Thera in 1450 B.C., it is difficult to find sources which apply to her reality, and much of what I pursued was by means of resonance, ie., material which fit the regression report.

Aspasia, Minoan Priestess, 1492-1455 B.C.:

Apollonius of Rhodes, *The Voyage of Argo,* New York, Penguin, 1959. Apollonius of Rhodes is third century B.C., and yet the names of the Argonauts and people in places they visited are totally familiar, as familiar as people in this lifetime.

Brindel, June Rachuy, *Ariadne,* New York, St. Marin's Press, 1980. The intensity that the author brings to this text and the way in which she reports the feelings of Ariadne is unusually genuine and reflective of direct experience by her.

Campbell, Joseph, *The Mysteries,*Vol. 2, Princeton, NJ, Bollingen, 1955. See "The Meaning of the Eleusinian Mysteries," and "The Mysteries of the Kabeiroi," for unusual resonance with the time of Aspasia.

Fontenrose, Joseph, *Python: A Study of Delphic Myth and Its Origins,* Berkeley, CA, 1980. This is the definitive modern work on Delphi. The place Aspasia went to read the oracle was called the "Oracle of Delphoi" by her, and this turned out to be a priceless detail. According to Fontenrose, the original oracle was 7 miles above the present Delphic Oracle, and it was called the Lycorean Oracle, or the oracle of the wolf.

Heidel, William, *The Frame of the Ancient Greek Maps,* New York, American Geographical Society, 1937.

Hoddinott, R.F.,*The Thracians,* London, Thames and Hudson, 1981.

Hood, Sinclair, *The Arts in Prehistoric Greece,* England, Penguin, 1978.

Jaynes, Julian, *The Origins of Consciousness in the Breakdown of the Bicameral Mind,* Boston, Houghton Mifflin, 1976. I cite this work because Jaynes assumes that seers before 1500 B.C. could actually hear the voice of the Gods in their heads. He begins with the premise that seers actually did possess presently unknown perceptual skills and that these skills gradually atrophied with the development of consciousness. Jaynes himself views such skills as "hallucinatory," while I view them as evidence of remarkable perceptual skill. But, as Jaynes traces "the breakdown of the bicameral mind," readers are treated to a broad and detailed panorama of the divination skill history of the ancients.

Rutherford, Ward, *The Druids,* Great Britain, The Aquarian Press, 1978. The author delineates the connections of the Indo-European peoples during the lifetime of Aspasia.

Severin, Tim, *"Jason's Voyage In Search of the Golden Fleece,"* Washington, D.C., National Geographic Magazine, Sept. 1985. This article is very interesting because while undertaking a modern voyage for the Golden Fleece, the author reports detailed folk memories of Jason's voyage by the people all the way along the route. Aspasia's home is a gold mining center, and Severin notes that the Golden Fleece was still being used recently as a cloth for panning gold. Perhaps Aspasia was extremely aware of this voyage because it had something to do with procuring gold.

Temple, Robert K.G., *The Sirius Mystery,* New York, St. Martin's Press, 1976. See "The Oracle Centers."

Taylor, Thomas, *The Eleusinian & Bacchic Mysteries,* San Diego, CA, Wizards, 1980. A reprint of the J.W. Bouton, 1875 edition.

Spanuth, Jurgen, *Atlantis of the North,* London, Sidgwick & Jackson, 1979. Spanuth posits that Heligoland is Atlantis, and Aspasia reports that it was one of the Atlantean theocracies along with Crete and Thera.

CHAPTER FOUR:

The focus of this chapter is the life of Lydia, the labyrinthian initiation of Aspasia, my own contact with the Native American spirits when I was a child, the deathly consciousness of the Victorian woman, and my birth and real embodiment in this lifetime. The books I have selected are mostly mythological because this chapter represents that special time when one moves outside the confines of the one lifetime sense and begins to let go of negative holds so that the identification with the larger whole can take precedence.

Brindel, June Rachuy, *Ariadne,* New York, St. Martin's Press, 1980. Already cited in the notes for Chapter Three, this novel comes closer to Aspasia's initiation in the Cretan labyrinth than any other source I've found.

Eliade, Mircea, *Rites and Symbols of Initiation,* New York, Harper Torchbooks, 1958. Eliade seems to be able to examine the meaning of initiation from the experience of the initiate in his/her culture. He avoids the supercilious attitude of most university scholars, and is an invaluable source for students of the spirituality of initiation.

_____, *Gods, Goddesses, and Myths of Creation,* New York, Harper and Row, 1967.

_____, *The Myth of the Eternal Return,* Princeton, Bollingen, 1974.

Jung, C.G., *Aion: Researches into the Phenomenology of the Self,* Princeton, Bollingen, 1979.

Kerenyi, C., *Goddesses of Sun and Moon,* Irving Texas, Spring Publications, 1979. Kerenyi's sensitivity about the goddess archetypes mostly coming from the time of Aspasia is very close to my feelings under hypnosis. Since this scholar is a male, it is hard not to conclude that he lived as a woman during those times.

Kubler-Ross, Elisabeth, *Death: The Final Stage of Growth,* New Jersey, Prentice Hall, 1975.

Lopez, Barry Holstun, *Of Wolves and Men,* New York, Scribners, 1978.

My totem animal is the wolf, and it turns out that the wolf was the totem animal of Aspasia, Ichor (as Anubis in Egypt), and Isaiah. It seems to be a soul connection. The wolves were annihilated in my section of Michigan by the time I was eight. I had the pleasure of hearing them howl in the winter night for the last time when I was about fifteen. As we annihilate the species, we end our soul connection with the animals and our own instincts are obliterated.

Matthews, W.H., *Mazes and Labyrinths: Their History and Develpment,* New York, Dover, 1970.

Renault, Mary, *The Bull From the Sea,* New York, Vintage, 1975. This is a good example of a childhood book which left me breathless. When your children are passionate about a period in history, they have been there before. And, how otherwise does a writer like Mary Renault recapture so much?

Sheldrake, Rupert, *A New Science of Life,* Los Angeles, Tarcher, 1981. I cite this work here for two reasons: 1) Sheldrake's theory of morphogenetic resonance which posits that animals can tune into the experience of their predecessors also can support the theory that they do so because they have returned; and 2) my inner psychic hologram altered when I reaccessed the Victorian Woman's decision to die when she decides to marry. If the inner psychic hologram can be altered by exploring the memory bank, then possibly one is clearing inner body blocks which might result in eventual disease?

Starhawk, *Dreaming the Dark,* Boston, Beacon Press, 1982. This is a powerful statement about the death of women from the patriarchal, mechanistic reality we live in.

Ulanov, Ann Belford, *Receiving Woman,* Philadelphia, Westminster, 1981.

Weigle, Marta, *Spiders and Spinsters,* Albuquerque, University of New Mexico Press, 1982. A great book on the feminine and spiders.

CHAPTER FIVE:

The focus of this chapter is very historical, because as soon as I rebirthed into this reality, I grounded myself into history. For many people, reincarnation can be most firmly established by historic verification. In my case, the firmest verification historically is my most previous life as the Victorian Woman. I have been able to talk to women who knew her, I have had the opportunity to identify her possessions, but I am not at liberty to identify her. Further back in time, the lifetimes which are the most verifiable are Erastus Hummell, the medieval merchant, and the Roman landowner. In fact, I suspect I could find historical or graveyard comfirmation of Erastus Hummell if I could go to Liepzig. The references and books suggested for this chapter are historically oriented.

Erastus Hummell (1561-1640):

Readers could consult any history of science or Germany who are interested in this period. After the regression, I checked some facts I had stated under hypnosis. I had said I was ruled by the Hapsburgs and that is correct. I described an instrument and drew it after regression which turned out to be a Gemmascope. Apparently Erastus adapted it for navigation. I checked to see if Giordano Bruno, Johannes Kepler, and Galileo Gallilei were contemporaries and they were. I mentioned that I studied with Kepler, and Kepler lived 1571-1630, so that is likely.

It is provocative to use Erastus as a consciousness model. He studies maps of the universe in the Count's library in 1600 A.D., and he possesses the memory bank of two Atlantean Enochian priests; the Minoan/Cretan mystery religions; Eighteenth Dynasty astrologer; the Hebrew prophetic tradition, plus a lifetime as an angel. And there he is at a point when the culture allows him to stretch his mind. Rudolph Steiner said, "Let us apply this (thought of possible remembering when one is inventing) to a particular soul what at that time acquired insight into the great cosmic connections, and let us imagine that there arises again before this soul what it had seen spiritually in ancient Egypt. This appears again in this soul . . ., and we have the soul of Copernicus. Thus did the Copernician system arise, as a memory-tableau of spiritual experiences in ancient Egypt. The case is the same with Kepler's system. These men gave birth to these great laws out of their memories." (From Egyptian Myths and Mysteries, See Chapter Two reference.)

Barraclough, Geoffrey, *The Origins of Modern Germany,* New York, Capricorn Books, 1963.

Eliade, Mircea, *Death, Afterlife, and Eschatology,* New York, Harper and Row, 1974.

Huizinga, J., *The Waning of the Middle Ages,* New York, Doubleday, 1956.

Head, Joseph, and S.L. Cranston, *Reincarnation: The Phoenix Fire*

Mystery, New York, Julian Pess, 1977. This is the best book on reincarnation history.

Maslow, Abraham, *The Farther Reaches of Human Nature*, New York, Penguin, 1971.

Moore, Marcia, and Mark Douglas, *Reincarnation: Key to Immortality*, New Harbor, Maine, Arcane, 1968.

Parry, J.H., *The Age of Reconnaissance*, New York, Mentor, 1964.

Smith, Lester E., *Intelligence Came First*, Wheaton, Illinois, Quest, 1975. An excellent book on consciousness, memory, and perception.

Spence, Lewis, *The Occult Sciences in Atlantis*, New York, Weiser, 1978. Possibly the best source on ancient racial memory.

The Medieval Merchant (about 1170-1240 A.D.):

Barraclough, Geoffrey, *The Crucible of Europe*, Berkeley, University of California, 1976. Mostly covering the Ninth and Tenth Centuries, this book lays the groundwork for the Eleventh and Twelfth Centuries.

Dawson, Christopher, *Medieval Essays*, New York, Image, 1959.

Ganshof, F.L., *Feudalism*, New York, Harper Torchbooks, 1961.

Heer, Friedrich, *The Medieval World*, New York, Mentor, 1961.

Knowles, David, *the evolution of medieval thought*, 1962.

Painter, Sydney, *Mediaeval Society*, Ithaca, Cornell, 1965. This is the best source for background on the life of the medieval merchant.

Petit-Dutallis, Charles, *The Feudal Monarchy in France and England*, New York, Harper Torchbooks, 1949.

Pirenne, Henri, *Economic and Social History of Medieval Europe*, New York, Harcourt, Brace, Janovich, 1933.

Tierney, Brian, *The Crisis of Church & State, 1030-1300*, New Jersey, Prentice Hall, 1964.

The Roman (74 -7 B.C.):

Angus, S., *Mystery-Religions*, New York, Dover, 1975. This is a good background book on the general religious fabric around the time of Christ.

Caesar, Julius, *The Battle for Gaul*, translated by Anne and Peter Wiseman, Boston, David R Godine, 1980.

Grant, Michael, *History of Rome*, New York, Scribners, 1978.

Rostovtzeff, M., *Rome*, London, Oxford, 1963. This work had the most information on taxation and land reform issues.

The Satyricon of Petronius Arbiter, translated by William Burnby, New York, Modern Library, no publication date.

CHAPTER SIX

This chapter focuses on transfiguration experiences which I believe almost all human beings have, but the mind shuts the memory down so completely that often we don't remember the ones we've had in this lifetime. For example, I was sure I had had a consummate mystical illumination experience when I was seven, but I could not recall it. Somehow in work with Greg, I became aware that this lost memory was part of my search, and we went back through the experience to examine it. It would appear that these experiences are too much for our normal consciousness; that must be the reason so many people forget the content. An example of an experience like this would be when you have climbed to the top of a mountain, your time sense seems distorted as if a minute is hours; you have gone someplace but you can't remember where; and all you are left with is a sense of the divine. You are a believer after that but you can't explain why. After recovering that memory, the memory of the angelic life, the life of Isaiah came back to me. It will take me years to assess the Isaiah regression, but at least I can list the books I've considered so far.

Next, this chapter moves right into the Horus initiation of Ichor. In actual regression order, the Horus initiation came way before the life of Isaiah. Both regressions have to do with the opening of the third eye or the ability to access very wide ranges of consciousness, and they both are concerned with the integration of the superconscious in the self and the use of superconscious energies. Readers will be surprised to see me cite many Gnostic sources. The Gnostics were various religious groups in the Holy Land, Egypt, all over the ancient world, who were declared systematically heretical by the Roman Church as it strengthened its politico/religio power base and claimed sole providence over the teachings of Jesus. The Roman Church also chose information from the Hebrew Bible which they felt strenthened their case for the Messianic Christ, and the Roman church especially liked the thought of Isaiah. I am attempting to interpret Isaiah in his own context, in view of what seems correct to me intuitively, and through other religious sources which seem close to his consciousness. Often, it seems to me that the Gnostics, especially the Jewish Gnostics, are close to the prophetic vision of Isaiah.

Isaiah in Eighth Century, B.C.:

Allegro, John,The Dead Sea Scrolls, New York, Penguin, 1964.

Anderson, Bernhard W., Understanding the Old Testament, New York, Prentice Hall, 1957.

Holy Bible, Revised Standard Edition, Nashville, Regency, 1952.

Buber, Martin, The Prophetic Faith, New York, Harper Torchbooks, 1960.

Crossan, John Dominic, Four Other Gospels, Minneapolis, Winston, 1985.

Eden, the Forgotten Books of and the Lost Books of the Bible, World Publishers, 1927.

Doresse, Jean, The Secret Books of the Egyptian Gnostics, New York, Viking, 1960.

Drake, Raymond, Mystery of the Gods—Are They Coming Back to Earth? 1972, no publisher given.

Franck, Adolphe, The Kabbalah, New York, Bell, 1940.

Graves, Robert and Raphael Patai, Hebrew Myths, New York, Greenwich, 1983.

Grollenberg, Luc. H., Atlas of the Bible, New York, Penguin, 1959.

Heschel, Abraham, The Prophets, New York, Harper Torchbooks, 1962. Heschel attempts to understand the impact of prophetic consciousness on the mind of the prophet.

Jonas, Hans, The Gnostic Religions, Boston, Beacon Press, 1963. A major source.

Heline, Corinne, Mythology and the Bible, La Canada, CA, New Age Press, 1972.

Laurence, Richard, The Book of Enoch, from the Ethiopian manuscript, San Diego, Wizards, 1973; photographic copy of the 1883 version.

Negev, Avraham, Archeology in the Land of the Bible, New York, Schocken, 1977.

Pagels, Elaine, The Gnostic Gospels, New York, Vintage, 1981.

Robinson, James M., The Nag Hammadi Library, New York, Harper and Row, 1977.

Scholem, Gershom, Major Trends in Jewish Mysticism, New York, Schocken, 1961.

_____, Kabbalah, New York, NAL, 1974. This is the best source I've found yet on the true consciousness of the Kabbalah.

Scheler, Gerald J., Enochian Magic: A Practical Manual, Minneapolis, Llewellyn, 1985. This is a very useful and thought provoking work on the contemporary applications of Enochian Science.

Szekely, Edmond Bordeaux, *The Discovery of the Essene Gospel of Peace,* International Biogenic Society, 1977. A thought-provoking source on the inner workings of the Vatican archivists.

Sitchin, Zecharia, *The Twelfth Planet,* New York, Avon, 1978.

_____, *The Stairway to Heaven,* New York, Avon, 1980.

_____, *The War of Gods and Men,* New York, Avon, 1985. So far, only Sitchin knows why Isaiah spoke as he did.

Wilson, R. McL., *The Gnostic Problem,* New York, AMS reprint of 1958 edition.

Ichor, Egyptian priest under Amenhotep II, references in relation to Horus Initiation:

Adams, W. Marsham, *The Book of the Master of the Hidden Places,* New York, Weiser, 1980. A very illuminated work on initiation.

Budge, E.A. Wallis, *Egyptian Magic,* New York, Dover, 1971.

Brunton, Paul, *A Search in Secret Egypt,* New York, Weiser, 1980.

David, A. Rosalie, *The Ancient Egyptians,* London, Routledge and Kegan Paul, 1982. This book is one of the best examples of the inability of scholars to understand what they are studying that I know.

de Lubicz, Isha Schwaller, *The Opening of the Way,* New York, Inner Traditions, 1981.

de Lubicz, R.A. Schwaller, *Sacred Science,* New York, Inner Traditions, 1982.

Eliade, Mircea, *The Sacred and the Profane,* New York, Harcourt, Brace, Janovich, 1959.

French, Peter J., *John Dee,* London, Routledge, & Kegan Paul, 1984. A good study of a great initiate.

Haich, Elisabeth, *Initiation,* Palo Alto, Seed Center, 1974.

Jung, C.G., *Psychology and the Occult,* Princeton, Bollingen, 1977.

Lamy, Lucie, *Egyptian Mysteries,* New York, Crossroad, 1981. This is the best book I have ever read on Egyptian sacred mysteries.

Spence, Lewis, *The Occult Sciences in Atlantis,* New York, Weiser, 1978.

Wilhelm, Richard, *The Secret of the Golden Flower,* New York, Harcourt, Brace, Janovich, 1962.

CHAPTER SEVEN

The chapter focuses on the point when I was able to go through the central negative experience, the place where I'm the most afraid, and confront my actual total connection with other human beings. And once that knot was removed, I plunged into channeling, into the connection with the angelic realms. I feel we all have been angels and will be again, but we will not know about it until we enter into the dark places first. I have no books to cite on this chapter because I have not found anything written about this subject which taught me anything. I have never read this chapter without crying.

CHAPTER EIGHT

This chapter focuses on the Osiris Initiation of Ichor, and the Egyptian references cited in Chapter Two and Six cover the background of the initiation. Then I moved into the priest of Enoch as he makes his connections to the divine plane. This regression came from a very deep place in my psyche, and after it I was more adept at connecting the divine plane to this reality. But, this regression goes so far back in time that there are no real sources to cite. Then, I moved into the vision of Aspasia of the eruption of Santorini-Thera. I have a lot of references and comments about this vision because I was driven to find out what I was seeing. Recovering the vision was very powerful, and it seemed like it had occurred just yesterday.

Priest of Enoch: first incarnation 6700 B.C. over Gobi Desert, Second incarnation about 5,000 B.C., location unknown. Here I am citing the research direction I am moving into and these are sources which may relate to these incarnations.

Baran, Michael, *Twilight of the Gods,* Smithtown, NY, Exposition Press, 1984.

Capt, E. Raymond, *Missing Links Discovered in Assyrian Tablets,* Artisan Sales, Thousand Oaks, CA, 1985. I am all too well aware that Christopher O'Brien, Raymond Capt, and others are not considered valid references by scholars. However, scholars have lost their prerogative on the judgment of correct sources because scholars are not asking pertinent questions. So, until they do, those of us who want answers will search all sources, and Raymond Capt is asking the right questions.

Chiera, Edward, *They Wrote on Clay,* Chicago, University of Chicago,

1966.

Churchward, James, *Understanding Mu,* New York, Warner, 1970.

Cory, I.P., *Ancient Fragments,* Minneapolis, Wizards, 1975. This is an indispensible source of ancient wisdom.

Daniken, Erich von, *The Gold of the Gods,* Great Britain, Souvenir Press, 1973. Von Daniken himself describes this book as "the incredible, fantastic story of this century." He is absolutely correct and he is completely ignored by historians and archeologists.

Doresse, Jean *The Secret Books of the Egyptian Gnostics,* New York, Viking, 1960; AMS 1970 reprint.

ascension   vision.

Graves, Robert and Raphael Patai, *Hebrew Myths: The Book of Genesis,* New York, Greenwich House, 1chitecture.

Hapgood, Charles H., *Maps of the Ancient Sea Kings: Evidence of Advanced Civilization in the Ice Age,* New York, E.P. Dutton, 1979.

Laurence, Richard, *The Book of Enoch the Prophet,* from the Ethiopian manuscript, San Diego, Wizards; 1973 photographic copy of the 1883 version.

Levi, *The Aquarian Gospel of Jesus the Christ,* England, L.N. Fowler & Co. Ltd., 1907; 1944 printing. I cite this work because of "Levi's Commission" by the higher forces. In it, he says, "Write full the story of The Christ who built upon the solid Rock of yonder circle of the sun-the Christ who men have known as Enoch the Initiate." (p.16).

LePlongeon, Augustus, *Sacred Mysteries Among the Mayas and the Quiches,* Minneapolis, Wizards, 1973. I cite this work because of the many parallels LePlongeon cites between the "Book of Henoch" or Enoch and the Mayas and Quiches. The second incarnation in 5,000 B.C. as Enochian priest felt like the location was where Mexico is now.

O'Brien, Christian, *The Genius of the Few,* England, Turnstone, 1985. This is an astonishing exploration of what really happened in the Garden of Eden. Enoch was the chronicler or scribe to the shining ones in the Garden around 7700 B.C., according to O'Brien. The time frame here is close to the 7600 B.C. visit of the twelfth planet according to Zecharia Sitchin.

Robinson, James M., *The Nag Hamadi Library,* New York, Harper & Row, 1977. See "The discourse in the Eighth and Ninth," where Hermes Trismegistus is instructing an initiate. He says, "For the entire eighth, O my son, and the souls that are in it, and the angels, sing a hymn in silence. And I, Mind, understand."

Scholem, Gershom G., *Major Trends in Jewish Mysticism,* New York, Schocken, 1941.

_____, *Kabbalah,* New York, New American Library, 1974. See section titled *Gematria.* In general, it would appear that Enochian wisdom is very numerological, and that eight is a key number for forming mastery tools.

Sitchin, Zecharia, *The Twelfth Planet,* New York, Avon, 1978.

_____, *The War of Gods and Men,* New York, Avon, 1985.

_____, *The Stairway to Heaven,* New York, Avon, 1980.

Spence, Lewis, *The Occult Sciences in Atlantis,* New York, Weiser, 1978.

Evans-Wentz, W.Y., *Cuchama and Sacred Mountains,* Chicago, Swallow, 1981. A great source on the transformative powers of sacred mountains.

Aspasia, Minoan priestess, 1492-1455 B.C.:

Bachofen, J.J., *Myth, Religion, and Mother Right,* Princeton, Bollingen, 1967.

Baines, John, *The Secret Science: For the Physical and Spiritual Transformation of Man,* Minneapolis, Llewellyn, 1980.

Baran, Michael, *Twilight of the Gods,* New York, Exposition Press, 1984. This book contains much on the Atlantean dispersal, and the author has an interesting way of tracing linguistics in ancient cultures.

Brown, Norman O., *Life Against Death: The Psychoanalytical Meaning of History,* New York, Vintage, 1959.

Bulfinch, Thomas, *Bulfinch's Mythology,* New York, Avenel Books, 1978.

Campbell, Joseph, *The Masks of God, Primitive Mythology,* New York, Penguin, 1959; reprinted 1981.

Campbell, Joseph, *The Mysteries;-"Papers from the Eranos Yearbooks,"* Princeton, Bollingen, 1978. See especially, C. Kerenyi on the mysteries of the Kabeiroi.

Cottrell, Leonard, *The Bull of Minos,* New York, Grosset and Dunlap, 1953; 1962 edition.

Doumas, Christos G., *Thera: Pompei of the Ancient Aegean,* London, Thames and Hudson, 1983. A superb and definitive book up to its publication date on the cataclysm Aspasia died in.

Eliade, Mircea, *The Myth of the Eternal Return,* Princeton, Bollingen, 1954.

_____, *Gods, Goddesses, and Myths of Creation,* New

York, Harper and Row, 1974.

Fox, Hugh, *Gods of the Cataclysm,* New York, Dorset, 1976.

Friedrich, Otto, *The End of the World: A History,* New York, Coward, McCann, & Geoghegan, 1982. Some discussion of the Santorini eruption in 1500 B.C.

Galanopoulos, A.G. and Edward Bacon, *Atlantis: The truth behind the legend,* Indianapolis, Bobbs-Merrill, 1969. This is the definitive work on the Thera eruption and its relation to the *Timaeus amd Critias* of Plato.

Graves, Robert, *The Greek Myths, vols I & II,* England, Penguin, 1955; 1981 reprint.

Graham, J. Walter, *"Notes on Houses and Housing-Districts at Abdera and Himera," American Journal of Archeology, Vol 73, #3, July 1972.*

Lantero, Erminie, *The continuing discovery of Chiron,* Maine, Weiser, 1983.

Luckerman, Marvin Arnold, *Catastrophism and Ancient History,* Los Angeles. This is a journal published twice yearly devoted to the examination of historical catastrophism.

Mavor, James, *Voyage to Atlantis,* New York, Putnam, 1969.

Nixon, Ivor Gray, *The Rise of the Dorians,* England, The Chancery Press, 1968. See Chapter Five.

Oliva, Pavel, *The Birth of Greek Civilization,* London, Orbis, 1981.

Patten, D.W., *The Biblical Flood and the Ice Epoch: A Study of Scientific History,* Seattle, Meridian Publishing Co., 1966.

Vogel, Martin, *Chiron: Der Kentaur mit der Kithara,* Germany, Bonn-Bad Goesberg, 1978, 2 vols. I am grateful to Dr. Kenneth Negus for his English translations of this work heard at the annual meeting of The American Federation of Astrologers in Chicago in 1982.

Pendlebury, J., *The Archeology of Crete,* New York, Norton, 1965.

Spanuth, Jurgen, *Atlantis of the North,* England, Sidgwick & Jackson, 1976.

Temple, Robert K.G., *The Sirius Mystery,* New York, St. Martin's Press, 1976. On page 162 Temple notes that the word Typhon can mean a "kind of a comet," and under hypnosis, I interchanged comet and Typhon.

Swimme, Brian, *The Universe is a Green Dragon,* Santa Fe, Bear and Company, 1985. Swimme works with the idea that gravity which holds the solar system together is "cosmic allurement."

Velikovsky, Immanuel, *Ages in Chaos,* New York, Doubleday, 1952.

_____. *Earth in Upheaval,* New York, Dell, 1955.

_____, *Worlds in Collision*, New York, Dell, 1950.

_____, *Mankind in Amnesia*, New York, Doubleday, 1982.

CHAPTER NINE

The focus of this chapter is on divination skill, technique, and the synchronicity principle. I live according to the Hermetic principle, "As Above, So Below," and this chapter shows how the priest of Enoch communicates with the other planes and utilizes alchemy; how the Druid channels with a crystal ball and another priest; and how Aspasia uses sheep entrail divination to protect her oracle. Much of this chapter is secret knowledge which can now be revealed. Many books have already been cited in relation to the Enochian, the Druid, and Aspasia, and so books cited here have only to do with divination skills and sources specific to the techniques each one of them worked with.

Priest of Enoch 5000 B.C. and 6700 B.C.

Albertus, Frater, *Alchemist's Handbook,* New York, Weiser, 1981.

Caron, M. and S. Hutin, *The Alchemists,* London, Evergreen Books, 1961.

Cockren, A., *Alchemy Rediscovered and Restored,* California, Health Research, 1961.

Jung, C.G., *Synchronicity,* Princeton, Bollingen, 1973.

King, Francis and Stephen Skinner, *Techniques of High Magic: A Manual of Self Initiation,* New York, Destiny. See especially "Divination as Magic."

Spanuth, Jurgen, *Atlantis of the North,* London, Sidgwick and Jackson, 1979.

Spence, Lewis, *The Occult Sciences in Atlantis,* New York, Weiser, 1978. See, "The Beginnings of Alchemy."

Steneck, Nicholas H., *Science and Creation in the Middle Ages,* Indiana, University of Notre Dame Press, 1976. A study on medieval scientist, Henry of Langenstein who died in 1397.

Trismegistus, Hermes Mercurius, *Divine Pymander,* Illinois, Yogi Publication Society; reprint of 1871 edition.

von Franz, Marie-Louise, *Alchemy,* Canada, Inner City Books, 1980. This is a brilliant work on alchemy which ends with the *Aurora Consurgens,* St. Thomas Aquinas's alchemical tractate.

Wilder, Alexander, *New Platonism and Alchemy,* Minneapolis, Wizards, 1975; reprint of Secret Doctrine Reference Series-1869.

Druid Priest in about 500 A.D.

Baer, Randall N. and Vicki V., *Windows of Light: Quartz Crystals and Self-Transformation,* New York, Harper and Row, 1984.

Dorland, Frank,*The Mystery of The Crystal Skull,* Taos, Wisdom Books, 1984. From a tape. This tape contains information on the darkest recesses of the brain where a substance called melanin is manufactured. The molecular structure of melanin is hexagonal and interfaces with similar hexagonal molecules in quartz crystal. Channeling is facilitated by visualizing the hexagonal forms in the melanin in the deepest recesses of the brain.

Sharkey, John, *celtic mysteries,* New York, Crossroad, 1975. Sharkey notes that the druids were stripped of their special priviliges as priests of old religion at the Synod of Drumceatt in A.D. 574. I remember it.

Tella, *The Dynamics of Cosmic Telepathy,* Aztec, New Mexico, Guardian Action Publications, 1983.

Readers may want to note that in the general Druid references listed for Chapter Two, the general information on the Druidic "Cult of the Head" is possibly elucidated by the remarkable lucidity in channeling of the Druid.

Aspasia, Minoan Priestess—1492-1455 B.C.

All works which focus on the spiritual and magical skill of the Minoan priests and priestesses note what a highly developed culture it was. Lewis Spence's *The Occult Sciences in Atlantis* has a chapter on prophecy and divination.

CHAPTER TEN

This chapter focuses on the domestic happiness of Erastus Hummel and there are no references. It moves into the personal life of Isaiah. I was so astonished after the first Isaiah regression, that I asked Greg Paxson to do another Isaiah regression focusing on his life as a normal man. The results are presented, but I can't reference it. The vision in the desert was the first Isaiah regression although it ends the book. Lastly, the text moves through the death of the Roman, and to his experience as an essence after death.

CHAPTER ELEVEN

This chapter focuses on the extraterrestial realm in relation to Egyptian death rituals. The previous Egyptian references will contain much information on the Egyptian funereal rites, and extra works cited here specialize in that area. The most unusual happening in the weighing of the heart ritual was the appearance of the Four Archangels. When I visited the Temple of Kom Ombo recently, the temple devoted to the crocodile or jaws of death, I noticed a relief in the back of the symbols for the Four Apostles. This temple is Ptolomeic or pre-Christian. Another experience I had in Egypt was also related to this regression. Before I went to Egypt, I could not figure out where this ritual took place. It never occurred to me that it would have been in the tomb of Amenhotep II although that seems obvious now. So, when I entered the tomb with my husband, Gerry, both of us immediately recognized the entrance and corridor. We became increasingly excited as we climbed closer to the funereal chamber. It is exactly the same room, and I can't really describe correctly how amazing the feeling was. It had all the intensity of a déjà vu experience with the knowledge added to it. Lastly this chapter moves to the final channeling at Delphi with Dionysius and Aspasia, and it ends with Aspasia's death at her oracle. Much has been cited on Aspasia's time, but a few more references will be given which specifically illuminate this part of her life.

Ichor in 1400 B.C. weighing the heart of Amenhotep II.

Budge, E.A. Wallis, *The Egyptian Book of the Dead,* New York, Dover, 1967. This version is from the Papyrus of Ani.

Campbell, Joseph, *The Mysteries; "Papers from the Eranos Yearbooks,* Princeton, Bollingen, 1978. See "The Mysteries of Osiris" by Georges Nagel.

Cory, Isaac Preston, *Ancient Fragments,* Minneapolis, Wizards, 1975. See second book of Manetho Chronology for Horus who was Pharaoh for 37 years right after Amenhotep II.

Grof, Stanislav and Christina, *Beyond Death,* London, Thames and Hudson, 1980.

Lamy, Lucie, *Egyptian Mysteries,* New York, Crossroad, 1981. See whole text and on pages 58-63 are photographs in Amenhotep IInd's tomb.

Reed, Bika, *Rebel in the Soul: a sacred text of ancient Egypt,* New York, Inner Traditions, 1978.

Schneweis, Emil, *Angels and Demons According to Lactantius,* Washington, Catholic University Press, 1944. This is a superb little book on the angels, and offers much illumination on what they might be doing anywhere including in a tomb in the Middle Kingdom in Egypt.

Sitchin, Zecharia, *The Stairway to Heaven,* New York, Avon, 1980. This is Sitchin's work on the passage rituals in Egypt as well as other issues. It is radical, brilliant, and should be read by anyone curious about Egyptian funereal rituals.

Aspasia, Minoan priestess, 1492-1455 B.C.

Fontenrose, Joseph, *Python: a Study of Delphic Myth and Its Origins,* Berkeley, University of California Press, 1959. In Chapter XIII concerning the pre-Apollonian information on Delphi, Dionysius is found to be present. The oracular cavern has not been found at Delphi, yet at the site of the Corycian Cave at the Lycoreian site, the more ancient oracle is described as "a small plain among the rocks, halfway up the mountain, a hole in the earth." p. 415. Fontenrose notes that Deukalion was the founder of Lycoreia, and that makes it difficult not to link up Deucalion's Flood with the tsunami or tidal wave after Thera eruption when the water would have risen 300-500 feet.

Friedrich, Otto, *The End of the World,* New York, Coward, McCann & Geoghegan, 1982.

Otto, Walter F., *Dionysus: Myth and Cult,* Dallas, Spring Publications, 1981.

Sherwood, Keith, *The Art of Spiritual Healing: A Practical Guide to Healing Power,* Minneapolis, Llewellyn Publications, 1985. This is one of the best books on the techniques of healing available at this time. Especially see p. 142 on the creation of a healing triangle of light.

Spence, Lewis, *The Occult Sciences in Atlantis,* New York, Weiser, 1978. See "the prophecy of the nameless seer of Atlantis." p. 87.

Taylor, Thomas, *The Eleusinian and Bacchic Mysteries,* San Diego, Wizards, 1980. A reprint of the 1875 Bouton edition.

Velikovsky, Immanuel, *Mankind in Amnesia,* New York, Doubleday, 1983. An underappreciated work on amnesia in relation to cataclysm.

CHAPTER TWELVE

This chapter focuses on the Druid priest and the place where Isaiah exists in his body. It seems apparent that the first incarnation after Isaiah in which the power of Isaiah could be felt was the incarnation as a Druid. The historical background of the king he was associated with, Sigebert, is correct, and the information the Druid channeled about the wife and brother of Sigebert is probably accurate. The thrill that I felt everytime I researched one of the regressions and found the dates, names, and historical circumstances to be accurate is a type of thrill which results in an ever-deepening fascination with life. Next I moved right into Isaiah. I have often noted that I am having difficulty integrating this energy into my present reality. This being Isaiah was absolutely centered in his power, and he was motivated by a knowledge about the meaning of human reality that few ever will attain. It is exciting to think that I might someday comprehend this center he embodied if I continue on my path. The scene at the end of *Eye of the Centaur* is fantastic, possibly shocking to some, and yet the drift of contemporary historical research is moving in the direction of considering the possibility, of and implications of, extraterrestial relations with humans within the last 12,000 years. So, references for the last chapter will attempt to lead the reader into considering this possibility. At this point in my life, I expect to know much more about extra-terrestial influences on human thought and behavior and it will be the subject of the next book of this trilogy, *The Mind Chronicles.*

The Druid Priest in the sixth century A.D.

Alcock, Leslie, *Arthur's Britain,* London, Penguin, 1971. This wonderful book has extensive information on the fourth through seventh centuries A.D. in Britain. He mentions a Sigeberht of Wessex who was listed in the *Anglo Saxon Chronicles* of Bede. This Sigeberht can be very accurately dated because he gave the derelict Saxon shore to Fursa for a monastery in 630. It seemed I was a hundred years off which would have created great difficulties because Anglia, Wessex, and Cornwall were in a state of near anarchy in the seventh century, and my regression did not reflect that. The other details around Sigebert gave the answer. See the Encyclopedia Britannica reference for the answer. Meanwhile this book gives much information on the sixth century. Bede often cites the monk Gildas as a major source, and Gildas reports fifty years of peace after the Battle of Badon which Alcock dates as 490 A.D. I believe that most of this regression falls into the historical period after the Battle of

Badon when travel to the Rhineland would have been feasible so that the Druid could be active at the sacred sites in Britain.

Baigent, Michael, Richard Leigh, and Henry Lincoln, *Holy Blood, Holy Grail,* New York, Dell, 1983. There is much information on the historical period in question, and the authors note that early Christianity absorbed most of Mithric theology.

Cumont, Franz, *The Mysteries of Mithra,* New York, Dover, 1956. A reprint of the 1903 Open Court version. This is a definitive source on Mithra and also notes the Christian swallowing of this sun cult.

Encyclopedia Britannica, *Eleventh Edition,* Vol XXV, England, Cambridge, p. 59. According to E.B., Sigebert was a king of the Franks who died in 575, and there is much evidence of close association between the Franks who were the consolidated federation of German States first united under Clovis and the Britains, 481-511. This consolidation was a major power factor until the 9th century, and one would expect the Druid to be very involved in this issue since his field of action moved from the Rhineland to Britainy. According to E.B., Sigebert married Brunhilda, a Visigoth, and his brother Chilperic (must be Childe in text) married Brunhilde's sister. But, this sister was murdered in 573 causing civil war. Sigebert was eventually assassinated by soldiers in the pay of Chilperic's second wife. So, obviously, I was channeling in a kingly fratricidal conflict of major proportions which was of extreme worry to me. It would seem that the Druid and Isaiah shared similar type frustrations with kings.

Wallace-Handrill, J.M., *The Barbarian West: The Eartly Middle Ages-A.D. 400-1000,* New York, Harper and Row, 1962. See "the Franks."

Isaiah in eight Century B.C.

Isaiah has been extensively referenced for Chapter Six. The vision of Isaiah was the end of the last regression, and I stopped work at that point because it was obvious that I was going to move into an entirely new dimension. The next book I write will take off at that point. References here are specifically related to extraterrestial considerations in the lives of the great prophets, mystics, the Gods, and all human experiences which have to do with "ascension" to a different level. Readers should realize that part of our cultural revulsion about this question comes from the fact that it is an official heresy of the Catholic Church to view fantastic events in the Old Testament as real. The heresy, Marcionism, has forced Church scholars to treat all this material as allegorical, which has caused people to stop questioning what is really being described in the ancient scriptures. Now we have a space technology which is causing many to read the ancient descriptions of the chariot, the Merkabah, the "wheel" of Ezekial, the statement in the Hebrew Bible and Book of Enoch, that "Enoch walked with the Gods" in a different light. Since the truth in the past will affect us if we find ourselves visited by or visiting extraterrestials, then the more we know about our possible ancient relations, the better.

Baines, John, *The Stellar Man,* Minneapolis, Llewellyn Publications, 1985. This is a very interesting work regarding the double nature of the soul experienced by the Enochian, by Isaiah, and myself in this lifetime. In the sequel to EYE, I will explore this issue in depth.

Baran, Michael, *Twilight of the Gods,* New York, Exposition Press, 1984.

Daniken, Erich von, *According to the Evidence,* Great Britain, Souvenir Press, 1970.

_____, *Miracles of the Gods,* New York, Delacorte, 1974.

_____, *The Gold of the Gods,* Great Britain, Souvenir, 1973.

Drake, W. Raymond, *Mystery of the Gods—Are They coming Back To Earth,* 1972; self-published.

Fox, Hugh, *Gods of the Cataclysm,* New York, Dorset, 1976.

Laurence, Richard, *The Book of Enoch the Prophet,* San Diego, Wizards, 1983; from the 1883 Ethiopian version. Simply put, I can find no other explanation for this work except an ascension off the earth and up into space.

Scholem, Gershom, *Kabbalah,* New York, Meridian, 1974. Because Hebrew scholars have not labored under the Vatican proscriptions for the last 2,000 years, Hebrew mystical literature is loaded with sources on extraterrestsial influences on humanity. The Merkabah literature is particularly rich. Scholem does not deal with the issue at all, but because he describes the mystical sources without prejudice, readers will find him a rich source for this question.

Schneweis, Emil, *Angels and Demons According to Lactantius,* Washington, Catholic University of America, 1944. An AMS reprint. a rich source on the behavior of these beings regardless of who they really are.

Shorter, Alan W., *The Egyptian Gods,* London, Routledge & Kegan Paul, 1937.

Sitchin, Zecharia, *The 12th Planet,* New York, Avon, 1976. Sitchin knows more about this question than anyone at the present time.

_____, *The Stairway to Heaven,* New York, Avon, 1980.

_____, *The Wars of Gods and Men,* New York, Avon, 1985. In this final volume of *The Earth Chronicles,* Sitchin theorizes that the Sinai had a nuclear detonation in 2024 B.C.

Velikovsky, Immanuel, *Worlds in Collision,* New York, Dell, 1950.

Temple, Robert K.G., *The Sirius Mystery,* New York, St. Martin's, 1976.

Trench, Le Poer, *The Sky People,* London, Neville Spearman, 1960.

ABOUT THE AUTHOR

Barbara Hand Clow is a noted astrological counselor, spiritual teacher, writer, and editor of books on New Age consciousness. Her first book, *Stained Glass: A Basic Manual* was published in 1976. She received her master's degree in theology and healing from Mundelein College in 1983 after writing a thesis on "A Comparison of Jungian Psychoanalytic Technique and Past-Life Regression Therapy."

Clow believes that everyone on Earth possesses memories of all times and places within their cellular matrices, and that anyone can remember everything that they have ever known if they have the courage to go deep within and experience themselves. She feels, as do many Native American and Mesoamerican spiritual teachers, that the purpose of the late twentieth century is to go beyond time, and beyond history. Her *Mind Chronicles* series is a journey into the archetypal memories of the human race. It is a redefinition of his-story to include and empower the experiences of women, animals, plants, and rocks.

As a result of her extensive personal work with ceremony at sacred sites and its role in the evolution of consciousness, Clow wrote the first volume of *The Mind Chronicles* trilogy, *Eye of the Centaur: A Visionary Guide into Past Lives*, in 1986. In this book, she embodies the shifts in dimensionality experienced by many people during the Harmonic Convergence in 1987. Her continued work on clearing the emotional body, and emptying the contents of the subconscious mind through shamanic journeying, compelled her to author *Heart of the Christos*, the second volume of the trilogy, which was published in 1989.

Clow is also the author of *Chiron: Rainbow Bridge Between the Inner and Outer Planets*, 1987, a definitive astrological work on the new planet Chiron, which rules the current redefinition of the species. She is married and the mother of four children: Tom, Matthew, Christopher, and Elizabeth.

Due to her continued commitment to her writing and her exploration of the subconscious, Barbara Hand Clow is not currently available for doing personal astrological readings.